FROM THE
COLD WAR
TO
ISIL

FROM THE
COLD WAR
TO
ISIL

ONE MARINE'S JOURNEY

BRIG. GEN. JASON Q. BOHM, USMC

Naval Institute Press
Annapolis, Maryland

Naval Institute Press
291 Wood Road
Annapolis, MD 21402

Library of Congress Cataloging-in-Publication Data

Names: Bohm, Jason Q., author.
Title: From the Cold War to ISIL : one Marine's journey / Jason Q. Bohm.
Description: Annapolis, Maryland : Naval Institute Press, [2019]
Identifiers: LCCN 2019011246 | ISBN 9781682474570 (hardcover)
Subjects: LCSH: Bohm, Jason Q. | United States. Marine Corps—Officers—Biography. | Marines—
    United States—Biography. | Military art and science—United States—History—20th century. |
    Military art and science—United States—History—21st century. | United States—History, Military—
    20th century. | United States—History, Military—21st century. | United States—Politics and
    government—1981–1989. | United States—Politics and government—1989–
Classification: LCC VE25.B64 A3 2019 | DDC 359.9/6092 [B]—dc23
LC record available at https://lccn.loc.gov/2019011246

♾ Print editions meet the requirements of ANSI/NISO z39.48–1992 (Permanence of Paper).
Printed in the United States of America.

27 26 25 24 23 22 21 20 19   9 8 7 6 5 4 3 2 1
First printing

This book is dedicated to the many Marines, soldiers, sailors, airmen, and Coast Guardsmen who have served, are serving, or will serve our great nation.

Contents

Illustrations

Foreword

The Marine Corps has an illustrious history, which parallels that of our great nation. Coming into being during the formative years of the United States, our Corps—like our country—adapted and grew in both war and peace through trial and error. Our nation shifted in both focus and commitments from a continental to a world power following World War I. Likewise, the Marine Corps used the years between the Great War and World War II as a period of heightened thought and innovation in order to better prepare for future conflict. We did not want to refight any previous conflict. The same dynamic as that of the interwar years took place following major changes in the strategic environment and advancements in technology after other prolonged conflicts, such as World War II, the Korean War, and the Vietnam War. Our nation and the world have changed radically since the early 1990s as well, with the fall of the Soviet Union, the rise of worldwide terrorism, and technological revolutions in computing, optics, targeting, and stealth. Jason Bohm, a colonel at this text's writing and now a brigadier general, has faithfully and courageously served our nation as a Marine during most of these latest periods of adjustment. His career and his insights provide us an invaluable look at changing missions for changing times.

Colonel Bohm tells the story of those changing missions that he and his fellow Marines and our joint service and allied partners confronted during the turbulent times between the end of the Cold War through the current fight against the Islamic State in Iraq and the Levant (ISIL). He provides candid and useful historical background on what shaped our nation's and our armed forces' actions during this period, as he uses a series of personal vignettes and deployment experiences to describe how he and others translated strategic and operational objectives into tactical actions on the ground. In addition, Colonel Bohm conveys what mission analysis almost always necessitated in terms of training and indeed recruiting and resourcing. In this unique way, he tells not only his story but also, more importantly, that of the Marine Corps during this significant and still-evolving time in our nation's history.

Second Lieutenant Bohm was fortunate to enter the Marine Corps during a period when one of our transformational leaders, the twenty-ninth Commandant, Gen. Al Gray, instituted maneuver warfare as the Corps' new warfighting philosophy, captured in the Corps' seminal doctrinal publication, *Warfighting* (Marine Corps Doctrinal Publication 1). Lessons learned in the schools of the Marine Corps and other services instilled in Lieutenant, and later Captain, Bohm the tenets of maneuver warfare that facilitated our nation's and our joint force's success during Operation Desert Storm in 1991, in the march to Baghdad during Operation Iraqi Freedom in 2003, and in numerous smaller operations around the globe. From actions on those and later battlefields and to the halls of Congress, Bohm describes how he and fellow Marines operationalized the principles found in *Warfighting* and how he applied them in numerous areas and many missions throughout his career.

Bohm's experiences at the tail end of the Cold War led him to gain renewed appreciation for the high end of conflict and understand better why America's armed forces must continuously prioritize and prepare for the most dangerous scenarios. Simply put and as we are constantly reminded, the cost of failure is too high. With that as backdrop, he relates that throughout our nation's history, major military operations have occurred at an average of only once every sixteen years, with the years in between replete with small wars or operations other than war (OOTW). Bohm's work outlines in vivid detail how thoughtful training and preparation for subordinate missions and operations below the level of armed conflict almost always enhance individual and unit readiness for subsequent tasks and more demanding operations.

Jason Bohm experienced many of these operations at first hand in places like Somalia, Haiti, Cuba, Bahrain, and Kenya—operations that our thirty-first Commandant, Gen. Chuck Krulak, described as the "Three Block War." Bohm did so while also training and leading General Krulak's "Strategic Corporals," those many young Marines who expertly operated across the full spectrum of conflict and whose tactical actions had then, and still have today, strategic implications in a faster and more globally connected world. Also, Bohm joined the Marine Corps at the height of the initial implementation of the Goldwater-Nichols Act of 1986. Thus, he has gained an appreciation for operating more effectively as a member of our nation's Joint Force on many of these operations. His generation of Marines and sister-service members are the first to be raised consciously "cradle to grave" in our post-Vietnam and post–Desert One era of jointness.

Throughout this eminently readable and thought-provoking chronicle, Bohm rightly places the reader alongside the men and women who answer our nation's call to service on the seas, in the air, and on the ground. He shares the sights, sounds, and smells of operating in distant lands, the joys of being a part of a "band of brothers," and the heartbreak of losing comrades in combat. The reader will experience what it is like to conduct boat raids, to fast-rope beneath helicopters, and to work beside coalition partners. His stories will take the reader on missions ranging from providing embassy security in Haiti to feeding starving Somalis, fighting insurgents and training Iraqi police in Al Anbar Province, and engaging ISIL fighters with some of the first forces sent back into Iraq as a Special Purpose Marine Air Ground Task Force (SPMAGTF).

This book will appeal to many audiences. Military historians and enthusiasts will gain an understanding and appreciation of an era about which relatively little is written. Veterans will reminisce and reflect on many of the operations, duty stations, and experiences they shared during their own periods of selfless service. Military families will recognize and relate to the lifestyle and sacrifices described. Those currently serving will gain better context and learn lessons they can apply to current and future operations. Aspiring service members will gain an appreciation for, and a better understanding of, life as a member of our nation's all-volunteer force (AVF). Americans in general will feel a sense of pride for the many accomplishments achieved by their United States Marine Corps, and indeed by all of America's armed forces over the last thirty years. All readers should be driven to ask themselves what kind of American servicemembers, technologies, and policies we need as we prepare to confront new challenges in the twenty-first century.

As a final "opening salvo," the reader should know that while then-Col. Jason Bohm was the author and narrator of this compelling work, he has also taken characteristic pains to imply that he could be "any Lieutenant" or "any Captain" as a Rifle or Fleet Antiterrorism Security Team (FAST) Platoon Commander, or Rifle Company Commander, or "any Lieutenant Colonel" as a Battalion Commander, or "any Colonel" as a Regimental or Marine Air Ground Task Force (MAGTF) Commander. Brig. Gen. Jason Bohm has proven himself much more over his three-decade-plus career. As Commander of Golf Company, 2nd Battalion, 1st Marine Regiment, he was selected as the Colonel William Leftwich Award recipient as our Corps' finest captain company commander. He was subsequently board-selected or personally selected on numerous occasions for subsequent critical commands and assignments, be they Commanding Officer, Marine Corps Recruiting Station (Charlestown, West Virginia); commanding officer of an infantry battalion (1st Battalion, 4th Marines); Senior Marine, Office of Legislative Affairs (OLA), U.S. House of Representatives; commanding officer of an infantry regiment (5th Marines); Commander Special Marine Air Ground Task Force Crisis Response Central Command; and, at the book's inception, the director of our Corps' Expeditionary Warfare School (EWS), wherein we train our captains. Brig. Gen. Jason Bohm knows that of which he writes. He has "walked the talk" and along the way learned much and then trained and led thousands of Marines, personally guiding many of them into and out of the crucible of battle. America and our Corps of Marines is fortunate to have Brig. Gen. Jason Bohm as a commissioned officer and Marine leader. Just as our Corps is better for his service, you, the reader, will be enlightened by the narrative he presents and the lessons that may be learned herein.

Semper Fidelis!
J. M. Paxton Jr.
General, U.S. Marine Corps (Retired)
Thirty-Third Assistant Commandant of the Marine Corps

--------------- ★ ---------------

Introduction

The smell of diesel fuel is strong as the Soviet Sixth Army continues its lightning strike across the northern Norwegian border from the Kola Peninsula. The T-72 main battle tanks with 125-mm cannons and laminate armor and BMP-2 infantry fighting vehicles with 30-mm automatic cannons and embarked infantrymen have made quick work of the Norwegian garrison of Sør-Varang. The garrison, responsible for guarding the 122-mile border with the Soviet Union, was no match for the onslaught.

It is only a few days since the Sixth Army staged in the vicinity of Murmansk—the world's largest city above the Arctic Circle and endpoint of both the railroad from Leningrad and the Arctic Ocean's Northeast Passage. Murmansk's strategic importance had been evident during World Wars I and II. The Allies had used its key port facilities to deliver tons of critically needed supplies to equip the Soviets. Its importance is just as great today. The ice-free port of Murmansk provides year-round access to the Barents Sea and is the home of the Soviet Northern Fleet.

A lifeline during World War II, Murmansk and the greater Kola Peninsula now serve a different purpose. What is arguably one of the most militarized regions of the world is now organized to defend the Soviet homeland from the very allies that once used this same area to assist it. More importantly, the area is now being used as a jumping-off point for a surprise attack against the northern flank of the North Atlantic Treaty Organization (NATO). The Soviets intend to use the region to control the Atlantic and prevent the Americans from coming to the aid of their European partners as they had in the past world wars.

Surprise and speed are critical to winning in this theater of what has become World War III. The Soviets know that the Americans' strategy requires a rapid reinforcement of Norway using U.S. Navy and Marine Corps amphibious forces and prepositioned Marine Corps equipment. The 4th Marine Expeditionary Brigade has the mission of reinforcing Norwegian airfields and ports as part of a larger naval campaign to defend Norway and the North Atlantic in the event of a Soviet attack.[1] After staging at airfields in the United States, the Soviets know, the brigade is expected to fly to Norway to marry with its prepositioned equipment and then redeploy rapidly to key locations throughout the country. The Soviets intend to beat the Americans in the race to secure those areas.

The United States established the Norway Air-Landed Marine Expeditionary Brigade (NALMEB) program in 1981. Gear and supplies to outfit up to 17,000 Marines is prepositioned in six climate-controlled caves in central Norway.[2] The caves hold 7,000 tons of ground and aviation ammunition, 1,000 vehicles, 40,000 cases of rations, 18 howitzers, and other items.[3] The Sixth Army's mission is to capture these caves and possible landing beaches prior to the arrival of the Marines.

Progress is good. The Soviets have quickly secured Finnmark County after crossing the border. They are surprised to see the Norwegians using the same scorched-earth tactics the Russians used so effectively against Napoleon's Grand Army in 1812 and Hitler's Wehrmacht in 1941 during the failed invasions of Mother Russia.[4] The Sixth Army's covering force met some resistance at Bardufoss, but quickly dispatched it.

The next objectives are the town and port of Narvik and the important rail line that connects Narvik to the iron mines in Sweden. Narvik also holds prepositioned gear for the United Kingdom's Royal Marines, who are to join their brothers from the United States and Norway in any fight against the Soviets.[5] Reports start to arrive at Sixth Army's headquarters about ambushes and harassment attacks occurring along the army's long column snaking its way through the restrictive terrain and stretching back to the border. This doesn't concern the Sixth Army commander. He keeps a laser focus on the prize; the Marines' prepositioned equipment and supplies appear within grasp . . . and then it happens.

The commander finds himself momentarily blinded by what seems to be a hundred fireworks exploding simultaneously on top of his column of tanks and personnel carriers. All units report they are under attack. The commander hears the roar of jet engines as he fully realizes what has just occurred. A section of the dreaded A-6 Intruders, the Navy and Marine

Corps all-weather medium attack aircraft, streaks past after dropping cluster bombs on the Soviet column. A Soviet ZSU-23-4 self-propelled antiaircraft gun blasts away at the Intruders with its quad 23-mm guns, but it is too late. The damage is done. The Americans have arrived ... *"Time!"*

The year was 1986. I was a freshman at the Illinois Institute of Technology and a midshipman in the Naval Reserve Officer Training Corps (NROTC) program. The Cold War deeply engulfed the United States and the Soviet Union. Capt. Marty Almquist, the Marine Officer Instructor at my NROTC unit in Chicago, had just ended the next turn in a war game in which I was serving as the commanding general of the Soviet Sixth Army. This war game was indicative of whom the United States saw as its most likely adversary. But the enemy, like many throughout America's history, would change in time, and the country would face new, uncertain, and evolving national security challenges. The character of war was also changing, requiring new strategies and a more flexible and adaptable military. To provide insight from my experiences as a Marine infantryman during these turbulent times, this book will take you on a thirty-year journey from the Cold War to the fight against the Islamic State of Iraq and the Levant (ISIL), covering many other operations in between.

Major shifts in U.S. domestic politics and the global geopolitical landscape between 1986 and 2016 forced America's armed forces to redefine themselves and codify their role as key elements of national power. This dynamic period began with President Ronald Reagan signing into law the Goldwater-Nichols Department of Defense Reorganization Act of 1986. The Goldwater-Nichols Act represented the first major shift in the U.S. national defense apparatus since the creation of the Department of Defense in 1947.

The Goldwater-Nichols Act instituted a number of major changes. It strengthened the position of the chairman of the Joint Chiefs of Staff and more clearly defined the roles and responsibilities of the joint chiefs and combatant commanders. It also forced the services to operate more effectively as a joint force,[6] an attempt to address the challenges and inefficiencies created by interservice rivalries during the Vietnam War, highlighted by the tragic events surrounding the failed Iranian hostage rescue attempt in 1980, and resulting in weaknesses that occurred in the invasion of Grenada in 1983. Implementation of Goldwater-Nichols had far-reaching impacts on how the U.S. armed forces organized, manned, trained, and equipped to meet future national security needs. It also directly influenced how my colleagues and I would prosecute the nation's military strategies.

Also, the evolving security environment influenced military doctrine and emerging operational concepts in how best to employ the military element of national power. The nation remained focused on confronting the only other superpower in the world as I prepared for commissioning as an officer of Marines. The National Security Strategy (NSS), the president's mechanism for sharing his strategic vision to Congress and the American people, at that time stated, "The United States shouldered the dual burden of facilitating the restoration of a world economic order and arresting the spread of the Soviet Union's peculiar brand of totalitarianism and communism."[7] This view drove the development of military strategy in the late 1980s and ensured an almost exclusive focus on the high-end range of military operations, to include major conventional combat and nuclear war, if required. It also called for large numbers of forward-based and forward-deployed forces, particularly in Europe and Korea.

The sudden downfall of the Soviet Union and collapse of communist control of the Eastern Bloc countries provided great opportunities, but also brought much uncertainty as to the direction the armed forces should take. The lack of a clearly defined enemy and of the relative stability once created by the checks and balances of two superpowers who both wanted to avoid all-out war created a void that all too many were willing to fill. Such was the world order in 1990, the year I received my commission as a second lieutenant with orders to The Basic School (TBS) in Quantico, Virginia. All new Marine lieutenants attend TBS to learn the art of leadership before being assigned their occupational specialties.

The United States had not fought a major conventional war since Vietnam, but it was ready to fight one with Iraq in 1990. Since its founding in 1776, the United States has conducted a major military operation only, on an average, once every sixteen years,[8] and it had been fifteen years since the United States had left Vietnam. Perhaps, then, it should not have been a surprise that the United States intervened when Saddam Hussein, Iraq's dictator, ordered his army to occupy Kuwait. There ensued a tumultuous relationship between the United States and Iraq that would consume much of my professional focus over the next twenty-six years. My military career began with maintaining stability in the Middle East during the 1990s, went on to multiple deployments in support of Operation Iraqi Freedom, and concluded with my commanding one of the first conventional forces to go back into Iraq to join our partners there in the fight against the Islamic State of Iraq and the Levant (ISIL) in 2015.

In 1990, training at TBS and excited about the prospect of going to war, I found fate had other plans. I was selected as an infantry officer, but amid training in the desert of Southern California in preparation for joining Operation Desert Shield, I found my orders canceled. The ground war designated as Operation Desert Storm ended almost as soon as it began, and I felt dejected and contemplated that another sixteen years would pass before I could hope to practice my chosen trade. However, I soon discovered the United States conducted hundreds of smaller operations between its major ones and therefore did not have to wait long for my first combat.

The National Military Strategy of 1992 took the armed forces in a direction vastly different from what it became accustomed since the 1950s. Calling for "a shift from containing the spread of communism and deterring Soviet aggression to a more diverse, flexible strategy that is regionally oriented and capable of responding to the challenges of this decade,"[9] it recognized America's role in providing leadership as the world's sole superpower following the fall of the Soviet Union and the recent victory in Desert Storm. The strategy provided four foundations for the nation's leadership role: strategic deterrence and defense, forward presence, crisis response, and reconstitution. It was under the rubric of crisis response that President George H. W. Bush deployed my unit to a country in Africa called Somalia.

Operation Restore Hope was an American-led humanitarian effort to deliver critically needed food and other supplies to alleviate a humanitarian crisis. Thousands of Somalis were dying from sickness and starvation by the summer of 1992. The United States had initially attempted to mitigate the tragedy by airlifting thousands of tons of emergency supplies into the country during Operation Provide Relief, but that effort proved insufficient. The lack of a strong, centralized Somali government and the prevalence of clan warfare resulted in an environment of anarchy, suffering, and lawlessness. Clan warlords became all-powerful at the expense of the population, and "food itself became a weapon."[10]

I was a platoon commander leading approximately fifty Marines in what initially seemed a straightforward mission. It quickly developed into a complex operation combining humanitarian efforts, peacekeeping, and combat. It was a situation Gen. Charles Krulak, the thirty-first Commandant of the Marine Corps, later described as a Three Block War, one in which Marines "may be confronted by the entire spectrum of tactical challenges in the span of a few hours and within the space of three contiguous city blocks."[11] Although my unit's mission in Somalia concluded before shifting U.S. policies and objectives led to the tragic events surrounding the Battle of Mogadishu,[12] the experience instilled lasting lessons and set the stage for other operations in which I soon participated.

The National Military Strategy (NMS) of 1995 defined the strategic environment as "unsettled" and as exhibiting both "opportunities and threats."[13] Increased regional instability, concerns about the proliferation of weapons of mass destruction, transnational dangers, crime syndicates, and terrorism became the norm as the globe continued to adjust to a world without the Soviet Union. I transferred to the Marine Corps' Fleet Antiterrorism Security Team (FAST) Company, where I would help confront these challenges and work toward achieving the NMS's objectives of "promoting stability and thwarting aggression."[14]

My tour with FAST began with reinforcing the U.S. embassy in Port-au-Prince, Haiti, as part of Operation Uphold Democracy. Our mission was to protect the American diplomatic mission during its efforts to return the legitimately elected government of Haiti to power, following a military coup. My platoon then supported Operation Sea Signal to return Cuban migrants from Panama to camps at Guantanamo Bay, Cuba. In addition, we supported Operation Fairwinds as part of the United States Support Group Haiti to help rebuild the infrastructure of the country and facilitate its further development as a stable democracy in the Western Hemisphere. We also provided security for the transfer of nuclear fuels, and concluded our tour together with an antiterrorism mission in Bahrain to protect American lives and property following a terrorist attack in Riyadh, Saudi Arabia, that killed nineteen U.S. service members and wounded five hundred.[15]

In 1997, I graduated from the U.S. Army's Advanced Infantry Officer Course as a captain and received command of a rifle company of approximately two hundred Marines and sailors. The strategic environment and our national military strategy continued to evolve. The 1997 NMS acknowledged a "lower threshold of global war," and identified the regional dangers represented by Iran, Iraq, and North Korea as the principal threats to our nation.[16] It also identified state and nonstate actors, such as terrorists and transnational dangers including extremism, ethnic and religious disputes, crime, and refugees, as asymmetric challenges to U.S. national security. It warned of wildcards, synergistic combinations of these threats employing new technologies. This new strategy called for the military to "shape" the international environment and "respond" to the full spectrum of crisis, while "preparing now" for an "uncertain future."[17] Although Goldwater-Nichols was already eleven years old, this strategy also called for "the greatest joint focus of any military strategy to date."[18]

My service continued to parallel the current NMS. Having prevented terrorist acts as a platoon commander with FAST Company, I unfortunately had to respond to a terrorist attack as a company commander when elements of my company deployed to Nairobi, Kenya. We were there in support of Operation Resolute Response following a deadly assault on the U.S. embassy that left more than two hundred dead and five thousand wounded.[19] The stark reality that there are those who want to kill innocent people and destroy the American way of life struck me as I walked the halls of the destroyed embassy.

Carrying this thought forward I prepared for other challenges and honed my amphibious skills on board ship as part of a Marine expeditionary unit (MEU). Graduating to the operational level of war, after serving at the tactical level for the first ten years of my career, I was assigned to Joint Task Force Skilled Anvil as a newly promoted major. My task was to plan for a military intervention in the Balkans to address a growing "regional danger."[20] Following this experience in learning the operational art on the job, I received a formal education on its nuances as a student at the Marine Corps Command and Staff College (CSC).

World events precipitated a dramatic shift in the focus of the military, as I graduated from CSC and the world entered the twenty-first century, with the terrorist attacks on 11 September 2001. The security environment again evolved and became more complex with the new war on terrorism, and there were profound impacts on the way the armed forces organized, trained for, and conducted military operations. The 2004 NMS now categorized security challenges as falling into four types: traditional, irregular, catastrophic, and disruptive.[21]

The days of a near-peer competitor for the United States appeared to be gone. The nation now prepared to engage adversaries from anywhere to include our own citizens in the continental United States and abroad. Technological advancements also expanded the battlespace to such new domains as cyber and space. Fate and timing worked against me again, as I began a three-year tour on recruiting duty just as this new war began. But it would be no short war, and I would get my opportunity to engage our nation's enemies.

After learning valuable lessons about recruiting, I deployed with another MEU as the executive officer of a battalion landing team. I was reminded that Mother Nature could be our greatest adversary; my unit responded to the devastating Indian Ocean earthquake and tsunami of December 2004, which killed more than 250,000 people.[22] Our unit rendered humanitarian assistance to Indonesia and Sri Lanka as part of Operation Unified Assistance. We then continued to Baghdad, Iraq, to participate in Operation Iraqi Freedom.

The insurgency there was expanding as we arrived. My experiences at that time would prove invaluable during my second deployment to Iraq, when I was a staff officer with the 1st Marine Expeditionary Force (Forward) and liaison to special operations forces in Fallujah. The skills and knowledge assisted me further when I commanded approximately 1,200 Marines, sailors, and soldiers, conducting counterinsurgency operations along the Syrian border during a third deployment to Iraq, as a lieutenant colonel. I was fortunate to receive the unwavering support of the American public during these deployments and learned to leverage their support not only to care for our Marines and their families but also to accomplish our missions by facilitating their relationship with our Iraqi counterparts and by supporting our development efforts.

In my tour, at the National War College (NWC) in Washington, D.C., I began to learn the art of making strategy. The courses there taught senior officers from all services and other federal employees how to develop broader approaches to strategic challenges and provided insight into interagency and other elements of national power. Upon graduation, I used my next assignment—to the Strategic Plans and Policies (J5) Directorate of how the Joint Staff at the Pentagon—to apply my newly acquired skills and see how the policies, directives, and decisions made at the strategic level translated into the development of campaigns at the operational level. Understanding how campaigns orchestrate tactical actions to achieve strategic ends also reinforces how tactical actions can have strategic implications in today's connected world.

A further tour in Washington as director of the Marine Corps Liaison for the U.S. House of Representatives continued my education in strategic leadership. I saw the synergistic relationship between the legislative and executive branches in defining national security requirements and how Congress authorizes military action by allocating resources. Our civilian leaders' commitment to national defense impressed me and helped prepare me for greater challenges.

Returning to the operational forces, I received the distinct honor of being given command of the nearly five thousand Marines and sailors of the Corps' most decorated regiment, the Fighting 5th Marines. The security environment, as recognized by the 2011 NMS, continued to evolve—as it has throughout my career. The NMS identified the need for a more flexible, agile, and adaptable force for the future, as operations in Iraq concluded and forces began to drawdown in Afghanistan.[23] The attack on 11 September 2012 reinforced this belief. On that date heavily armed Islamist militants launched an organized attack on the U.S. diplomatic mission and CIA compound in Benghazi, Libya, killing four Americans including Ambassador Chris Stevens.

The military's inability to provide an adequate response during that crisis prompted the armed forces to develop methods and units to ensure this type of tragedy would not be repeated. The Marine Corps established a new organization, called the Special Purpose Marine Air Ground Task Force Crisis Response (SPMAGTF-CR), to meet this need. The first SPMAGTF-CR was established to support operations in Africa and Europe. I received the task of leading the 5th Marines in establishing another SPMAGTF to support the Central Command commander in the Middle East. This new unit was designated Special Purpose Marine Air Ground Task Force, Crisis Response, Central Command (SPMAGTF-CR-CC). The 5th Marines led the effort in building, equipping, training, leading, and deploying this force to respond rapidly to crisis or contingency.

The SPMAGTF-CR-CC did not have to wait long for a crisis to occur. The Islamic State of Iraq and the Levant (ISIL) attacked in northern Iraq in June 2014, just as our unit made final preparations for deploying that September. The ISIL forces quickly captured the key city of Mosul and launched another attack from the west. It quickly defeated Iraqi Security Force (ISF) units or forced them to retreat, though some heroically fought back and held on. The pending deployment of the SPMAGTF-CR-CC took on increasing importance.

As a Marine Air Ground Task Force (MAGTF), our unit was task organized with organic command, ground, air, and logistics combat elements to prosecute a full range of military operations. For crisis response, SPMAGTF-CR-CC operated in eleven different countries performing a number of varied missions. We reinforced the U.S. embassies in Baghdad, Iraq, and Sana, Yemen; provided the theater's Tactical Recovery of Aircraft and Personnel (TRAP) to rescue downed pilots and conduct theater-wide casualty evacuation; and established a crisis response force able to react within six hours of notification. We also assisted partner nations with building their capabilities and capacities to confront security challenges. Our unit conducted active air strikes to destroy ISIL forces in Iraq and Syria. We supported special operations forces in Iraq and established a task force in Iraq to partner with Iraqi Security Forces in degrading and defeating ISIL in the western Euphrates River valley. We conducted these tasks in support of what became known as Operation Inherent Resolve.

Since returning from my fourth deployment to Iraq, I have had time to reflect on serving our great nation in uniform over the last thirty years. My career journey has been often like a roller-coaster ride, with peaks and valleys of shifting priorities, fluctuating defense budgets, and corresponding changes in personnel and equipment levels, all resulting from an evolving strategic environment, emerging adversaries, and shifts of political power and worldviews from one extreme to another. But, as has always been the case, it is the duty of American men and women on the ground to make do and undertake their nation's bidding in peacetime and war. It is our responsibility to place mission accomplishment above all else, regardless of personal feelings toward policies, the amount of resources available, or the potential sacrifices required.

This book is about one Marine's experiences from the Cold War to the fight against ISIL. It provides some operational and strategic context to the operations described above, but its focus is on the tactical actions taken and some of the lessons learned. These lessons were learned by the Marines, soldiers, sailors, airmen, and international partners with whom I have had the privilege to serve in achieving operational objectives and national strategic ends. It is a compilation of sea stories—some funny, some sad, all evocative of the sights, sounds, and adventures of the American serviceman as seen through my eyes. I hope you enjoy the journey.

★

Marine Culture, Warfighting, and Desert Storm

In order to appreciate better many of the characters in the following chapters, one must first understand the culture of the Marine Corps. It is an organization like no other. Born on 10 November 1775, the Marine Corps is older than the nation it defends. Initially established to fight at sea and conduct military operations ashore, it has a role that has changed little over the past 241 years.

Many over the years have questioned why our nation needs a Marine Corps—smallest of all the services and professing to fight on land, sea, and air—when it has an Army, Navy, and Air Force just as capable in these domains, but on a grander scale. Lt. Gen. Victor Krulak answered this question when he stated, "The United States does not *need* a Marine Corps[:] . . . the United States *wants* a Marine Corps."[1] General Krulak's book *First to Fight* is worth reading—it provides a great historical perspective and rationale for this "want." I offer enduring cultural perspectives in the following section as examples of what drives the strong desire for a Marine Corps and helped convinced me to devote a lifetime within its ranks to our country's service.

Marine Culture

Marines are *fighters and winners*. Marines have an illustrious history of victory in battle and success in any assigned mission across the range of military operations. Whether feeding a starving child or defeating an enemy in combat, Marines have proven time and again that they can "get it done." They are either fierce fighters or compassionate people, depending on the circumstances. Phrases such as "Send in the Marines," "First to fight," "Ready," and "Nobody likes to fight, but someone needs to know how" are more than catchy recruiting poster slogans; they stand on the fact that every Marine is a fighter regardless of his or her military occupational specialty. The Marine Corps follows an ethos of every Marine being a "rifleman." This mind-set and the skills associated with it begin in boot camp and officer candidate school, to be reinforced throughout a Marine's time in service.

Marines are always *ready*. The Marine Corps' reputation as "America's 911 Force" rests on law reinforced by countless examples of its rapid response to crises and contingencies around the world. When deliberating on the roles and responsibilities of the armed forces in 1952, the Eighty-Second Congress defined the Marine Corps as the nation's shock troops and wrote into Public Law 416 that the Marine Corps "must be the most ready when the nation is generally least ready . . . to provide a balanced force in readiness . . . a ground and air striking force ready to suppress or contain international disturbances short of large-scale war."[2]

The nation demanded, and still demands, a relevant force that can successfully address crisis and contingencies today. The Marine Corps achieves this high state of readiness by maintaining forward-deployed and forward-engaged operational forces, keeping forces in the United States on high alert for rapid deployments, and maintaining an institutional, expeditionary mindset that is understood by all Marines and sailors serving with Marines.

Marines are *expeditionary*. They are accustomed to conducting operations in foreign lands and under normally austere conditions. Known for effectiveness in "every clime and place," Marines are comfortable moving into environments with little or no services, support, or resources. Marine units operate as Marine Air Ground Task Forces with their own organic command, ground, air, and logistics combat elements. This affords the ability to be self-mobile, self-supporting, and self-sufficient. MAGTFs can operate independently for set periods of time without being tied to external support, which enables them to respond rapidly, move quickly, and adapt to changing situations on the fly. Marines are built purposely to win battles, not wars. They are the nation's middleweight force, heavier than special operation forces but lighter than the Army. Marines' close tie to the Navy facilitates their expeditionary capabilities.

The Marine Corps has a *naval character*. The Corps was created to serve with the U.S. fleet. From the days of fighting from the riggings of sailing ships during the Revolutionary War to executing a range of military operations from today's amphibious warships, the complementary capabilities of the Navy/Marine Corps team have been a winning combination. Deployed Marines derive strength from their close integration with the Navy and the inherent security, survivability, and flexibility provided by amphibious warships partnered with MAGTFs. The Navy also provides medical, dental, and religious support to the Marine Corps for its most precious asset—its people.

Above all, the Marine Corps is a *people-oriented* organization. Where the Navy prioritizes ships, the Air Force planes, and the Army tanks, artillery, and other inanimate objects, the Marine Corps focuses its efforts and resources on its people. While understanding that technology and weapons are important and have their place, the Marine Corps internalizes the concept that "war is a violent struggle between two hostile, independent, and irreconcilable wills, each trying to impose itself on the other."[3] The Marine Corps therefore instills in its people a mentality and belief that there is no challenge too great and no obstacle too high for them to overcome. It trains its people to be flexible and adaptable problem solvers, comfortable operating in uncertain and chaotic environments. Sixty-one percent of all Marines are twenty-five years old or younger; the Corps conditions Marines to lead even at the most junior levels.[4] Past experiences in war indicate that senior leaders often become casualties in combat and that it will often fall on junior Marines to accomplish the mission. Marines will do this because they refuse to let each other, or the Corps, down.

Marines are *faithful.* The Marine Corps' motto is *Semper Fidelis,* Latin for "Always Faithful." They are faithful to their God, country, and Corps, and their Corps consists of their fellow Marines. There is no such thing as an ex-Marine. Once an individual earns the title "Marine" through the crucible of Marine Corps boot camp or officer candidate school, that identity remains for life—once a Marine, always a Marine. Marines derive strength in combat through an inseparable bond and esprit de corps fostered through shared experiences of hardship, sacrifice, and loss. Known for doing more with less and always accomplishing their mission, Marines take great pride in being disciplined, smart, and physically and mentally tough. They refuse to let past generations of Marines down by blemishing the reputation of the Corps.

Marines are *frugal.* This is a result of the Marine Corps being the smallest service, falling under the Department of the Navy and needing to equip itself to fight in the air, on land, and at sea, thus Marines finding themselves lacking sufficient resources. Moreover, the Marine Corps traditionally has received hand-me-down equipment from the Army and has had to prioritize its limited resources on "beans, bullets, and Band-Aids" rather than creature comforts. In fact, as of February 2016 the Marine Corps provided America with 21 percent of the infantry battalions, 15 percent of the fighter and attack aircraft, and 19 percent of the artillery battalions of the armed forces for only 7 percent of the total Department of Defense budget. Marines like to think they provide the nation with the biggest bang for the buck. The Marine Corps must consistently reinforce the knowledge of its value to the country, because its existence has been under attack since its founding.

Marines maintain a healthy *institutional paranoia*. Interservice rivalries, jealousies, and fighting over roles, responsibilities, relevance, and resources have resulted in endless battles among the service branches. The Marine Corps has often had to defend itself from annihilation—not from an enemy on the battlefield, but from the other services and politicians at home. Unfortunately, the glowing reputation earned by Marines in battle, sometimes at the expense of other services in the same operation, has caused some jealousy. This factor combined with the belief that the Marine Corps provides capabilities duplicating those in the larger services has led to attempts to reduce its size or disband it altogether. Powerful American leaders, such as Presidents George Washington, Harry S. Truman, and Dwight D. Eisenhower (all former Army officers) attempted to reduce the size and scope of the Corps. Ultimately, the superior performance and successes by Marines over the years have sustained the American people's desire for a Marine Corps. Its leaders understand that it cannot rest on its laurels, so they are constantly seeking improvement.

Marines are *visionary*. Although the nature of war is enduring, the character of war is not. Marines understand this. They are never content with being able to fight the *last* war but look to remain one step ahead of potential adversaries by developing the operating strategies and technologies needed to win the *next* war. Small wars concepts, amphibious warfare, close air support, and the employment of the amphibious tractor, helicopter, and tilt-rotor aircraft are all examples of Marines leading in new and innovative ways. The post–Vietnam War era presented major challenges for the Marine Corps but also provided a period of increased budgets and the impetus to redefine itself with a new vision for a post–Cold War world with new challenges.

Warfighting Doctrine

The Marine Corps entered a period of self-assessment and reflection following the Vietnam War. American national security interests shifted focus to the NATO alliance and defeating the Soviets on the plains of Europe with large mechanized forces. Just as the Air Force had reigned supreme with its strategic bombers in the post–World War II nuclear age, the Army became the force of choice with its large conventional mechanized forces. Many critics saw no role for the lightly armed, seaborne Marines in this new fight. However, the Marines found their niche in the defense of NATO's northern flank. Understanding the importance of maintaining the sea lines of communication between the United States and its allies in the North Atlantic, Marines focused on the defense of Iceland, Norway, and Denmark—hence my early lessons as a midshipman.

However, world events again drove change. A revolution in Iran, civil wars in Central America and Lebanon, Soviet intervention in Afghanistan, and other events broadened the opportunities for the Marine Corps. The transition to an all-volunteer force and the inauguration of President Ronald Reagan brought a period of drastic personnel changes and increased defense budgets that enabled the modernization of Marine Corps weapons, vehicles, and aircraft and recruitments of higher-quality personnel. The only missing ingredient was a warfighting doctrine to define how Marines would think and operate successfully on future battlefields.

Gen. Alfred Gray became the commandant of the Marine Corps in July 1987, one year after I first donned a uniform and began lessons on how to defeat the Soviets. His appointment was timely. The Marine Corps was still reeling from multiple blows—the loss of 241 Marines in the bombing of the Marine Barracks in Beirut in 1983, the alleged divulging by two Marine embassy security guards of sensitive information to the Soviets, and Lt. Col. Oliver North's implication in the Iran-Contra affair. General Gray was what the Marine Corps needed as he led the Corps in a "crusade of self-improvement and plotted a course to redefine the Marine Corps for the post–Cold War era."[5] He established a warfighting doctrine that drove my future actions in peace and war.

General Gray's Fleet Marine Force Manual 1, *Warfighting*, first published in 1989 and updated as Marine Corps Doctrinal Publication 1, *Warfighting* in 1997, remains the definitive document that shapes the way Marines think, prepare, and conduct operations.[6] Marines have a bias for action, and *Warfighting* provides broad guidance to direct these actions.

It utilizes concepts and values to describe the philosophy through which Marines form their approach to success on and off the battlefield. Its four chapters describe the nature and theory as well as the preparations for and the conduct of war.

As an expeditionary force and the smallest service, the Marine Corps must fight in a way in which it can "win quickly against a larger foe on his home soil with minimal casualties and limited external support."[7] *Warfighting* labels this concept "Maneuver Warfare." Maneuver Warfare represents "a warfighting philosophy that seeks to shatter the enemy's cohesion through a variety of rapid, focused, and unexpected actions, which create a turbulent and rapidly deteriorating situation with which the enemy cannot cope."[8] It calls for focusing on the enemy, bypassing his strengths, and striking his weaknesses with a faster tempo against which he cannot respond effectively. The goal is to present adversaries with dilemmas from which there is no escape.

Independent-minded Marines, bold of thought and action, are necessary to operationalize this concept. The Corps fosters a philosophy of command that enables decentralized action based on a commander's intent and mission tactics that encourage initiative and freedom of action. This mindset is ingrained along the entire chain of command from private to general. I first discerned this approach as a newly commissioned second lieutenant in 1990 when attending The Basic School.

The Basic School

The Basic School is where all newly commissioned Marine officers and appointed warrant officers receive their introduction to the science and art of being officers of Marines. It is located on Marine Corps Base (MCB) Quantico, otherwise known as the "Crossroads of the Corps," in northern Virginia. Established in 1917, MCB Quantico was the principal training base for Marines deploying to fight in World War I. It earned its title as the "Crossroads" due to the many diverse organizations it houses, including TBS.

Following the ethos of "every Marine a rifleman," TBS trains and educates lieutenants in the individual and collective skills necessary to lead a platoon of riflemen. All lieutenants go through a six-month period of instruction broken into four phases. The first phase consists of individual skills and includes such tasks as leadership, rifle and pistol qualifications, land navigation, water survival, martial arts, and communications training. This phase sets the conditions for transitioning to the collective skills

MCDP 1

Warfighting

U.S. Marine Corps

PCN 142 000006 00

Marine Corps Doctrinal Publication 1 (MCDP 1), *Warfighting*, is the definitive document that shapes the way Marines prepare for and conduct operations. It provides broad guidance and utilizes concepts and values to describe the philosophy through which Marines form their approach to success on and off the battlefield. *Author collection* required for training later at the level of the squad, thirteen Marines. Training in the second phase includes decision making, combined-arms operations, offensive and defensive operations, scouting, patrolling, and other squad tactics. The third phase consists of combining the efforts of three squads to operate as a platoon and includes crew-served weapons, convoy operations, engineering training, and other advanced skills. The final phase conditions lieutenants to think beyond the basic unit to understand their roles as part of an integrated MAGTF, the Marine Corps' principal organization for conducting all missions across the range of military operations. In addition, lieutenants learn the Marine Corps organization, history, and traditions; drill and ceremonies; administration; intelligence; logistics; first aid; legal; and much more.

Performance at TBS determines a lieutenant's future military occupational specialty (MOS), but only after the instructors have made it emphatically clear that it is the title of "Marine," and not what one does as a Marine that matters most. All events at TBS possess different weights and grades, and they each fall under one of four categories: leadership, military skills, academics, and physical fitness. The school evaluates lieutenants in different leadership positions and expects them to perform well throughout the course. It also tests them in physical fitness and military skills events to determine their overall aptitude for being successful leaders. The cumulative average of each event determines the lieutenant's class standing in a class of approximately 250.

I found TBS to be an exhilarating and enjoyable experience. The knowledge learned and friendships forged during this formative period prepared me well. I consider my brothers in Fox Company Class of 1990 ("Fox 90") to be some of my best friends even today because of our shared experiences. One particular episode at TBS stands out. Our company was split into two opposing forces for an exercise, and my unit had the mission of conducting a night ambush in a cold and wet midwinter. We had been in the field (the woods) all week, and every piece of gear we had was waterlogged after days of snow, sleet, and rain. We tried to stay warm by putting on every layer of clothing we had, but this only reduced our mobility and made us look like Michelin—or Stay Puft Marshmallow—men.

Our mission was to ambush a resupply convoy, and we settled in around midnight to wait. Everyone was nodding in and out of sleep, shivering a mile a minute, and one of my peers was lying on top of me to conserve body heat. After approximately two hours, I heard a whimper, which grew louder, and then I felt my buddy's body begin to quiver.

I knew he was miserable, and I heard him start to pray, "Oh God, please let the trucks arrive so we can kill them and get out of here." At that point I told my buddy to shut up. The trucks arrived; we dutifully engaged them with blank ammunition and artillery simulators and then withdrew. Having grown up in upstate New York and attended school in Chicago, I know what it means to be cold, but that night in Quantico was the coldest of my life, so I can't blame my buddy too much for crying, although I was still glad when he became a pilot and not an infantryman. That night, however, cemented Fox 90 as a unit and began our transformation into officers of Marines.

This experience and others at TBS provided the foundation for my goal of becoming a leader of Marines, a goal I had had since my youngest days. In fact, my mother still has a letter from a Marine major in her scrapbook that states, "Dear Jason, thank you for your interest in the Marine Corps, but seeing as though you are only 12 years old, we can't help you at this time." The major recommended I remain in school and contact him when I was ready to graduate. Little did I know that I would follow in his footsteps and eventually become "that major" as the commanding officer of my own recruiting station, but that's a story for a later chapter.

TBS also holds a warm place in my heart because I married my best friend at the Marine Corps Memorial Chapel at Quantico, while attending the school. I would be lying if I said our relationship has always been smooth; we have had our ups and downs over the years. For example, my wife was not happy when I told her to never make me choose between her and the Marine Corps, because she would not like the outcome. I will admit I was young and dumb at the time and can honestly say I would hang up my uniform willingly to spend the rest of my life with her if given that ultimatum today.

Military families, and particularly military spouses, are heroes. They often sacrifice more than the uniformed member in a relationship. My wife often found herself keeping the home fires burning, being a mother, father, financial manager, disciplinarian, taxi driver, housekeeper, and every other role required to maintain our household and raise our children alone while I was off training or on deployment for months at a time.

Spouses are critically important to the military. My wife provides me with much-needed balance between my personal and professional lives and sustains me through the good times and bad. She has always been a confidante with whom I can share my joys, concerns, frustrations, and achievements, and has enabled and helped guide me as we have traveled through our life's journey. My joy at being a newlywed at TBS was amplified when I heard I had received my first choice, that of becoming an infantry officer following graduation.

The Infantry Officer Course

It is recognized in the Marine Corps that every asset in the operating forces exists to support the infantryman on the ground. This belief is an extension of the ethos that every Marine is a rifleman. However, being riflemen and infantrymen are two separate and distinct functions. Infantry is a specific MOS, one that requires more advanced skills than that of a basic rifleman. Although traditionally considered hard and disciplined, but not necessarily the sharpest tools in the shed, the infantrymen of today must be masters of both the science and art of warfighting. They must conduct myriad complex operations across the spectrum of conflict, as not only fierce warriors but also humanitarians, peacekeepers, culturists, city managers, and diplomats.

Today's infantrymen operate on the world stage where their tactical actions on the battlefield can be immediately broadcast across the globe and have strategic implications. General Krulak understood this when he coined the phrase "strategic corporal" to accompany his concept of the Three Block War.[9] He identified all Marines as requiring unwavering maturity, judgment, and strength of character so they could make well-reasoned and independent decisions under extreme stress as visible symbols of American foreign policy.

The strategic corporals of today receive this training at one of two Marine Corps Schools of Infantry (SOI)—one at Camp Lejeune, North Carolina, the other at Camp Pendleton, California. Just as all officers go through TBS to forge a common bond as MAGTF officers before they receive specialized MOS training, all enlisted Marines receive Marine Combat Training (MCT) prior to attending their respective MOS schools. Those Marines designated for the infantry field remain at the SOIs to learn the advanced skills required for an infantryman. Enlisted specialties within the infantry field include rifleman, machine gunner, mortarman, assaultman, reconnaissance man, and light armored vehicle crewman. Infantry officers are generalists and have expertise in each of these specialties. All infantry officers receive additional training at the Infantry Officer Course (IOC) in Quantico, following graduation from TBS.

At the time I attended, IOC was a ten-week, MOS-producing school consisting of intensive classroom instruction, practical application, and field training.[10] Instruction occurred in weapon operation and employment and the conduct of a plethora of ground combat tasks—offense, defense, patrolling, and reconnaissance among others. The mission of the school continues to be to prepare infantry officers to serve as platoon commanders in the operating forces.

Graduates of IOC can expect assignments as commanders for rifle platoon, reconnaissance platoon, weapons platoon (60-mm mortar, squad multipurpose assault weapons, and medium machine guns), or heavy-weapons platoon (81-mm mortar, antiarmor, and heavy machine guns) within an infantry or reconnaissance battalion. Infantry officers can also be selected to serve in a Light Armored Reconnaissance (LAR) battalion after completing an additional six-week LAR crewman course conducted at the School of Infantry. LAVs are eight-wheeled vehicles of different configurations that provide highly mobile and lethal ground reconnaissance capability.

Students attending IOC spend most of the ten-week course living in the field while learning how to shoot, move, and communicate as infantrymen, also affectionately known as grunts. I became so accustomed to living in the field that one day while in "the rear" and having to relieve myself, I actually started to undo my fly in public, before I caught myself.

Operation Desert Shield

The training I received at TBS and IOC in Quantico in 1990 took on increased urgency as it appeared the nation was heading for war. Iraq invaded Kuwait on 2 August 1990, just two days before my wedding and a year after the fall of the Soviet Union. Iraq faced a declining economy exacerbated by massive foreign debt incurred during its eight-year war with Iran and dropping oil prices brought on in part by the decision by Kuwait and Saudi Arabia to overproduce oil. Saddam Hussein, Iraq's president, also believed that he was destined to unite the Arab people and that the United States and Israel were conspiring against Iraq with the assistance of the Kuwaitis and Saudis. Iraq possessed the fourth-largest military in the world in 1990, with over 1 million troops, 6,000 armored personnel carriers, 5,000 tanks, 3,500 artillery pieces, 600 surface-to-air missiles, and 500 fixed- and 500 rotary-winged aircraft.[11] Hussein did not believe the United States possessed the resolve to respond to conflict in the region. These factors convinced him that Iraq could invade and annex Kuwait successfully.[12]

Iraq's supposedly elite Republican Guard led the invasion, using four columns attacking from the north and west to seize Kuwait quickly.

Saddam Hussein directed the immediate construction of formidable defensive works consisting of tank ditches, berms, and minefields along two defensive belts covered by strongpoints equipped with tanks and artillery stretching from the coastline across Kuwait and oriented toward Saudi Arabia. By taking Kuwait and its Persian Gulf coast, Saddam would dominate oil production and the Middle East, a goal the international community refused to allow.

The United Nations acted quickly in condemning the invasion, and the United States formed a coalition that included partnered western and friendly Arab countries. As diplomats worked to find a peaceful solution, President George H. W. Bush put the military into motion in what would become the largest employment of U.S. military power since the Vietnam War. The immediate requirement was to defend Saudi Arabia from further Iraqi aggression.

This first phase of a larger operation became known as Operation Desert Shield. The Air Force 1st Tactical Fighter Wing deployed to Saudi Arabia and began conducting combat air patrols on 9 August, just as elements of the U.S. Army 82nd Airborne Division began arriving in Saudi Arabia. The cruisers, destroyers, and frigates of the U.S. Navy's Joint Task Force Middle East were already on station in the Persian Gulf. On 10 August, Gen. Norman Schwarzkopf, the commander in chief of U.S. Central Command, requested three Marine Expeditionary Brigades (MEB), the Marine Corps midlevel Marine Air Ground Task Forces.

Marine Air Ground Task Force

As discussed earlier, the MAGTF is the Marine Corps' principal organization for all military operations. Each MAGTF consists of four elements: command (CE), ground combat (GCE), air combat (ACE), and logistic combat (LCE). MAGTFs are tailorable and can be organized by task with specific capabilities to accomplish any mission across a range of military operations, including forcible-entry amphibious assaults. They can project combat power ashore in measured degrees to conduct operations or secure staging areas as a base for follow-on forces. MAGTFs provide senior leaders a "rheostat" of options and force packages.[13]

MAGTFs come in three standard sizes: the Marine Expeditionary Force (MEF), Marine Expeditionary Brigade (MEB), and Marine Expeditionary Unit (MEU). The MEF is the largest of the MAGTFs. It is commanded by a lieutenant general (three stars). A MEF normally consists of between

20,000 and 90,000 Marines and sailors organized into a division for the GCE, a Marine Air Wing for the ACE, and a Marine Logistics Group for the LCE. There are three standing MEFs: I MEF based at Camp Pendleton, California; II MEF at Camp Lejeune, North Carolina; and III MEF at Okinawa, Japan. Each MEF normally deploys with sixty days of sustainment.

The MEB is the middle-sized MAGTF. Either brigadiers (one star) or major generals (two stars) command MEBs. A MEB normally consists of approximately 17,000 Marines and sailors organized into a Regimental Landing Team (RLT) for the GCE, Marine Air Group (MAG) for the ACE, and Combat Logistics Regiment (CLR) for the LCE. There are currently four standing MEBS that correspond with the MEFs. The 1st MEB is part of I MEF, 2nd MEB is part of II MEF, and 3rd MEB is part of III MEF, and there is a newly formed 5th MEB established in the Middle East as of 2015. MEBs normally deploy with thirty days' sustainment.

The MEU is the smallest of the MAGTFs. It is commanded by a colonel. An MEU normally consists of approximately 2,200 Marines and sailors organized into a Battalion Landing Team (BLT) for the GCE, composite squadron for the ACE, and Combat Logistics Battalion (CLB) for the LCE. There are seven standing MEU command elements; the 11th, 13th, and 15th MEUs are part of I MEF and based in Camp Pendleton; the 22nd, 24th, and 26th MEUs are part of II MEF and based in Camp Lejeune; and the 31st MEU is part of III MEF in Okinawa. MEUs normally deploy with fifteen days of sustainment. All MAGTFs are scalable and organized by task to meet mission requirements.

Maritime Prepositioning Force

In response to General Schwarzkopf's request for three MEBs, the 7th MEB (subsequently disbanded) began to arrive in Saudi Arabia on 14 August 1990 to join up with equipment forward deployed as part of a new concept called the Maritime Prepositioning Force (MPF). Then–Secretary of Defense Harold Brown had first proposed the MPF concept in 1979 in response to a perceived weakness in America's ability to project power.[14] Although the United States maintained large bases in Europe and the Pacific during the Cold War, it had little combat power forward deployed in the Middle East.

The MPF concept was part of the newly developed Rapid Joint Deployment Task Force. It consisted of embarking a mechanized MEB's worth of gear, equipment, and thirty days of sustainment for 17,000 Marines on board a squadron of U.S. Military Sealift Command vessels.[15] Three squadrons (only two—more capable—standing squadrons exist today), each carrying an MEB's worth of gear, were created. Navy officers commanded each squadron, while civilian merchant marines manned the MPF ships. The three squadrons deployed to the Mediterranean Sea and Indian and Pacific Oceans.

The concept called for deployed Marines from the United States using Air Force strategic airlift or Civilian Air Fleet aircraft to meet an MPF squadron at secured airfields and ports. It took approximately three days to unload the MEB's gear and equipment before employment.[16] The prepositioning program also included the land-based Norway Air-Landed Marine Expeditionary Brigade (renamed the Marine Corps Prepositioning Program—Norway) program described in the introduction.

Operation Desert Storm

The 7th MEB was the first ground element to arrive in theater with enough tanks, armored personnel carriers, organic aircraft, and sustainment to pose a serious threat to the Iraqis. Although elements of the 82nd Airborne had arrived in Saudi Arabia approximately a week before, they had deployed with only two days of sustainment and no heavy weapons or vehicles. The 1st MEB, which deployed from Hawaii at the time, and a second MPF squadron joined the 7th MEB by the end of the month.

The two MEBs consolidated and reorganized as part of the 1st Marine Division when Lt. Gen. Walter Boomer deployed with his I MEF Headquarters and took command of all Marine forces in theater on 3 September 1990. Boomer had been commissioned in 1960 after graduating from Duke University and served as an infantry officer with distinction, earning several combat decorations in Vietnam. He commanded units at every level prior to assuming command of the I MEF and went on later to be assistant commandant of the Marine Corps. As commander of the I MEF, he received the task for the ground offensive phase of the campaign, which would become known as Operation Desert Storm.

Ninety-four thousand Marines had deployed to the region by February 1991.[17] This was more than had been employed during the famous Marine battles of World War II to seize Okinawa and Iwo Jima. By the time the ground offensive began, I MEF consisted of the 3rd Marine Air Wing, the 1st and 2nd Marine Divisions, and 1st Force Service Support Group (later renamed Marine Logistics Group). Not all Marines fell under the Marine component in-theater; there were two additional sea-based MEBs and a MEU deployed under the command of the Navy component commander.

Marines achieve greater operational and strategic flexibility by maintaining ties to the sea. It was common practice in 1990 for the Navy/Marine Corps Team to maintain three forward-deployed MEUs on a constant basis. An East Coast MEU deployed to cover the Atlantic and Mediterranean Sea; a West Coast MEU covered the western Pacific, Indian Ocean, and Persian Gulf; and the single Okinawa-based MEU covered the Asia-Pacific region. The 13th MEU from I MEF left on a scheduled six-month West Coast deployment from Camp Pendleton in June 1990. After training and earthquake relief in the Philippines, it conducted a port call in Hong Kong before being ordered to the Persian Gulf in response to Iraq's invasion of Kuwait. Upon arriving in theater, the 13th MEU provided security at the airfields and ports where the MEB collected MPF equipment and later moved to theater reserve with a larger amphibious force formed to respond to the crisis.

In August 1990, the 4th MEB was preparing to deploy from the East Coast to Europe for two exercises with NATO forces when it received orders for the Persian Gulf. The 4th MEB had been the Marine Corps' designated unit to protect NATO's northern flank from Soviet invasion during the Cold War and had remained focused on the area following the collapse of the Soviet Union. On receiving orders to shift focus, the MEB traded in its cold-weather gear for desert uniforms and embarked on board naval amphibious warships bound for the Persian Gulf. Only twelve of the twenty-four ships needed were available, which required the MEB to deploy its assault equipment and supplies using civilian-operated Military Sealift Command ships.[18] The shortage of required amphibious warships is a problem that continues to plague the naval services.

The 4th MEB joined with the 13th MEU to form a theater reserve. They received the "be prepared to" missions to reinforce ground forces defending Saudi Arabia and to conduct raids and assaults against the Iraqi flanks and rear, if needed. It was also hoped their presence would divert Iraqi forces to defend against a possible amphibious assault.[19] In October 1990, the 5th MEB relieved the 4th MEB in the Persian Gulf, but its mission was subsequently changed to reinforce the 4th MEB, as Boomer kept both MEBs in theater. In late November President Bush made the decision to increase the U.S. military presence in theater to approximately 500,000 personnel in preparation for a ground offensive to liberate Kuwait.

Not surprisingly, the lieutenants of Fox 90 watched the military buildup in the Middle East with great interest. The opportunity to prove ourselves in the crucible of battle appeared to be coming sooner than any of us envisioned. The notion that the lessons we were learning in the woods of Quantico would likely be applied on the battlefield in Kuwait in a few short months was exhilarating. Nevertheless, we had plenty of concerns. I particularly focused on three likely scenarios that could have grave consequences for me and the Marines I might be fortunate enough to lead. Intelligence indicated that Iraqi engineers were experts at constructing extensive defensive works based on their experience in the Iran-Iraq War. "Intel" reports identified two formidable Iraqi defensive belts—with minefields, tank ditches, berms, wire obstacles, and strongpoints—covered by large concentrations of artillery that would no doubt rain down on any forces attempting to breach them.

The second threat was Saddam Hussein's possible employment of nuclear, biological, and chemical (NBC) weapons against our forces. He already demonstrated his willingness to employ these weapons against the Iranians and his own Kurdish population during the Iran-Iraq War. There was no reason to believe he would not do the same when attacked by "infidels" from the West.

My third concern was the possibility of having to fight in the urban sprawl and metropolis of Kuwait City, where as many as a million people were living at the time. History demonstrated that combat in urban areas such as Seoul during the Korean War and Hue during the Vietnam War usually resulted in high casualty rates. A complex attack into Kuwait City had the potential of becoming another great chapter in Marine Corps history, but at a high cost. Paying particular attention to the classes on these topics during TBS, thirty-one fellow students and I then crossed the road to begin our advanced infantry training at IOC.

Opportunity Lost

The Infantry Officer Course prepared us well for the inevitable fight that was brewing in the Persian Gulf. The seriousness of our trade became apparent, when we heard rumor, with or without merit, of loss projections of 198 Marine infantry platoon commanders in the first forty-eight hours of the pending war. Our "pucker factors" increased exponentially, though, when we heard IOC was planning to increase its student throughput of the school, expanding the normal class size of approximately thirty to upward of ninety students for the next three courses.

The anticipation of battle increased on 16 January 1991 when a thirty-two-day aerial campaign to degrade and destroy Iraqi forces commenced prior to the expected ground offensive. As we continued to train, IOC's capstone training event, a nine-day "war," shifted from the Virginia woods of Quantico to the Marine Corps' premier live-fire training center in the Mojave Desert at Twentynine Palms, California. With this news came the realization that my class would likely receive orders to join the forces in the Middle East. The shift provided us with an opportunity to acclimate to a desert environment, while dramatically increasing the level of our live-fire combined-arms training. We also tested new desert gear that the Marine Corps intended to field in what was expected to be a protracted war.

The training at Twentynine Palms was outstanding, and my fellow students and I were riding high as the ground offensive in the Persian Gulf commenced on 24 February 1991. Orders were being prepared, and it looked like I would receive an assignment to the 5th MEB. I looked forward to participating; however, the campaign was over almost immediately. Often referred to as the Hundred-Hour War, the ground offensive phase of Operation Desert Storm lasted only five days. At 0400 on 24 February, the 1st and 2nd Marine Divisions attacked along two avenues of approach into Kuwait (wearing NBC suits for fear of chemical attack), while the Army's VII and XVIII Corps conducted envelopments to the northwest to cut off retreating Iraqi forces. The 532 amphibious assault vehicles, 268 tanks, 301 light armored vehicles (LAVs), and 216 artillery pieces manned by Marine divisions made quick work of the Iraqi defenders.[20]

The bubble of enthusiasm my IOC peers and I felt quickly deflated as we waited for our flight back to Quantico on 28 February and discovered that President Bush had just ordered a cease-fire. The Marines in Kuwait had performed superbly. For the loss of nine aircraft, twenty-four killed, and ninety-two wounded, the Marines captured more than 23,000 prisoners and destroyed over a thousand tanks, six hundred armored personnel carriers, four hundred artillery pieces, and countless enemy soldiers.[21] The tenets of Fleet Marine Force Manual I *Warfighting* had proven their worth, even though no orders to the Middle East were forthcoming for me. I received instead orders to Camp Pendleton to join the 3rd Battalion, 9th Marines, which had just fought its way through the obstacle belts of Kuwait as part of the 1st Marine Division.

★

The Infantry, Okinawa, and "Bohm's Bastards"

The Infantry

Although disappointed that I had missed Operation Desert Storm, I remained excited about joining my first unit. The 3rd Battalion, 9th Marines (3/9) was part of a larger hierarchy of warfighting units organized into the 1st Marine Division. A division is the largest ground combat element in the Marine Corps. The smallest maneuver unit is a fireteam. A fireteam consists of four men: a fireteam leader, a rifleman, an automatic rifleman, and an assistant automatic rifleman. The fireteam leader is normally a corporal, armed with a M16 service rifle. It has an M203 grenade launcher attached, so he can also act as a grenadier.

The fireteam organizes and trains for maneuver warfare in its most basic form. The rifleman engages enemy forces with direct fire. If the enemy finds cover for protection against direct fire, the fireteam leader engages the enemy with indirect fire, which produces a blast effect and shrapnel that reach behind the cover. This places the enemy in the horns of a dilemma. Whether he exposes himself to direct fire in the open or to indirect fire behind cover, he loses. The fireteam also possesses an automatic rifleman who provides a large volume of fire to suppress and destroy enemy forces to allow the other members of his team to maneuver.

The application of maneuver warfare, with the tools and capabilities to employ it, increases in complexity as units get larger. A Marine squad consists of three fireteams, led by a sergeant. Three thirteen-man squads combine under a platoon sergeant and platoon commander to create a platoon. Squads have Navy corpsmen to provide medical aid during combat, but a single corpsman per platoon during peace. Platoon sergeants are normally staff noncommissioned officers, and platoon commanders are normally lieutenants, the first officer in the chain of command. Platoons can vary in size but are usually between thirty-five and fifty Marines.

Three rifle platoons and a weapons platoon combine to create an infantry company. A captain with a first sergeant as his senior enlisted adviser commands a company. Companies can vary in size, but generally range between 150 and 250 Marines and sailors.

Three rifle companies, a heavy weapons company, and a Headquarters and Service company combine to form a battalion. A lieutenant colonel with a sergeant major as his senior enlisted adviser commands a battalion. Battalions also vary in size, but generally range between 850 and 1,200 Marines and sailors depending on how the unit is organized.

Three or four battalions and a headquarters company form a regiment. A colonel, with a sergeant major as his senior enlisted adviser, commands a regiment. Regiments too can vary in size, ranging from 3,000 to 5,000 Marines and sailors. The regiment is the largest all-infantry unit in the Marine Corps.

Three infantry regiments combine with an artillery regiment and headquarters battalion and separate tank, light armored reconnaissance, ground reconnaissance, combat engineer, and assault-amphibian-vehicle battalions to form a division in the Marine Corps. A major general with a senior sergeant major as his senior enlisted adviser commands a division. Divisions can also vary in size, generally between 20,000 and 25,000 Marines and sailors. All Marine Corps units have a baseline-task organization, but can detach, or attach, Marines and capabilities to reorganize as the mission requires.

Camp Pendleton

At the time I joined 3/9, it was one of four infantry battalions constituting the 7th Marine Regiment (see below for why not the 9th). Although the 7th Marines' headquarters and its other three battalions (1/7, 2/7, and 3/7) permanently transferred to the Marine Corps' desert training center at Twentynine Palms, 3/9 remained at Camp Pendleton, in California, along the Pacific coast.

Camp Pendleton is the Marine Corps' premier amphibious training base on the West Coast. Its history goes back to 20 July 1769, when a

Spaniard, Capt. Gaspar de Portolá, led an expeditionary force to establish Franciscan missions throughout California.[1] He baptized the land, where the base now stands, on that day in the name of Santa Margarita. The land became private property granted by the governor of California following Mexico's independence from Spain in 1821. Its owners used it as a cattle ranch, Rancho Santa Margarita y Las Flores, for many years until the U.S. government purchased most of it in 1942.

The beauty of the 122,798 acres of Camp Pendleton is both a blessing and a curse for Marines fortunate enough to be stationed there. Although pleasant most of the year, weather in Camp Pendleton can be deadly. Torrential downpours can cause sudden flooding, resulting in swelling rivers and grave consequences. The Santa Margarita River, which runs parallel to the Marine Corps Air Station, overflowed and carried helicopters away in 1993. A battalion commander was killed when a dry river bed near the School of Infantry quickly became a roaring river and carried him away when the ground collapsed. Although sunny and in the 70°–80° Fahrenheit range most of the year, it snows and sleets at the higher elevations on base, and Marines can experience hypothermia. Wildfires can spread quickly during the dry seasons.

My sergeant major and I had a close call with a wildfire while I was a regimental commander responsible for one of the base's subcamps in 2014. We had gone to one of our barracks to investigate how close a major fire was getting to the camp when a three-story-high wall of flame erupted in front of us just as we arrived. It was quickly hard to see beyond the smoke and fire. Just as I was starting to get concerned, I heard the distinct sound of the dual rotors of one of the last operational CH-46 helicopters in the fleet. The helicopter swooped in and dumped a huge bucket of water right on top of the wall of flames, my sergeant major, and me, dousing the flames and us in the process. Although wet, I was more than grateful.

Many Marines who had to hike or run up them since Camp Pendleton first opened have cursed its many high and rolling hills and peaks. In fact, the Marines have hated the hills so much they have immortalized them with names like "First Sergeant," "Sergeant Major," and my favorite, "Mount Mother F—er."

Victory Parade and Community Support

The local community in Oceanside, California, was preparing for an extravagant event—the largest West Coast victory celebration since World War II—as my wife and I checked into Camp Pendleton in April 1991.[2] One thousand Marines, representing the 94,000 who served in Desert Storm, marched in a victory parade through the city before approximately 100,000 spectators. One of my first official duties as a platoon commander was to march in the parade. My battalion was being recognized as one of the units that had gone through the breach   in Kuwait. The task troubled me at first, because I didn't feel that I deserved the recognition that those who had fought in Desert Storm so rightfully earned. As our formation of twelve columns marched abreast through downtown Oceanside, and the cheers, applause, and shouts of support became deafening, I felt less troubled. The euphoria of patriotism demonstrated by the public overcame me. I found myself lifting my chest a little higher and marching a little taller as the pride of being an American swelled within me.

It was not lost on me, or on the thousands in attendance, that the thousands of Marines and other service men and women who returned from Vietnam had not received this outpouring of love and support. There were no war protesters present on this day, as Lee Greenwood's "God Bless the U.S.A." blared over the loudspeakers. Many understood that this parade was being held as much for our Vietnam veterans as it was for the present-day Marines. The many celebrations held across the nation to welcome our warriors home, like this one in Oceanside, were therapeutic for a nation that recognized how it had mistreated those returning from Vietnam. The overwhelming support demonstrated by the local community that day has been sustained and, in fact, strengthened following the tragic events of 11 September 2001. I was later able to leverage it in helping to accomplish missions in places like Haiti and Iraq.

Okinawa and the Unit Deployment Program

Life in Camp Pendleton was good but short-lived; my battalion prepared for deployment. I was now the 3rd Platoon Commander, Lima Company, 3/9. Lima Company was an infantry company filled with highly motivated young Marines confident in their abilities. That some of them were too confident became evident in one of our first training events together, trench clearing (that is, clearing an enemy-held trench of its defenders). Marines had not focused much on trench clearing since World War I, but the extensive defensive positions erected by Iraq during Desert Storm convinced many of the necessity to become proficient in this tactic once again.

My announcement to the platoon that we would be conducting this training received a less-than-enthusiastic response and pleas of, "Come on, sir, we just spent the last seven months in the desert rehearsing this." I saw their point but needed to determine our level of proficiency, so I responded, "Show me." The result was enlightening for me and humbling for the Marines. Although many had participated in Operation Desert Storm, these Marines failed to understand in the desert that they had all held billets with less responsibility. Many of the seasoned leaders from the war had since transferred, leaving the remainder in charge. The world looks much different when you're the one in the hot seat and now have to lead. Simple lessons like this are important to learn in garrison before having to execute in war. Having established the fact that we could all learn from each other, my platoon became a tight and cohesive unit by the time we deployed to Okinawa, Japan.

Okinawa is a small island located 340 miles from the Japanese mainland. Originally an independent kingdom made up of people of Chinese, Malay, and Ainus descent, Okinawa had paid tribute to China until invaded and annexed by Japan in 1875.[3] Sixty-seven miles long and three to twenty miles wide, the island is part of the Ryukyu Archipelago. A series of ridges, cliffs, and caves dominate the geography.

Strategically, Okinawa possessed three airfields and two bays that in late World War II had been considered suitable for development as advanced naval bases for the expected invasion of mainland Japan. Okinawa was the last of a long list of islands invaded by the United States in its island-hopping campaign; it took eighty-two days to secure at the cost of over 75,000 American dead and wounded and 110,000 Japanese killed.[4] This was the bloodiest battle in the Pacific theater during World War II, in part due to the Japanese use of fanatical Kamikaze suicide air attacks—akin to the Islamic fundamentalists suicide bombings faced by Marines today.

Third Battalion, 9th Marines deployed to Okinawa in 1991 as part of the Marine Corps' Unit Deployment Program (UDP). Marines have maintained a presence on Okinawa since its capture in 1945. The number of Marines on the island has risen and fallen over the years, experiencing a peak during the Vietnam War, after which units received permanent assignments to the island. These included the 4th and 9th Marine Regiments and their respective battalions, one of which was 3/9. Marines on one-year assignments away from their families, who remained in the United States, predominately manned these units.

The Marine Corps established the UDP in 1977 to reduce the number of unaccompanied tours to Okinawa and strengthen unit cohesion. The program consisted of maintaining the 4th and 9th Marines' regimental headquarters in Okinawa but permanently assigning their respective battalions to regiments stationed in the United States. Infantry battalions would deploy as cohesive units on six-month deployments to fill the ranks of the 4th and 9th Marines on a rotational basis. This had been the reason for 3/9's assignment to the 7th Marines in the United States, and why my battalion was sent to the 4th Marines on Okinawa in 1991.

The deployment proved an action-packed UDP for 3/9. Although stationed in Okinawa, the battalion deployed elements across the Pacific on exercises and training in Japan, the Philippines, Korea, Thailand, and other areas. Unfortunately, I was unable to participate in these events, because a platoon and I received orders to support the III MEF Maritime Special Purpose Force (MSPF). The MSPF was a specially trained, low-profile unit with precision skills to perform enhanced, conventional, maritime special operations such as direct-action raids against high-value targets and in extremis hostage rescue. MSPFs possess five elements: command, reconnaissance and surveillance, security, assault, and support; I was assigned as the security platoon commander. The MSPF had to remain on Okinawa throughout the 3/9's deployment in order to rapidly respond to developing crises throughout the region if required.

I found assignment to the MSPF brought some outstanding training opportunities and a corresponding allocation of ammunition. My platoon and I spent countless hours on the range shooting thousands of rounds, honing advanced marksmanship and close-quarters battle skills taught by the III MEF Special Operations Training Group (SOTG). SOTG reinforced the seriousness of our mission by making the Marines dig graves and hold funerals for any "friendly" targets that were shot during room-clearing exercises.

My platoon also learned various methods of insertion and extraction, involving foot, vehicle, helicopters, and boats. Two of the more memorable training exercises were Special Patrol Insertion/Extraction (SPIE) training and a long-range boat raid. The SPIE system was developed during the Vietnam War as a means to insert or extract small units from areas unsuitable for landing helicopters. The system consists of lowering from a helicopter a rope with metal connectors to penetrate jungle canopy or reach to rough terrain or water. A Marine wearing a harness with attached carabiners hooks up to the metal connectors on the rope and attaches a second safety line to a second connector. The helicopter then lifts vertically, avoiding any obstacles, prior to moving forward to a secure landing zone. One cannot help but feel like Superman, dangling hundreds of feet above ground with the wind blowing through one's hair.

Operating in the open seas on a Zodiac rubber raiding craft is also exhilarating. The MSPF conducted a long-range boat raid, traveling from

Marines from the 3rd Battalion, 9th Marines Maritime Special Purpose Force conducting Special Patrol Insertion/Extraction (SPIE) training over Okinawa, Japan, in December 1991. The SPIE system was developed during the Vietnam War to insert or extract small units from areas unsuitable for landing helicopters. *Author collection*

The author rehearsing small boat operations with the 3rd Battalion, 9th Marines Maritime Special Purpose Force at Orowan Bay, Okinawa, in preparation for the "Raid from Hell" in December 1991. *Author collection*

one side of Okinawa to the other, following countless hours of swimming and boat drills in the calm waters of Orowan Bay. Little did those on the raid know when we departed in calm waters, that this exercise would forever be known as "the boat raid from hell!"

No one expected this to be a difficult training mission. We were to ride the boats to the open seas and follow a route a few miles off shore parallel to the coastline until reaching a predesignated staging point. While holding the boats at sea, we would send in scout swimmers to conduct a quick reconnaissance of the beach for enemy activity and suitability for landing. The raid force would push into the beach when signaled and stage the boats on the beach with security. We would then move inland, destroy the designated target, and return to the boats for extraction. It was all fairly straightforward, or so we thought.

All was going well, as we headed out to sea in a wedge formation (oriented like an arrow head) of ten boats. When riding in a Zodiac, Marines straddle its gunwales with one leg inside and one outside, and lean forward onto the Marine in front of them; all gear and equipment is strapped down in the center of the boat in case it broaches. I settled in for the long trip straddling the right gunnel with my head resting on the side of the right butt cheek of Lance Corporal Bryant, a bright kid from Olympia, Washington, who took well to the water. This configuration had its disadvantages, particularly on long trips. After a few hours of bouncing off the waves, with my head still resting on Bryant, the strong scent of urine overcame me, and I asked, "Bryant, did you just piss on me?" Bryant never answered, but the uncontrolled shaking of his laughter answered my question. It didn't really matter, since we were already soaking wet from the ocean, and Bryant didn't have a choice, anyway.

We continued to make periodic navigational checks using key terrain features along the coast. All seemed to be going as planned until a "fairly easy" trip became a monumental test of our boating skills and perseverance. The calm seas quickly turned heavy as an unexpected storm rolled in. Rain started to come down in torrents, degrading our ability to navigate; we lost sight of the shoreline. Sea swells increased in intensity as the night dragged on. We were wet, cold, and starting to shake in and out of sleep as the forward movement of our formation slowed in the rough seas.

Waves were breaking over the sides of the boats. At one point, starting to doze off, I quickly came to my senses as I heard, and then felt, a loud swoosh as a wave completely covered the boat. Startled, I sat upright from my crouched position and was surprised to see the boat completely filled. We were awash, and our engine had died. The coxswain yelled, "Holy shit! Start bailing!" The only things we had available to use were the knit watch caps we were wearing. Those of us in the boat started frantically bailing what water we could as the coxswain tried to start the engine. The rest of the raid force continued to push on unaware that our boat was dead in the water.

We eventually got things moving in a positive direction and caught up with the rest of the raid force, but the sea swells continued at dangerous levels. The leadership discussed the possibility of aborting the mission for safety reasons, but we had passed the point of no return. It made just as much sense to continue on as it did to turn around and return to base. As we pushed on, the swells were so high that it seemed, looking at the boats on our flanks, like we were on a roller-coaster ride. As we hit the crest of each swell, the boats on either side were down in the trough, with a twenty-foot difference in height between the boats as we constantly shifted positions up and down. I recall picturing myself jumping down into the boat on our side. In all, we spent approximately sixteen hours in the water during that exercise for the forty-five minutes it took us to destroy the target on the ground. Those of us who were on that training raid still talk about the adventure twenty-five years later.

It is exciting experiences like this boat raid that drive many Marines to want to become reconnaissance (recon), force reconnaissance, or Marine Corps Special Operations Command (MARSOC) critical-skills operators. Marines are men and women of action. The adrenaline rush experienced in performing many of the special skills they execute suits them well. It meets their appetite for adventure. I, like most of my peers, had to confront the decision to follow the conventional infantry path or pursue one of these special units.

Recon and special operations forces normally operate as small light units and are made of more senior and mature operators with advanced skills. General-purpose conventional forces consist of the full spectrum of Marines from the newly joined eighteen-year-olds to the crusty, old staff noncommissioned officers. They normally fight as larger units with heavier organic firepower than their brothers in recon and MARSOC.

I loved being an infantryman, and although I contemplated joining recon, I made my final decision while a member of the MSPF. I enjoyed leading my Marines in the many training events we conducted on Okinawa and was always riding high when we returned from our missions. However, each time I returned to the command post I would see the recon platoon commander sitting in a room in front of a bay of radios monitoring his teams that were out executing their parts of the mission. Although he got to conduct great training, the recon platoon commander's mission was to monitor the progress of his teams from the rear and report the information they provided. I preferred to participate in the missions. To be fair, recon and MARSOC officers often physically participate in missions too, but I was happy with what I was doing at that time and looked forward to the opportunity to command an infantry company in the future.

After nearly six months on Okinawa, 3/9's deployment was almost complete. However, our battalion commander had one more treat in store for his MSPF Marines. Sympathetic to the fact we had not been permitted to leave the island when the rest of the battalion traveled across the Pacific, our battalion commander scheduled a KC-130 Hercules tanker to fly the MSPF to Korea for a week of liberty (time off). We flew the platoon to Osan Air Force Base, just outside Seoul, and billeted the Marines at the Osan Inn. My Marines were pleased to hear that the Osan Inn was a coed barracks, unlike those found in the Marine Corps. I received quarters in officer billeting. This is where I received one of my first lessons in the cultural nuances between the different branches of military service.

Upon arrival in Okinawa, the officers of 3/9 had been billeted in Bachelor Officers Quarters, affectionately known as the Crack Houses. When I first opened the door to my room, I found a lamp smashed across the floor, a sandbar stretching across the floor left by a wave from a past typhoon. Even better, the desk I was given to use in my office space had no drawers. When I arrived at the Osan Inn on liberty, I received an entire townhouse in which to stay. It was fully furnished with updated furniture and a full kitchen shared with a neighbor in the adjacent townhome. I was shocked to find out my neighbor was a "full bird" Air Force colonel. When I became a Marine, even captains were thought of as gods, and a lowly lieutenant like myself did not engage with captains, let alone colonels. When I first met my neighbor, I walked up to him, stiff and proper, held out my hand, and said, "Good afternoon, sir, Lieutenant Bohm, United States Marines." He looked at me, smiled, and said, "Hey, Paco." Being an anal-retentive Marine, I was a little surprised. A Marine officer would surely never be this informal, but I was game. I looked him in the eye and responded, "Hey, sir, Kato," which was my radio call sign at the time.

We were from different worlds, but as I soon found out, that was okay. Each of the services brings its unique cultures, roles, and responsibilities to the fight. Goldwater-Nichols ensured the armed services would operate as a joint team. This concept proved to be effective throughout my career.

As we prepared to redeploy home, I was transferred from Lima Company to the battalion's Weapons Company to lead the 81-mm Mortar Platoon.

"Bohm's Bastards"

The 81-mm Mortar Platoon was one of the tightest units I have had the privilege to serve in, but it took some work in building the team and my relationship with it. While I was working with the MSPF in Okinawa, the 81s were building a reputation for themselves as a group of misfits, troublemakers, and malcontents. This was the result of a platoon commander who had made known his disappointment in assignment to the 81 platoon, and his intention of resigning from the Marine Corps. It is no surprise these Marines had issues when they perceived their leader cared little for them or their mission.

Upon returning to the United States, I led the platoon the only way I knew how, the way my company commander from Lima Company, Capt. Fred Padilla, had trained me. Captain Padilla was a stellar officer who came from an Air Force family. He was a recent graduate of the Marine Corps Amphibious Warfare School in Quantico, and I have had the good fortune to have him as my company commander then and mentor to this day. Padilla pursued a successful career that brought eventual promotion to general officer. Under him, we conducted hard, realistic training that replicated combat to the best of our ability and instilled a mind-set that one's mission always came first. Understanding that this standard often brings hard work and sacrifice, we also emphasized the critical importance of caring for the Marines and their families.

Things were a little rough at first when I joined the 81s. I informed the platoon they were going to park their vehicles and hike, start using camouflage paint, dig in at all positions, and provide for their own defense every time we went to the field—all tasks to which they had become unaccustomed. We worked long and hard, and the platoon coalesced. I knew they had finally accepted me one day after a long hike carrying the mortars. As part of my plan to help strengthen the platoon by giving it an identity in which to take pride, I pulled the Marines into a tight "school circle" and explained to them that I wanted them to come up with a name for the platoon. The Marines instantaneously, and in unison, yelled out "Bohm's Bastards!" That floored me, but I could not have been prouder. By taking my name, the Marines demonstrated their acceptance and appreciation for my being a firm, but fair, leader whom they could trust. This trust and our cohesion continued to grow as we developed our gunnery skills.

A mortar platoon's primary mission is to provide suppressive and, when necessary, destructive fire against enemy forces in support of friendly maneuver. The 81-mm mortar is an indirect-fire asset, normally employed from behind covered positions concealed from the enemy. Firing from behind cover provides protection to the platoon, because the enemy is unable to employ direct-fire weapons against targets they cannot see. Successfully employing the mortar platoon in this manner requires a team effort.

The mortar platoon requires three elements to accomplish its mission of delivering timely and accurate fires. The gun line, consisting of the gun crews and mortar systems, is the muscle. Forward Observers (FOs) are the eyes. They position themselves forward of the gun line to gain visibility on, and report the location of, the enemy. The Fire Direction Center (FDC) represents the brains. It takes the information provided by the FOs and translates it into data that are applied to the fuses and mortars to achieve desired effects. All three components are essential to the functioning of the fire support team.

"Bohm's Bastards," the 81-mm Mortar Platoon, Weapons Company, 3rd Battalion, 9th Marines. This platoon provided the Battalion Commander's "hipocket artillery" and the battalion's quick-reaction force during Operation Restore Hope in Somalia. *USMC Photo, 3/9 UDP cruisebook*

Mortars can also provide "marking rounds," to direct aircraft to targets. Bohm's Bastards had the mission of supporting a Tactical Air Control Party (TACP) live-fire training event in this capacity. A TACP handles airspace deconfliction and terminal control of aircraft providing close air support to ground forces.[5] The Expeditionary Warfare Training Group Pacific, based out of Coronado, California, was responsible for teaching these skills to all students west of the Mississippi River. Observation Post (OP) X-Ray at the Marine Corps' Marine Air Ground Task Force Training Center at Twentynine Palms was the site of the live-fire portion of the course. The 81s Platoon set up two guns firing to the east and two guns firing to the west of the OP, with the FDC in the center. The FOs positioned themselves with the TACP students on higher ground overlooking the target area.

The mortar platoon provided "mark" and "suppression" missions in support of students synchronizing the employment of close air support with indirect fire. One fires a mark on or near a target to provide pilots a visual reference, using either white phosphorous rounds that produce a white plume of smoke or illumination rounds set to ignite on the ground, a bright glowing point. Suppression missions consist of firing high explosive

A gun crew preparing to fire the M252 81-mm mortar in support of a Tactical Air Control Party shoot on Observation Point (OP) X-Ray, Twentynine Palms, California. The platoon was on OP X-Ray when a Navy F-14 negligently dropped a bomb near its position. *Author collection*

rounds onto notional enemy air-defense positions to protect aircraft during bombing runs as they fly toward, and away from, marked targets.

Students were evaluated in how well and safely they orchestrated this combined-arms dance. A Navy F-14 Tomcat squadron with the call sign "Hobo" provided the air support for this course, with sections of two F-14 Tomcats for each bomb run. Students worked closely with our FOs to ensure suppressive fires started to impact enemy positions sixty seconds prior to the "time on target" (TOT), the exact time an aircraft's bomb must hit a target. This suppression continued for thirty seconds, at which time the mortars would mark the target. This gave the pilot thirty seconds to acquire the target and line up the aircraft for bomb release. Pilots were not authorized to drop their bombs until the student reported "cleared hot." When two planes were providing support, students could use either the original mark or the explosion from the lead plane's bomb to talk the second aircraft, known as Dash-2, onto the target. Dash-2 also required a "cleared hot" before dropping. This procedure is used as a safety precaution to ensure the aircraft, prior to releasing its bomb, is lined up against the proper target and not friendly forces prior to releasing its bomb. Suppressive fires could commence again to protect the aircraft once the bomb dropped, if desired.

The shoot was going well. The mortars were firing effectively. Time hacks were met, and the guns were on target. Missions were occurring simultaneously on both the east and west sides of the OP. I walked the line to ensure all was as it should be and stopped in a central location to apply some sunscreen. As I rubbed the lotion on my arm, I saw a black blur race across my field of vision. Suddenly, the OP erupted and shook like a 6.0 earthquake. I looked into the sky above to see a mushroom cloud of black smoke rising high into the air.

Dash-2 had just dropped a Mk 82 five-hundred-pound bomb right on our position. I immediately ran to the Forward Observer's position, where the explosion originated. I jumped under the camouflage net they were using for shade and saw Corporal Webb seated with a dazed look on his face and blood streaming down his forehead. "Corporal Webb, are you all right?" There was no response; the corporal continued to look into space. "Corporal Webb, Corporal Webb, are you all right?" Corporal Webb came back to his senses, felt the blood on his face, and began to comprehend what had just happened. The lead aircraft on the last mission had dropped its bomb right on target. However, Dash-2 had not aligned his aircraft correctly, and the forward air controller had not cleared him to release. The pilot had dropped his bomb anyway. This mistake injured Corporal Webb and three students. We were lucky it was not worse.

The Mk 82 is an unguided, low-drag, general-purpose bomb. During this training shoot, the safe distance, or "Danger Close," for dropping this ordnance near troops in the open was one thousand meters. Hobo's bomb impacted only 120 meters from our position. I measured it using an aiming circle, a survey tool used to lay in the gun line. Fortunately, the bomb had exploded on a counterslope, facing away from us, which caused the bomb fragment upward and away from our position. God was watching over us that day. Unfortunately, not all Marines have been as lucky, evident in other "blue-on-blue" friendly-fire incidents during other conflicts and training exercises. Military operations are inherently dangerous whether in peace or war. This somber thought set in as we received the call to respond to a developing crisis in Somalia.

CHAPTER

★

Restore Hope and the Three Block War

Somalia is a country replete with a history of turmoil, war, and lawlessness with only short bouts of stability and growth. The emirates that facilitated trade between the Horn of Africa and the Arabian Peninsula in the nineteenth century loosely controlled the area that would become Somalia. Then Western countries moved in to colonize the region.[1] The French, Italians, and British all staked claims to portions of this strategically significant area with its approaches to the Red Sea, Suez Canal, and Indian Ocean. The British defeated the Italians in the region during World War II and assumed responsibility for administration of the area until 1949, when the United Nations assigned Italy trusteeship of the area.[2] Somalia formally received recognition as a sovereign state in 1960.

The nascent country struggled to unify the people, including six major clans, into a single nation. Nepotism and corruption became rampant as clan alliances took priority over a centralized government, with the result that a military coup followed the assassination of the president. Maj. Gen. Mohammed Siyad Barre assumed control of the country and immediately arrested members of the old government. Barre favored the Soviet style and established his own political philosophy, which he called "scientific socialism";[3] he based it on the Quran and Marxism.[4] Barre embraced the Soviet Union and China and strengthened his position by offering the Soviet Union air and naval bases in Somalia in exchange for foreign assistance. This included financial support, fighter aircraft, tanks, artillery, and thousands of smaller weapons, but the relationship soured when the Soviets attempted to spread their influence in the Horn of Africa by siding with

Ethiopia in its conflict with Somalia. This opened the door for the United States to assume a supporting role in Somalia in 1980 and control of the port and airfield, first established by the Soviets. Somalia maintained its relationship with the United States throughout the 1980s, until the clans ousted Barre in 1991.

Somalia grew more dangerous after Barre's overthrow. Three main opposition groups from the clans took control of the country and created their own political parties; the most powerful was the United Somali Congress (USC), formed by the Hawiye clan. An interim government was established but did not last as feuds and infighting developed quickly between factions in the Hawiye clan led by General Muhammad Farah Hassan Aideed and Ali Mahdi Muhammad. Aideed, the former head of Barre's bodyguard was considered the most powerful warlord in Somalia with 5,000 troops and 30,000 followers.[5] It was Aideed whom U.S. forces pursued in 1993 when their mission shifted from one of simple humanitarian assistance to that of pursuing Aideed in order to provide a more secure environment for its humanitarian mission. This shift resulted in the Somali killing of eighteen Americans from Task Force Ranger and wounding seventy-three in the Battle of Mogadishu in October 1993.

Mahdi was a former member of parliament and controlled a smaller but still powerful force. He became the new president with the toppling of Barre. I would soon find myself in the crosshairs of these two warlords.

The deteriorating situation in Somalia resulted in the removal of all U.S. personnel from the country in January 1991. Ambassador James Bishop ordered the evacuation following increased fighting in the area and small-arms fire around the U.S. embassy. Elements of the 4th Marine Expeditionary Brigade, already deployed in support of Operation Desert Shield, were detached with two amphibious warships to conduct a noncombatant evacuation operation (NEO), Operation Eastern Exit.[6] This ended U.S. presence in Somalia for nearly two years.

As clan fighting continued, Mother Nature also added to the humanitarian crisis in Somalia. A three-year drought exacerbated by confiscation of crops by feuding warlords and bandits with no clan affiliation resulted in a food shortfall across the country. The United States attempted to help the masses of people by delivering 48,000 tons of food and medical supplies to international humanitarian organizations over a six-month period, in Operation Provide Relief, but it was not nearly enough.[7] Warlords and bandits continued to hijack critically needed supplies intended for distribution by relief organizations. By November 1992, 350,000

Somalis had died of starvation and other related diseases, and these numbers looked to increase.[8]

On 3 December 1992, the United Nations (UN) unanimously passed Resolution 794. It authorized military intervention in Somalia and allowed the use of whatever military force was necessary to accomplish the humanitarian mission.[9] This was the first time in UN history that it chose to intervene in the internal affairs of a country without a request from the host nation to do so.[10] The United States formed and led a coalition of twenty-three countries in what became Unified Task Force Somalia (UNITAF) to provide a secure environment for the distribution of humanitarian supplies.

The operation was designated Operation Restore Hope. Commander of the force was Lt. Gen. Robert Johnston, the commanding general of I Marine Expeditionary Force (MEF) in Camp Pendleton. A Scottish immigrant to the United States, Johnson graduated from San Diego State College, served with distinction as a company commander in Vietnam, and was Gen. Norman Schwarzkopf's chief of staff during Desert Storm. (He retired from the Marine Corps in 1995.) Commander of the Marine component of the task force was Maj. Gen. Charles Wilhelm, the commanding general of the 1st Marine Division, also from Camp Pendleton. Wilhelm, a North Carolina native, also served with distinction in Vietnam and later served as a deputy undersecretary of defense and as the commanding general of the Southern Command before retiring with four stars in 2000 after thirty-seven years of service. The major ground combat element of the Marine component was the 7th Marines, from Twentynine Palms. My unit was one of the battalions forward-deployed under 7th Marines.

To secure the port and airfield before we could arrive in Somalia from the United States was the responsibility of the 15th MEU (Special Operations Capable). In the early morning hours of 9 December 1992, elements of the 15th MEU conducted rapid landings in Mogadishu using a combination of helicopters, armored amphibious vehicles, and rubber raider craft to secure the port, airfield, and U.S. embassy. The SEALs (Sea, Air, Land) and recon Marines who paved the way for the force were surprised to see a media circus with lights blazing and cameras rolling to meet them as they came ashore— an indicator of how the twenty-four-hour news cycle and future social media storm could place the tactical actions of U.S. service men and women at center stage for viewing across the globe. Just as in Operation Desert Shield, Maritime Prepositioning Force (MPF) ships would soon follow into the port to begin offloading the gear and equipment needed by my battalion and other forces flying in from the United States.

The 3rd Battalion, 9th Marines began arriving in Mogadishu during the second week of December 1992. My platoon and I boarded a commercially chartered Boeing 747 at March Air Force Base in Riverside County, California, and settled in for the long flight to Somalia. I found it strange to be wearing war gear and carrying an M16 service rifle while boarding a civilian airline and being greeted by flight attendants, who knew where we were going. As we made our final approach into Mogadishu, I looked out the window to see a reinforced artillery position shaped like a triangle with howitzers positioned at each of the corners providing 360-degree coverage. The sharp contrast of disembarking a pristine and modern aircraft and entering into the devastation and pungent smells of Somalia was not lost on me as the door opened and a wave of hot, humid air engulfed us.

My battalion had the mission to relieve our sister battalion, 2/9, that had landed with the 15th MEU the previous week. The company and battalion commanders of the two units commenced the actions required to conduct a relief in place at the airport. I moved to the port to conduct a turnover with 2/9's 81-mm Mortar Platoon. The tragic history of Somalia was evident as I made my way to the port facility with my counterpart. I listened intently and took notes as Lt. Andy Milburn briefed me on his experiences in the area since landing. Andy was a unique character. He had graduated from the University of London in the United Kingdom in 1985 with a degree in philosophy and from the Polytechnic of Central London (now the University of Westminster) with a law degree prior to enlisting in the U.S. Marine Corps in 1987, later receiving a commission. While trying to decipher Andy's thick British accent, I could not help but take in the sights and sounds of the city. Mogadishu was a wreck; what had clearly once been a beautiful, cosmopolitan, coastal city had become a war zone. The city reminded me of a Caribbean setting, with open-air buildings of exquisite, but simple, architecture. However, bullet holes now pockmarked the once-attractive buildings, and rubble and trash littered the streets. The once-large businesses and their stone structures appeared closed and were replaced by small markets of wooden huts sprawling along the roads in front of the ghostly buildings.

The smells were intense. The aroma of drying carcasses of camels hanging and festering in the sun outside butchers' huts punctuated the ever-present smell of wood burning for cooking, or trash burning. One could also catch the occasional wisp of salt air coming off the nearby Indian Ocean. Young thugs were seen everywhere gnawing on khat, a plant native to the Horn of Africa that provides a druglike euphoria when chewed. We quickly learned to be on high alert when fresh stocks of khat arrived; it often meant increased activity and danger would follow.

Upon arrival at the port, I quickly found out there was no room at the inn. The place was busting with activity as units and gear in support of UNITAF arrived, and everyone was looking for billeting. My platoon was to take over the spaces being vacated by the platoon from 2/9, but a military police unit had already staked claim to the old administration building. I spent a good part of the day exploring the port with Lieutenant Milburn in search of a place to bed down the Marines and begin operations.

My platoon sergeant, GySgt. Frank McGill, coordinated collecting vehicles from the MPF ships. McGill was an old-school artilleryman who was assigned to the 81s platoon to train and lead infantrymen in the fine art of providing indirect fires. He was a godsend; I could not have asked for a better right-hand man.

As I continued the search, Lieutenant Milburn showed me a firing position he had established with a portion of his 81-mm mortars. The 81-mm mortar is an indirect-firing system that launches a seven- to twelve-pound projectile at a high angle through the air to provide high-explosive, illumination, screening, or marking effects, depending on the type of round and fuse employed.[11] The 81-mm mortar has the nickname "battalion commander's hip pocket artillery" because it is the largest indirect-fire asset organic to the infantry battalion. Since this was a humanitarian mission, with limited combat-related activity at the time, 2/9 only had three of its eight mortars positioned to provide illumination in support of night operations. Brilliant light came from firing an illumination round at high angle into the air. Once at the desired elevation, a propellant attached to a parachute was ejected from the mortar round and burned at 500,000–600,000 candlepower. The illumination lasted approximately one minute as the round slowly drifted toward the ground.[12] It was not likely during this operation that the 81-mm mortars would ever be called to fire high-explosive rounds into a built-up area such as Mogadishu, with its innocent civilians.

The thought of having to dedicate a portion of my platoon to fire missions that would likely never come to pass was not appealing. I believed we could be far more useful to the battalion in a more traditional infantry role. I addressed this with our battalion commander, Lt. Col. J. P. Walsh, at the first opportunity. Walsh was another old Vietnam vet who listened to common sense. I explained that handheld pop-up flares, M203 40-mm illumination grenades launched by fireteam leaders, and 60-mm mortars found in the weapons platoons of the rifle companies could provide any required illumination. I also argued that although the 81s could fire illumination over the urban areas, the nine-pound body of a spent illumination round would be falling out of the sky with the risk of landing on and injuring innocent civilians. The colonel accepted my reasoning and assigned Bohm's Bastards to become the battalion's Quick Reaction Force (QRF), since we possessed our own High Mobility Multipurpose Wheeled Vehicles (HMMWVs).

Having no luck finding an appropriate space for use inside the confines of the port facility, I expanded my search beyond the fence line of the port and found a perfect location—a blessing in disguise. The Somalia Fruit Company had a compound located just outside the port's main gate with access to a main road, designated "Route Red," that ran through the city. The compound offered hardened buildings, warehouse and office spaces, a fence, two entry and exit points, and sufficient parking to support our unit's vehicles. However, the greatest treasure was what might have been the only air-conditioned space in the city and became an oasis of relief after long hot patrols. It didn't take my company commander, Captain Padilla, long not only to agree to make the Somalia Fruit Company 81s Platoon's new home but also to designate it as the new Weapons Company 3/9 command post.

Weapons Company secured the Somalia Fruit compound, as the remainder of 3/9 relieved 2/9 in defensive positions along the perimeter of the airport two miles to our west. In addition to the 81-mm Mortar and Headquarters Platoons, Weapons Company also included a heavy–machine gun platoon armed with .50-caliber and Mk 19 40-mm grenade machine guns mounted on HMMWVs, and a "Dragon" Platoon. The Dragon was a man-portable, wire-guided, antiarmor missile that could destroy tanks, fortified positions, and armored vehicles to 1,500 meters. Although we had little fear of facing tanks in Somalia, the clans employed civilian vehicles referred to as "technicals" that had machine guns and other heavy weapons mounted on them. I was thinking about how best to address this threat as I dropped my pack at the new command post and looked toward the perimeter fence. There I found myself overcome by a sad sight.

A small boy dressed in rags with deep sunken eyes was looking at me with an outstretched hand. As our eyes connected, he said, "*Cunto, cunto*," the Somali word for food. He raised his hand in a motion like he was putting food into his mouth.[13] Higher headquarters had previously passed guidance for the Marines not to share our processed rations, "Meals Ready to Eat" (MREs), with the locals. The MREs were so high in calories that it could shock the systems of some Somalis and actually kill them. Although

I felt sorry for the boy, I did not want to harm him further and responded, "No, no cunto." The young kid who I thought a moment before was on his deathbed, immediately perked up and yelled at me, "F—k you, bitch! George Bush number ten, Saddam Hussein number one!" I thought *What the heck*? as the young boy pulled out a homemade dagger and pointed it at me in a threatening gesture. I couldn't help but smile as I pulled my KA-BAR fighting knife out of its sheath and held it in front of me. The boy flipped me the middle finger and ran away. This was going to be one heck of a deployment.

Gunnery Sergeant McGill did well in acquiring the vehicles we were to employ throughout the deployment. Ten high-back HMMWVS came rolling down the ramp from Motor Vessel *1st Lt. Jack Lummus* (T-AK 3011), a MPF ship carrying the prepositioned gear those arriving from the United States would operate. The Marines performed operational checks to ensure the vehicles were in order after arriving at Somalia Fruit. I was surprised to see three AK-47 assault rifles crashing to the ground when two Marines opened a bag and shook out a camouflage net; we surmised that some departing Marines, who had used these vehicles recently in the Middle East, had likely been trying to hide the "souvenir" AK-47s not realizing they would separate from the vehicles. The Marines continued to op-check our gear and equipment as the leadership planned the way forward.

Although we had conducted some rudimentary language and cultural training in the United States in the little time we had prior to deploying, Weapons Company and the rest of our battalion had to learn mostly on the job. To be most effective in a humanitarian setting, it is best to first understand the local language. This enables the people you intend to help to convey directly what they need, instead of receiving what someone from another country thinks they need. Understanding the culture is also important to ensure that those you plan to help can, and will, accept the assistance you are trying to provide. Although the Marine Corps later established cultural learning institutions, we gathered our cultural intelligence the same way Marines had since 1775—we patrolled.

Patrolling in Mogadishu was an interesting prospect. All our patrols initially remained within a one-kilometer radius of the port and airfield in an area called the "Green Zone" and were on foot or used vehicles. The 81s Platoon conducted our first patrols dismounted, due to the confined area in which we were working. There was also no better way to get to know the terrain and people inhabiting it than engaging them face-to-face. The daily interaction with the local population was invaluable for gathering information about the residents, businesses, mosques, clans, and nuances and patterns that helped to identify when something, or someone, was out of the ordinary.

Our patrolling was as much a force-protection issue as it was an intelligence-gathering tool. In addition, our daily engagements with the locals increased their trust and confidence in our ability to see to their well-being, thus lowering their inhibitions and resulting in more information sharing. We became accustomed to having children join us for portions of the patrols and grew alert when they would fade away, a clear indicator that we were about to take fire. We also began to recognize Aideed's information-collection network of young men who trailed us and reported our movements. This was particularly noticeable when we operated in the vicinity of the Olympic Hotel and Bakara Market, which we referred to as the "gun market." Both areas were Aideed strongholds and would be the scenes of the Battle of Mogadishu less than two years later.

It was during one of these patrols I had my first taste of combat. All was going well as I led a foot patrol east out of the Somalia Fruit compound, then north up a road designated the "Green Line." The Green Line was an agreed-on neutral zone that separated Mogadishu between two factions; Aideed controlled everything to the west, and Mahdi controlled everything to the east. As we made our way on the Green Line, machine-gun fire erupted from Mahdi's area and began hitting near us. A number of thoughts immediately raced through my head, as I turned and started to yell for the Marines to get down and return fire, but nothing had to be said. Before I could open my mouth, I watched with satisfaction as muscle memory took control, and the value in conducting countless battle drills at home prior to deploying became evident here in Somalia. The Marines reacted in exactly the way they had been trained. I was so pumped up at that moment that I wanted to jump up and yell, "Yes!" However, prudence took over, and I decided to seek cover before I got shot. Incidents like this violation of the neutral Green Line were of grave concern to Lieutenant General Johnston and Ambassador Robert Oakley, appointed special envoy to Somalia by President Bush, due to his experience in Africa. They worked together to develop a weapons control plan to foster a more secure environment and facilitate the humanitarian mission.

Weapons were an integral part of life in Somalia. Warlords derived their power and influence through possessing the largest and deadliest weapons. Their most popular weapon was the technical. Criminal bandits and thugs also relied on weapons for their livelihood to rob humanitarian

"Bohm's Bastards" respond to sniper fire outside the Somali parliament building in Mogadishu, Somalia, during Operation Restore Hope, December 1992. *Author collection*

organizations and innocent civilians. Humanitarian organizations hired locals for personal "protection" and the security of their supplies. Often times, this protection was supplied by the very factions and thugs who were perpetrating the robberies, when not provided protection money. At the end of this chain were the innocent civilians trying to protect their families and personal belongings.

Realizing they could never fully disarm the population, Ambassador Oakley and General Johnston devised a plan to control the most dangerous weapons. They met with faction leaders and came to an agreement, starting with Aideed and Mahdi, to secure their heavy weapons in designated cantonment storage areas approved by UNITAF. This plan worked for a while, but later violations resulted in coalition forces' having to engage in kinetic operations to exert control and put the warlords in check. The increased tension threatened the warlords' power and prestige and was the start of the downward spiral with Aideed that eventually resulted in the Battle of Mogadishu.

In this complex and chaotic environment that General Krulak later referred to as the Three Block War, UNITAF struggled with identifying metrics. Was success to be measured by the number of starving people fed, by the prevention of conflict between warring factions, or by the defeat of adversaries challenging the authority of the force? The answer in all cases was yes. We had to do it all simultaneously. UNITAF eventually developed a "transition matrix" to identify quantitative criteria to measure progress in five categories: resistance, humanitarian relief, infrastructure, populace, and transition actions.[14] Although the matrix helped to shape the actions of the force, one must be careful with what is asked for, because one may get it. An example of how this manifested itself in Somalia was the drive for increased "weapons counts."

Just as "body counts" became an artificial measure of success in Vietnam, weapons counts became a measure in Somalia. There was a push to get weapons off the streets and out of the hands of the "wrong" people, who might use them for bad purposes. Marines were to demonstrate judgment and discernment in allowing the "right" people to maintain their weapons for protection. Unfortunately, that was not straightforward, as became evident when we had units coming through our area who were not familiar with the populace and confiscated weapons from those who we would have allowed to keep them. Technical vehicles and crew-served weapons became prized catches, while small arms were generally left alone. In later operations, such as in Haiti, I saw organizations establish weapons-buyback programs, only to have people use the money they received from turning in decrepit old weapons to purchase newer and more capable ones.

As we continued patrolling our area in Somalia and seeking out crew-served weapons, Major General Wilhelm established an ad hoc unit to improve security further. Task Force Mogadishu consisted of elements of 1/7, 3/9, 3/11, the 3rd Light Armored Reconnaissance Battalion, and 3rd Amphibious Assault Battalion (AAB). The commander of the newly formed unit was Col. Jack Klimp, who was scheduled to take command of our parent regiment, the 7th Marines, but found himself delayed pending the completion of the regiment's participation in Operation Restore Hope. (The delay did not affect him professionally; he would retire years later as a lieutenant general following a distinguished career.) Colonel Klimp devised a four-phased plan to address the security issues in Mogadishu.[15] Although distinct, each phase developed and informed the others simultaneously. The first phase consisted of gathering information to further assess the environment and situation on the ground, similar to what we had been doing to this point. The second phase called for an increased presence in the city through actions like patrolling and manning checkpoints, which resulted in my personally leading four patrols on Christmas Day. (Someone

Weapons cache discovered by "Bohm's Bastards" during a patrol in Mogadishu in support of Operation Restore Hope. Weapon counts became the new measure of success, like body counts were in Vietnam. *Author collection*

had the bright idea that the troops would not think about missing home during the holidays if they were kept busy.) The third phase consisted of conducting direct actions when firm intelligence indicated the location of threats or weapons caches. (Bohm's Bastards took advantage of this phase soon afterward.) The final phase consisted of evaluating the task force's actions to assess their effectiveness and inform the development of improved tactics.

Just as the task force was forming, 3/9 received orders to relieve 2/9 in the interior of the country, at the city of Baidoa. The tasking split our company into two units with our commanding officer and half the company traveling to Baidoa with the battalion and regimental commanders. The company executive officer (XO) and 81s Platoon were assigned temporarily to the 3rd AAB and Task Force Mogadishu. Our active patrolling and information gathering was about to pay off. I found myself pulled into a meeting with the commanding officer of 3rd AAB and informed that I would lead the first formal patrol outside the Green Zone, in Operation Lucky Strike.

The purpose of Operation Lucky Strike was to expand the presence and influence of Marine forces in Mogadishu while gathering key information about designated locations. The patrol received much attention, because this was one of the first times Marines would venture beyond the Green Zone. In addition to elements of my platoon, attachments from reconnaissance and counterintelligence units and the assistant division air officer joined the patrol, which consisted of seven HMMWVs with two mounted heavy machine guns and a section of Marines from 81s riding in HMMWVs. I received a predesignated route, with a number of checkpoints in Aideed's and Mahdi's areas. I also received a number of requirements to collect specific information about key aspects of the city. These included the road conditions of major routes and possible landing zones for casualty evacuation or the insertion of quick-reaction forces. After receiving my order, I asked if I could deviate from the established route to investigate an area that our patrolling had indicated was likely housing heavy weapons but was not on the approved list of cantonment sites. I received permission.

The operation started off well with the vehicle patrol maintaining good control through the busy streets. Checkpoints were being called in without incident. I observed a food convoy of five trucks pass us at an intersection. Armed men sat guard on top of the piles of rice stacked in the back of the trucks as other men with whips slashed at teenage boys trying to grab the bags off the trucks as they drove by. I turned the patrol to follow the convoy. Suddenly, the radio became alive with reports of "I got a technical vehicle," "crew-served, crew-served," "RPG [Rocket Propelled Grenade]!" Unbeknownst to us, we had just crossed from Aideed's to Mahdi's territory in an area where the Green Line was not distinguishable. The street was lined with armed men on both sides of the road every ten feet for as far as I could see.

I instructed the patrol to remain calm and turned the convoy around to investigate the location where the technical was reported. Mahdi's men knew the rules and were hiding the technical vehicle; I glimpsed its front just as it backed into a driveway and a gate closed behind it. I called in a report to Task Force Mogadishu and spoke to my XO, 1st Lt. James "Mac" McArthur. A Seattle native, Mac had graduated from the University of Washington with a degree in communications and a commission from the Naval Reserve Officers Training Corps (NROTC) program. Mac serves as a colonel on the Joint Staff. We continue to be close friends today. That day in Mogadishu, Mac told me to stand by as he conveyed our sightings to higher headquarters. I waited for a response, assessing the situation in the meantime. We had stumbled into a gauntlet of potential bad guys, we were on their turf, and they had us vastly outnumbered and outgunned. I

"Bohm's Bastards" prepare to depart on Operation Lucky Strike in support of Task Force Mogadishu. This was the first formal patrol authorized outside the Green Zone separating Aideed's and Mahdi's clans. *Author collection*

judged, however, that the fighters were likely on the road to protect the rice shipment and not to do us harm, unless we asked for trouble. Mac came back on the radio and said, "Higher wants you to confiscate the technical and crew-served weapons." This was the proverbial test we always talked about back in The Basic School, "What now, Lieutenant?"

I thought about it for a few seconds and responded, "Negative, not a wise call at this time, pushing on." Luckily, the task force trusted the judgment of the man on the ground and let us go. As we continued down the road the line of armed men extended for over a mile, and we had to pass through a number of road blocks with crew-served weapons. There is not a doubt in my mind that we would have fought an entire neighborhood if we had attempted to confiscate their weapons that day, and it would not have gone well for us. Once we crossed back into Aideed's territory, I diverted our convoy off the given route and vectored into the area that our patrolling had informed us was likely hiding weapons.

We pulled up outside a walled compound housing a three-story red building with a smaller single-story dwelling to its side. The patrol quickly dismounted, made entry into the compound, and began to sweep through the area to secure the perimeter before searching the buildings. Following behind Cpl. Scott Robinson as he cleared the front of the main building, we turned the corner at the far side. Robinson (who would later get out of the Marine Corps and serve as a fireman in Beaufort, South Carolina) almost jumped out of his boots as he dove backward yelling, "Crew-served, crew-served!" I peeked around the corner to find myself looking down the double barrels of a ZSU-23-2 mounted in the back of a dump truck. The ZSU-23 is a Soviet-made, towed 23-mm antiaircraft gun that can fire armor-piercing or high-explosive rounds up to 2.5 kilometers. Luckily, the gunners manning this weapon—and the .50-caliber machine gun also mounted on the truck—had gotten spooked and run when we entered the compound. Upon investigating the weapons, we found the ZSU locked and loaded with 400 rounds and the .50-cal loaded with 200 rounds. This got our attention, and we began a systematic search of the compound, which I later found out was the site of Radio Mogadishu. The radio station had shut down due to clan fighting in 1991 but was currently being used by Aideed.

We felt we had hit the jackpot when a search of the buildings exposed overwhelming numbers of weapons of many different makes and models. It was like walking into a museum with exhibits of the best-known weapons of the twentieth century. There were scores of modern weapons such as the M-16, AK-47, and G-3. We found a French Milan Missile and Italian radios, and also confiscated weapons from our past, like the M-1 Garand rifle used by U.S. forces in World War II and Korean and Japanese 40-mm knee mortars used so effectively against the Marines during the war in the Pacific. Our most prized find was a mint-condition Lewis machine gun, the same gun fired by Allied biplanes of World War I. I called for reinforcements to assist with hauling the load back to the base camp and for AH-1 Cobra attack helicopters to provide overhead cover in case Aideed decided he didn't want to give up these weapons. The patrol concluded without incident.

We were feeling good about ourselves when some bad news arrived. One of the rifle companies securing the airport had just lost a weapon. There are few crimes as grave as a Marine losing a weapon. Believing in the ethos of every Marine a rifleman, we are fanatical about the connection between a Marine and his weapon. This is evident by the Rifleman's Creed—memorized by all Marines since 1942—which begins, "This is my rifle. There are many like it, but this one is mine."[16] We were told that the Marines guarding the airport were in two-man fighting holes around the perimeter of the airfield and were at 50-percent alert status that evening.

ZSU-23 Shilka antiaircraft weapon captured by "Bohm's Bastards" at the Radio Mogadishu compound during Operation Lucky Strike in support of Operation Restore Hope. This weapon was armed and manned, but the gunner ran when the platoon made entry into the compound. *Author collection*

This means that one of every two Marines at the post is awake and on watch at all times, while his partner eats or rests.

A fireteam of four was manning two holes, and the fireteam leader had shared a hole with his automatic rifleman (AR) armed with a M249 Squad Automatic Weapon (SAW). The fireteam leader had the watch as the AR man slept. Trying to supervise his Marines properly, the fireteam leader had gone to his team's other hole to ensure the Marine on watch remained alert. Unfortunately, he had failed to wake the AR man before he departed. A Somali infiltrated through the defensive wire and grabbed the M249 SAW as the AR man continued to sleep.

Our battalion commander was not amused. In fact, the incident so angered him that he had every Marine "dummy-cord" his weapon to his body. A dummy cord is a rope or line used to ensure any small item that may be accidentally dropped or left behind remains connected to the Marine and is not lost. Dummy cords were never meant to be used for weapons other than pistols, which are normally secured with a standard lanyard made for this purpose. Rifles or crew-served weapons are too large and unwieldly for use with dummy cords, but that did not stop Lieutenant

Colonel Walsh from directing their use. Some Marines thought the order so silly that they exaggerated the size and length of their dummy cords to include chains ten to thirty feet long, and the colonel eventually got the message and relented. A later raid recaptured the M249 SAW. However, the stress added by the dummy-cord order had a longer-lasting impact.

With the conclusion of Operation Lucky Strike, Bohm's Bastards and the remainder of 3/9 joined the rest of the battalion in Baidoa. It didn't take long for staff officers operating from the port to hear of our impending departure and the secret of our air-conditioned space at the Somalia Fruit Company. Groups of them started to hover around our command post like vultures waiting to pounce the minute we left. I was amused one day as I watched a group of them depart the compound and drive past the Somali kids who used to sit on the fence and talk with our Marines guarding the entry point. As their vehicle drove up to the gate, I watched as one of my Marines nodded to the kids, who all blurted out, "F—k you, pogues!" Pogue, or POG, is a pejorative military slang term for noncombat, staff, and other rear-echelon or support units. It is also short for "people other than grunts." This was a fitting end to our time in Mogadishu, as we prepared for the long haul to Baidoa.

The battalion executive officer led our convoy on the 150-mile trek to Baidoa. The convoy consisted of the remainder of Headquarters and Service (H&S), India, Lima, and Weapons Companies mounted in HMMWVs, five-ton trucks, and armored amphibious vehicles (AAVs). What would have been a three-hour drive in any Western country took our convoy fifteen hours to complete. Of the nearly 13,000 miles of roads in Somalia, only 11 percent of them were paved, and the Somalis failed to maintain those roads that were.[17] Huge potholes pocked what asphalt we encountered during the trip. The road conditions wreaked havoc on the weak tires of the trucks and HMMWVs and the stiff suspensions of the AAVs. The convoy stopped countless times to make repairs. Clan fighting further exacerbated the trip: the convoy had to push through an active firefight between two groups vying for control of a bridge that we needed to cross. The Marines were hot, hungry, and exhausted by the time we arrived in Baidoa that evening.

Our company commander, Capt. Fred Padilla, met us when we arrived at the airfield designated as our base camp. It was dark, there was no power for lights, and we were used up. Captain Padilla had our HMMWVs form two lines facing inward, with their headlights on and enough space in between for the Marines to establish a tight perimeter in which to rest before daylight. It did not take long after the headlights were turned off for the Marines to pass out cold.

As I had become accustomed, I arranged my gear in such a way that it was all within arm's reach in case I needed to grab it quickly in the dark. I was just starting to doze off when Pfc. Manuel Bibian Gomez screamed. Bibian Gomez was one of the junior members of the platoon, but he had been pulling his weight. No one knew what was going on. Flashlights shone in all directions, and Captain Padilla screamed, "Grab him!" as the sound of 150 rifles simultaneously chambering rounds rang out. The company prepared to repel what many of us thought were Somalis infiltrating the perimeter. It took a few minutes before my platoon sergeant figured out that Bibian Gomez had had a nightmare. The stress and fatigue of the long trip, combined with the fear of losing another weapon, had the Marines on edge. After a good laugh and much razzing of Bibian Gomez, we all settled in for a few hours of sleep.

Elements of the U.S. Army and French Foreign Legion in a combined operation with Marines from the 15th MEU had originally secured Baidoa on 15 December 1992. The 7th Marines, under Col. "Buck" Bedard, assumed responsibility for the city and its surrounding areas on 22 December. A 1967 graduate of the University of South Dakota, Emil "Buck" Bedard served honorably in Vietnam and as the assistant operations officer for the 7th Marine Expeditionary Brigade (MEB) in Desert Storm. Bedard retired in 2003 as a lieutenant general.

Although an important hub for the distribution of humanitarian supplies to Somalia's interior, Baidoa did not promise the level of action experienced in Mogadishu. However, its nickname, the "City of Death," was the result of massive starvation in the area.[18] Visible manifestations of death lay in small mounds of dirt that acted as graves for the thousands who had died. There was no rhyme or reason to their placement; it was almost as though people were buried right where they dropped. Shortly after we arrived, we learned that President Bush intended to visit the troops. In anticipation of the president's arrival, 3/9 saturated the area with security and presence patrols to learn our new surroundings and ensure a safe and stable environment.

I learned an invaluable lesson about remaining calm during one of these operations. I was leading an uneventful dismounted patrol through the city when I received a call giving me the location of a suspected weapons cache and orders to check it out. We pulled the Marines in, plotted a new course for the target building, and stepped off with a greater sense of urgency.

On arriving at the designated location, we cordoned off the building and entered without warning to achieve surprise. The Marines moved swiftly through the building using their room-clearing techniques. We found some military-aged males in the first rooms, and we came upon a gathering of men, women, and children in a larger room. A woman, whom I assumed to be the matriarch, was cutting something with a military-style camouflage knife with a serrated edge. Our arrival obviously agitated her, and she started screaming at us as she pointed the knife at me. The Marines nearest me pointed their weapons at her, yelling for her to put down the knife. Tension increased as the Marines found a room secured with a brand-new, large padlock, which raised further suspicion that the reported weapons cache was inside. We told the woman, who continued to scream and wave the knife, to open the door. The language barrier made matters worse, but I made clear through body language that if she failed to unlock the door, I was going to kick it in.

This further irritated her. She moved into my personal space with the knife, and my Marines placed the muzzles of their weapons close to her face. Children began to cry on the other side of the room. I took a deep breath and paused, then put my hands together like I was praying, slowly bowed my head to the woman and held out my hand toward the locked door. I said, "Please" as calmly as I could. This had the desired effect. The woman dropped the knife, took out a key, and opened the door. Nothing of significance was found in the room; the report of a weapons cache was incorrect. Luckily, we averted what could have been a tragic event.

This was not the first false report we received in Baidoa. On another occasion, we followed up on information that a weapons exchange would occur that evening at a local camel market, with a second exchange at a nearby water plant. The weapons company devised a plan where the company commander would establish a jump command post (CP) in a central location, the Dragons Platoon would address the exchange at the water plant, and the 81s would have responsibility for the camel market. We would move in after dark to mask our movement in order not to spook the weapons dealers and go to predesignated rendezvous points for extraction following the operation. I asked if we should pack gear to remain in the field overnight but was told not to worry about it because we would return to the base camp that evening.

The insertions at all three sites went as planned. My force moved stealthily into position around the camel market at approximately 9:00 p.m. I positioned myself inside some bushes, which offered concealment and a good view of the surrounding area. The night-vision goggles (NVGs) that nearly every Marine infantryman and soldier possesses today were in short supply then, and I was the only member of my unit with a pair. As I settled into my hide site, I turned on the NVGs. Over the next few hours I watched a group of men chewing on khat, had a dog walk up and urinate on my bushes, and even saw a couple make love under the stars. However, the expected weapons exchange never materialized.

When I called the company jump CP at the designated time and reported no activity, I requested the trucks meet us at the rendezvous point for extraction. Instead, I was told to move my unit by foot to link up with the jump CP at its position. I assumed that the trucks were in the process of transporting the Dragons Platoon, who also had no luck, back to the base camp at the airfield and that we would follow next. I turned my NVGs off as I approached the jump CP and found out otherwise. The company commander expressed his disappointment with the result of the evening's operation and directed that 81s conduct a predawn sweep of the village for weapons. The time was about 2:00 a.m., the sweep scheduled to start at 4:30 a.m. My platoon sergeant posted security and directed the Marines to grab a piece of ground and get some sleep.

After ensuring the Marines were bedded down, I joined them by propping my war gear against a small rise in the ground and lying down in the dirt. The air was cool and moist that evening. After a quick nap, I got up, put my gear back on, and conducted an operation check on my NVGs. As the hazy green screen of the NVGs came into focus, I was horrified by what I saw. We were all lying in a field of human feces. Because there was no running water in most homes and few latrines, people relieved themselves outside. As humanitarian supplies began to flow into the area, and a staple meal of rice and beans was given to the population, people defecated wherever they happened to be when their systems needed to purge, since local digestive systems had not yet adapted to the new food. The consistency of the excrement was like pancake mix that had cooked in the African sun. Marines, with their unique sense of humor, referred to the result as "Somali Pancakes," which could be found everywhere. To make matters worse that morning, when I looked down at the patch of ground on which I had propped my head, I realized it was another shallow grave—such is the life of a grunt.

As directed, the 81-mm Mortar Platoon swept through the village toward our base camp. The tally for our efforts was a single AK-47 confiscated from a man who was acting squirrely when questioned. I was disappointed when we moved to the front of the building just as the sun was rising and saw a sign marked "Concern" hanging on the wall. Concern Worldwide was one of the humanitarian organizations operating in the area, and the man was a hired guard. We gave the weapon back and made our way to the base camp empty-handed and without further incident.

Weapons Company's home while in Baidoa was an old airfield littered with abandoned Soviet weapons. Bohm's Bastards took over an old hangar with no roof and two decrepit Chinese Shenyang J-6 fighter aircraft parked in the rear. The J-6 was the Chinese-built version of the Soviet MiG-19 Farmer. The two aircraft had loaded weapons but had clearly not flown for years. The Marines had affectionately named our hanger "Hotel Kato," after our radio call sign, Kato. We were sticky, tired, and smelled from the crap that we had slept in the night before; I gave the Marines time to clean up. I grabbed a bucket and five-gallon water can and shed my nasty uniform. Cleaning up the best I could, pulling ten ticks off of my body, I broke out the only clean uniform I had. Little did I know it would be forty days before we took our only shower in Somalia using a field expedient facility before we got on the plane to head home.

Having cleaned up, we prepared for the arrival of President Bush. Weapons Company, mechanized for the event, was to establish a cordon along the road on which the president would travel to visit a local orphanage. The company parked amphibious-tracked vehicles to block each intersection along the route to form an inner ring of security, as our Marines conducted dismounted patrols in an outer ring of security a block beyond.

As I sat on top of one of the AAVs, I saw a small crowd gathering around a young boy holding something. He had an MRE packet in his hands. I was amused to see he did not quite know what to do with it. He smelled it, licked it, and bit it, but he couldn't figure out how to get to the food inside of the foil packet. I called out and waved for him to pass it up to me. It was a potatoes au gratin meal—hated by most Marines. Although originally told not to give the Somalis MREs, that concern appeared exaggerated, and I couldn't resist, so I ripped the packet open, pushed some of the food toward the top of the packet, and handed it back to the boy. He took a sniff and tasted the food with his tongue. Immediately reeling back with a look of distaste on his face, he tried to give it back to me. I waved my hand no, and he passed it on to one of the onlookers. It was passed on to three other people each with a similar response. The last finally threw the food to the ground and walked away. It seemed that even starving people wouldn't eat some of the lousy meals we were being fed.

President Bush's visit went off without a hitch. He rode by in the back of a Marine AAV with the hatches thrown open and gave us a thumbs up, the last highlight of Operation Restore Hope for the Marines and sailors of 3/9. Originally scheduled to return to Okinawa before this crisis occurred, the Marine Corps wanted to get us back on track, so we returned to Camp Pendleton.

Homecoming was a bittersweet event. The Marines couldn't wait to get home to their families, but many wanted to remain in Somalia to see the mission through. These thoughts vanished, though, as we pulled into Camp Margarita, the location of our headquarters and barracks on Camp Pendleton. We could hear the 1st Marine Division Band playing and got a quick glimpse of our families and friends on that beautiful sunny day as we drove by them on our way to the armory. Mission always comes first, so the families waited until we turned in, and accounted for, our weapons and serialized gear. This time it took far longer than it should have, because a single Marine had misplaced an item; we had to search everyone's gear to locate it. By the time we were finally released, the women outside, who looked radiant in their summer dresses when we had driven by hours earlier, were now freezing because of the cool and humid evening air. No one cared as couples embraced and families reunited.

4

★

Steel Rain, Amphibious Operations, and Korea

The 3rd Battalion, 9th Marines was not home long before preparations began for its next deployment to Okinawa, which would consist of conducting bilateral and multilateral exercises, training, and cultural events throughout the Pacific to build and strengthen partnerships and to assure friendly nations of the American commitment to peace and stability in the region while deterring would-be adversaries. These activities are what joint doctrine refers to as "Phase 0" operations, in which the joint force "shapes" the environment.[1] In a perfect world, forward-engaged, military forces conducting shaping operations mitigate crises and contingencies that otherwise would require increased military intervention. Many believe investing in Phase 0 operations during peace can prevent war and cost far less in the long run.

Steel Rain

Once on Okinawa, the 81-mm Mortar Platoon worked to increase its lethality. We established a forward observer course for all infantry squad leaders so they could augment the calls for fire by our organic FOs. The course consisted of giving each squad leader hands-on experience on the gun line, in the Fire Direction Center (FDC), and as FOs calling in live-fire missions. We conducted the course in the Camp Schwab impact area approved for live-fire training on the north side of the island.

Live-fire training was challenging on Okinawa. The scarcity of usable land causes tension between the military and the local population; the military and locals compete for the use of land for military training, agricultural use, housing communities, and public roads. The employment of indirect-fire assets caused even greater challenges since their high angle of fire put them in competition for the limited airspace above the island. Unfortunately, the Schwab impact area was in the direct flight path of commercial airlines approaching the Naha International Airport. These land and air factors restricted the area authorized for indirect-fire training to a confined area including a single hill and road leading to another range that would close for the duration of our shoot. The platoon received approval for using the range after briefing the officials at Range Control who authorized such training.

With space so limited, many areas in Okinawa had approval for dual use by both the military and local population. Since sensitivities to inflicting property damage were high, the United States wanted to maintain a good-neighbor status with our island hosts and went to great lengths to facilitate this relationship. For example, there were rumors of fines of up to $500 imposed on any Marine caught cutting down small trees outside impact areas. Such was the setting as Bohm's Bastards hiked to the field and established its firing positions to run the FO Course.

It was a beautiful day, and the course was running smoothly, or at least it started out that way. The platoon set up a section of four guns, and students received targets and worked the data needed to call for fire. They used radios to pass this information to the FDC, who translated it into data called down to the gun line. We would use one of the four guns for adjustment, by firing a single round using this data. The student would observe the impact of the round and call in any corrections to get the next round on target. This process would continue until a round landed within the thirty-five-meter effective-casualty radius. Once on target, the student would call in "Fire for effect," which resulted in each of the four guns firing two rounds using the corrected data from the adjusting gun. The result was devastating, as eight seventy-meter rings of death exploded nearly simultaneously, raining steel on the target area.

I stood behind each student and observed our FOs coaching them through their calls for fire. They completed one mission after another successfully. It was a thing of beauty. Each mortar round had a fuse that Marines could adjust to achieve different results when the round impacted; they could set fuses for point detonating, proximity, or delayed effects. A point-detonating fuse will explode at the point of impact, the normal configuration of the fuse. It results in a fragmentation pattern that spreads laterally at ground level. A proximity fuse explodes approximately ten feet above ground level, raining shrapnel down on the target. This fuse is ideal for attacking troops in the open or firing into trench lines or behind covered positions. Delayed fuses explode approximately a half-second after impact. This delay causes rounds to penetrate targets with overhead cover before exploding.

We employed all three fuse settings during the FO-course shoot, starting with point-detonating fuses. The only distinguishable target on the approved range was a single hill covered with trees and jungle canopy, a few thousand meters away. The effects were impressive. The first rounds hit the thick treetop canopy, causing the point-detonating fuses to function like proximity fuses. Trees shuddered, branches shattered, and leaves flew in all directions as the rounds exploded above ground. We then shifted to delayed fuses after a few missions, and the results were spectacular. Large geysers of dirt, root, and tree limbs sailed high into the air with each explosion. The devastation rendered by the exploding shells covered the hill top, which soon looked like a scene out of no-man's-land during World War I.

We fired the next mission and watched as something new disrupted the familiar brown cloud of dirt and debris and the muffled sound of an explosion being absorbed by the soft ground. Instead, there was a sharp crack, and a distinctly gray cloud of smoke rose as the exploding rounds walked off the hill and onto the nearby road. The eyes of every Marine immediately shifted toward me. I saw the concerned looks on their faces and knew they were thinking, "What now, Lieutenant?" We were all well aware of the problems with damaging infrastructure used by the Okinawans, and I did a quick assessment. I thought we would be all right since Range Control had approved the impact area, so I grinned and said, "Continue." However, a feeling of uneasiness settled in my gut. The next mission was fired with the same result, except this time two rounds exploded on the road. All eyes focused on me again. I'm sure the Marines saw the sweat forming on my brow, but I said, "We're OK, continue."

The mission continued, but things got worse. The data being called in was correct, and squad leaders checked and double-checked the data on the guns. Gunners ensured sights were "bubbled up" and level prior to firing every round. The issue was that the mortar was living up to its reputation as an "area suppressive" weapon, not a precision direct-fire weapon. The mortar was not designed with "one shot, one kill" accuracy in mind.

The next mission had the same effect. This time, we could all distinctly see large chunks of the concrete drainage system on the side of the road flying through the air. I immediately thought, *OK, now I'm screwed!* I asked Gunnery Sergeant McGill for a round count and determined it was best to fire out our remaining rounds rather than go through the monumental task of turning in unexpended ammunition. I authorized a final mission and watched with horror as the rounds flew across the road and hit an Okinawan outhouse. The explosion sent its roof twirling through the air, and shrapnel ripped through its walls. I thought, *Now I'm dead. My career is over.*

I made my way back to base and knocked on my commanding officer's (CO's) door to report what happened. Luckily, we had played by the rules, and the CO was understanding. He took me to the battalion commander to explain the situation, and I subsequently drove to Range Control to report the damage. Range Control was concerned and pulled out our range request and map overlays to confirm we had not fired outside the approved limits. To my great relief we were cleared of any wrongdoing, with the only result being that Range Control asked that we provide a working party to help make repairs, which I was more than willing to do. I would live to serve another day, next time on board ship.

Amphibious Operations

Marines have operated from Navy ships since the Marine Corps first formed. On 3 March 1776, 234 Marines and 50 sailors under the command of Capt. Samuel Nicholas, the first Commandant of the Marine Corps, conducted an amphibious raid to capture British cannons and supplies on New Providence, in the Bahamas.[2] This was the first amphibious operation conducted by U.S. Marines but certainly not the last.

From 1775 to 1998 Marines routinely served on sea duty as part of Marine detachments (MarDets) permanently assigned to ships' companies.[3] MarDet duties over the years included providing security, running ship's brigs, providing orderlies to ship's commanding offices, manning naval guns, and in later years guarding special weapons. MarDets were also used to form landing parties in pursuit of national interests, when required. Although one could find them on most U.S. Navy ships in the eighteenth and nineteenth centuries, MarDets eventually only served on capital ships, such as heavy cruisers, battleships, and aircraft carriers, before the detachments ceased to exist in 1998. To conduct the large-scale amphibious operations, which visionaries, like Lt. Col. Pete Ellis,[4] envisioned for future conflicts,[5] a different configuration was needed.

The Marine Corps had found its niche in amphibious operations and put full weight behind its development in the 1920s and 1930s, initiating a multipronged campaign to establish an amphibious doctrine while building the force to execute it. The Marine Corps Schools in Quantico received the tasking of studying amphibious operations and drafting a doctrinal publication for future landings. The result was the *Tentative Landing Operations Manual*, begun in 1931 and completed in 1934. The *Tentative Manual* identified the crucial elements of an amphibious operation: command relationships, naval gunfire and aerial support, ship-to-shore movement, the securing of the beachhead, and logistics.[6]

Simultaneously, Headquarters Marine Corps worked with Congress and the Navy to establish formally the Fleet Marine Force (FMF), which they approved in December 1933. The FMF was to serve with the fleet, a mission that ran counter to the thoughts of many Marines who had fought in ground units in World War I and more recently in the Philippines and the Banana Wars in the Caribbean. Regardless, the commandant gave his marching orders, and the Corps moved out smartly. The only missing components were the amphibious warships and connectors needed to test the new concept and conduct future operations.

Navy preparations for conducting amphibious operations were seriously lacking in the early 1930s following an almost complete absence of funding during the post–World War I depression, which lasted until 1938. The Navy maintained only two troop transports in this period. It had no purpose-built amphibious warships until the eve of World War II.[7] The Navy also lacked adequate connectors to move troops and equipment to and from the beach. Providing adequate naval gunfire in support of a landing force also proved problematic. However, the development of naval aviation in support of ground troops at the time was promising; Marine pilots had developed the concept of close air support earlier in Haiti and Nicaragua. The Navy/Marine Corps team worked together to test new capabilities against the new *Tentative Manual* in six fleet landing exercises conducted from 1935–41.[8] The fruition of these efforts was the successful execution of U.S. amphibious operations throughout World War II, Korea, Vietnam, and beyond.

Fleet Marine Force units, partnered with purpose-built amphibious warships, provide unique capabilities and opportunities for national leaders. Marine-Air-Ground-Logistics teams derive strength from their close integration with the Navy and the inherent security, survivability, and flexibility provided by amphibious warships. The forward-deployed, ready-made, advanced bases provided by amphibious warships afford operational maneuver advantages to Marine Air Ground Task Forces (MAGTF), and barriers to would-be adversaries. There are no sovereignty concerns when operating at sea. The Navy/Marine Corps Team provides self-mobile, self-supporting, and self-sustaining tailored forces that can rapidly deploy and easily be retrieved. Amphibious forces have been a force of choice for years, owing to the lift capacity, loiter time, sustainment, and forcible entry capabilities these integrated teams provide.

The Navy/Marine Corps team will be relevant only as long as their combined capabilities exist. Budget constraints, conflicting priorities, and increased technologies have resulted in a loss of available amphibious warships in recent years. Whereas thousands of amphibious ships, boats, and vessels were available at the height of World War II, the number of amphibious warships today hovers around the mid-thirties. Today's amphibious warships are far more capable than those of World War II, but numbers still matter.

The geographic combatant commanders, who are responsible for executing U.S. national military strategies, routinely identified during the 2010s a requirement for amphibious forces in excess of forty amphibious warships. The Marine Corps' requirement to execute its part of existing war plans at the time was thirty-eight ships, but it has accepted risk with as few as thirty-three. The Navy, under agreement with the Corps, was to maintain a minimum of thirty operationally available amphibious ships. Unfortunately, the number with maintenance issues usually exceeded the agreed-on 10 percent. This is an issue with which the Navy/Marine Corps team continues to struggle.

In September 1993, Bohm's Bastards received the mission of forming a Special Purpose Marine Air Ground Task Force (SPMAGTF) to test the feasibility of employing infantry Marines from aircraft carriers. Aircraft carriers are capital ships designed to project combat power through the use of the over seventy aircraft constituting their air wings. They are not amphibious warships, nor are they configured to support ground forces. This experiment was designed in part to expand the flexibility and types of missions that aircraft carriers could perform to increase their relevance as multipurpose ships. SPMAGTFs form to conduct specific missions that remain limited in scope, focus, and often duration.[9] SPMAGTF "Indy" derived its name from our ship, the USS *Independence* (CV 62). Our task was to conduct a heliborne mortar raid on Iejima Island off the northwest coast of Okinawa using Marine CH-53 helicopters to prove the feasibility of such operations.

We successfully conducted the raid, but the Navy was not happy. Navy officers watched in horror as the Marines dragged mud, small stones, pieces of foliage, electrical tape, and other items commonly found on infantrymen across the flight deck upon our return. These items are collectively known as "foreign object debris" (FOD) and can do enormous damage to jet engines if sucked into their air intakes. (I never received feedback on the experiment but found it interesting to later see U.S. Army helicopters and Special Operations Forces operate from an aircraft carrier off the coast of Haiti during Operation Uphold Democracy.) The 81s Platoon would soon apply its newly acquired shipboard skills in other ways.

Bohm's Bastards boarded the USS *Dubuque* (LPD 8) in October 1993 and set sail for Korea. The *Dubuque* was an amphibious warship designed to transport 840 Marines. Commissioned in 1967 and named for the city of Dubuque, Iowa, it was classified as an amphibious transport dock; the ship had a flight deck able to carry two to four helicopters and a well deck to support seaborne ship-to-shore connectors.

Connectors to get Marines from ship to the shore include any combination of Armored Amphibious Vehicles (AAV), Landing Craft Air Cushion (LCAC), and Landing Craft Utility (LCU). The AAV is a tracked vehicle that operates on land and sea and carries a squad of Marines.[10] The LCAC is a hovercraft designed to avoid many obstacles that hinder traditional surface craft, and it carries any combination of ground vehicles weighing up to sixty tons.[11] The LCU is the heavy-lift connector that can carry up to four hundred troops or 125 tons of vehicles or cargo.[12] These connectors can operate from any ship with a well deck. Bohm's Bastards landed in Pohang, Korea, using LCUs in support of Exercise Valiant Blitz 1993.

Korea

The Korean Peninsula has a varied climate and topography. It experiences extreme heat in the summer, followed by monsoon rains, then bitter cold in the winter. Korea is half the size of California and mountainous in the north and along the east coast. Northern Korea is an industrial area owing to its rich resources and rough terrain, while southern Korea historically focused on agriculture because of its abundant flatlands. These differences, and foreign intervention, resulted in a history of turmoil and unrest, like most countries that attract Marines. Originally known as Choson, the "Land of the Morning Calm," Korea has a history that demonstrates that it has oftentimes been anything but calm.[13] The strategically located peninsula rests 125 miles east of China's Shantung Peninsula and 120 miles west of Japan. It is only eighty miles southwest of the key Russian port at Vladivostok and just south of the Manchurian region of northern Asia. Korea's central location ensured the Chinese, Japanese, Mongols, Americans, and later Soviets would often clash over its control.

U.S. Marines and sailors landed on its shores and destroyed a fort in 1871 in an attempt to coerce the Koreans into treaty and trade negotiations, and America would remain involved in Korean affairs ever after.[14] Following World War II, the Soviets and Americans agreed on an arbitrary line along the 38th Parallel to facilitate the surrender of Japanese forces.[15] Both countries maintained an influence on the peninsula. Unfortunately, the withdrawal of approximately 50,000 American occupation troops from Korea in 1948, and U.S. secretary of state Dean Acheson's statement in January 1950 that "neither Korea, nor Taiwan were within the U.S.'s security cordon in the far east,"[16] led the North Koreans to believe they had implicit approval for an attack south to unify the country through the use of force.

The Korean War began in June 1950, with North Korean forces attacking across the 38th Parallel. They quickly pushed aside South Korean troops and the first American advisers and captured the capital, Seoul. Gen. Douglas MacArthur, the senior American commander in the region, deployed a hastily formed force to slow the North Korean advance and buy time for a larger force to land on the peninsula. The 1st Provisional Marine Brigade, a MAGTF, arrived at Pusan just in time to assist the U.S. Eighth Army in blocking North Korean penetrations at what became known as the Pusan Perimeter. The brigade quickly became known as the Fire Brigade, because of its ability to quickly shift focus to react to new threats. The Marines' reputation grew, as their presence increased to include the entire 1st Marine Division.

General MacArthur requested that the 1st Marine Division conduct an amphibious assault at Inchon to cut off, and ultimately defeat, the North Koreans around the Pusan Perimeter. The successful assault resulted in the recapture of Seoul and the severing of North Korean supply lines. North Korean forces in the south folded, with the Marines in their rear and the Eighth Army assaulting their front. American forces, now part of a larger United Nations force, reestablished the 38th Parallel and continued the attack north. General MacArthur's insistence on a total victory, and his own hubris, contributed to China's entering the war and snatching victory from MacArthur's hands. Chinese and UN forces slugged it out for two more years in what became known as the Outpost War.[17] By the time it was over, the fighting ended close to where it all began, near the 38th Parallel. The resulting armistice ended what had been America's first experiment with the Cold War concept of "limited war" but would not be its last.[18]

Tension remained high in Korea following the signing of the armistice. The United States maintained a strong military presence on the peninsula, having learned its lesson in the prelude to the Korean War. This presence continues today. Annual U.S. and South Korean combined exercises demonstrate American resolve to defend South Korea, improve interoperability between the two military forces, and provide a deterrent to North Korea. Exercise Valiant Blitz 1993 was one such exercise.

Exercise Valiant Blitz was part of a larger program developed to maintain the readiness of the Combined Forces Command (CFC). The CFC is an integrated Korean-American headquarters created in 1978 to be responsible for the defense of the Republic of Korea.[19] Valiant Blitz focused on conducting amphibious operations, and the exercise in 1993 consisted of elements of 3/9 in an combined amphibious assault at Pohang, Korea. Located on the east coast of the peninsula, Pohang was part of the northern boundary of the Pusan Perimeter during the Korean War. The combined force was to engage in a force-on-force exercise with one of 3/9's rifle companies acting as the "aggressors."

The 81-mm Mortar Platoon landed across Pohang Beach on a dreary, wet, and cold November morning. The assault companies had already landed in AAVs and were pushing inland. The 81s landed in LCUs and moved off the beach to establish a firing position to support the assault companies' maneuver. It was dark, a heavy rain was falling, and visibility was poor.

We set in just past a built-up area off the side of a road. I laid the gun line in, and Gunnery Sergeant McGill established the Fire Direction Center. Our FOs moved forward with the rifle companies. It was a quiet morning, and there were no requests for missions as the sun began to rise. As the roosters started to crow, I saw a small Korean woman hobble toward my vehicle. She was not happy. She started to flail her arms and yell at me in Korean, and I had initially no idea what she was saying. I began to understand once she reached to the ground and picked up a sapling. Unbeknownst to us, we had established our firing position right in the middle of her garden. I tried to apologize, as she waved her arms in the air and walked back toward her house. Gunny McGill got the platoon ready to move.

The author while leading his platoon in Exercise Valiant Blitz, Pohang, Korea, November 1993. *Author collection*

The exercise went well. We learned many lessons concerning the execution of amphibious operations and follow-on operations ashore. The 81s Platoon displaced numerous times to provide continuous "fires" to the maneuver elements and defended its position against "aggressors" often. We began to appreciate the beauty of the rolling hills, rice paddies, and small villages as the rain cleared and the weather became more bearable, even if the smell of feces being used as fertilizer in some areas offset the view. The arrival of the Moon Pie Man broke the monotony of our "dry" missions.

Military field rations have not been well liked over the years. Whether it was hardtack during the Revolutionary and Civil Wars, Spam in World War II and Korea, C-Rations during Vietnam, or MREs from the 1980s to today, military personnel often try to supplement military chow with other delights.[20] The MREs of the early 1990s were not very good. Many older dehydrated meals that tasted like cardboard were still being distributed, and newer experimental meals were not much better. We saw this with the Somalis' response to potatoes au gratin. One enterprising Korean gentleman recognized the discontent and established a bartering system to trade meals with the Marines. He was known as the "Moon Pie Man."

The Moon Pie Man traveled from one Marine position to the next across the exercise "battlefield" to trade one MRE for a ramen noodle soup, a bottle of Coca-Cola, and a tasty moon pie dessert. Moon pies consist of marshmallow squeezed between two graham crackers dipped in chocolate. They are delicious and a heck of a lot more appetizing than the old MREs. Not only did the Moon Pie Man provide warm soup, cool drinks, and tasty desserts, but he also proved to be a good source of intelligence on the aggressor force. He had normally just come from their position when he visited us. Only the owner of our favorite hangout following the conclusion of Valiant Blitz—the ROK (Republic of Korea) Hard Café—surpassed the Moon Pie Man owing to his offerings of warm pizza and a pretty face.

The ROK Hard Café was located at Camp Mujuk, outside Pohang. Camp Mujuk is the only U.S. Marine Corps Installation in South Korea.[21] It is the base camp for Marine units conducting live-fire training at the nearby Su Song Ri Range and mountain-warfare training at the ROK Marine Corps' Division Mountain Warfare Training Center. The 81s Platoon enjoyed training at both sites and concluded each day with a visit to the ROK Hard. The Marines did this for two main reasons. First, the café served some pretty decent pizza, which provided more relief from MREs. Second, and perhaps more important to many of the young Marines, the owner had a pretty daughter who worked the cash register; most Marines asked her out on a date. No one succeeded in getting a yes—at least none I am aware of. The Marines also got to enjoy Pohang.

The term "liberty," or "liberty call," is music to a Marine's ears. Liberty is time off granted to a Marine after a hard day's work, as opposed to "leave," which is vacation time a Marine earns through his or her service. Our battalion received liberty in Pohang at the conclusion of our time in country. As luck would have it, I had the assignment of shore patrol duty.

Shore patrols have the mission of ensuring the good order and discipline of naval personnel while in a leave or liberty status. In layperson's terms, it means you are working when everyone else is enjoying themselves. To make matters worse, your appointed place of duty normally consists of the bars and other establishments where Marines tend to get in trouble. This trouble normally follows the heavy consumption of alcohol.

I didn't mind standing the duty, because I was married and had just welcomed the birth of our first child. The maturing effect allowed me to let someone else have fun that night, and I had a good time watching the Marines cut loose in places like Club Love after nearly a straight month of hard training. My shore patrol partner and I found the Marines well behaved and professional as we continued to walk our beat.

A Korean gentleman approached us as we crossed a street. He asked probing questions about our unit, what we were doing in Korea, and how long we expected to remain. We had been told to be on the lookout for North Korean sympathizers trying to collect information but did not think anyone would be so bold as to ask such pointed questions. After excusing ourselves from the man, we reported his presence to a nearby South Korean military post as directed. The South Koreans did not hesitate to grab the man and start issuing a "wood shampoo" by slugging him over the head with wooden batons as they "led" him away. This incident reminded me that the war, and potential for another war, was still very real to many Koreans. Although the Cold War was technically over, elements of it were still alive and well.

Bohm's Bastards concluded their time in Korea with another reminder of the past war. We visited an orphanage built by Navy Seabees and Marines in 1953—the final year of the Korean War. The children there in 1993 were starving for attention. I took great satisfaction in watching the Marines play with them, proving once again that Marines are not only the fiercest warriors when needed but can also be the most compassionate of people. I also reflected on the fact that my own child had been born one week after we departed for deployment and would be six months old before I laid eyes on her for the first time.

Elements of 3rd Battalion, 9th Marines boarded the USS *San Bernardino*, Landing Ship Tank (LST) 1189, and set sail for Okinawa. Knowing I was due for orders upon return from deployment, I requested assignment to the Marine Corps Security Force Battalion (MCSFBN) for duty with a Marine Detachment (MarDet) on a battleship or aircraft carrier. I received orders to the MCSFBN, but not to a MarDet. Instead, I was assigned to the Fleet Antiterrorism Security Team (FAST) Company. Little did I know that this new assignment would take my operational experience to new levels.

CHAPTER

★

Antiterrorism, Haiti, and Embassy Reinforcement

Fleet Antiterrorism Security Team (FAST) Company

Terrorism has existed since man first walked the earth and used violence and intimidation to coerce others. The methods, lethality, and scope of terrorist attacks have evolved over the years, but the desired ends have generally remained the same. Terrorists threaten civilian populations, organizations, or governments to influence policies, practices, or conduct.[1] They also use violence, or the threat of violence, as a retaliatory tool.

Concerns with terrorism increased in the late 1970s and 1980s. Over fifty American citizens, including the Marine security guard detachment, became hostages when militant students seized the U.S. embassy in Tehran in November 1979.[2] Sixty-three people died when a car bomb exploded outside the U.S. embassy in Beirut, Lebanon, in April 1983. Two hundred twenty U.S. Marines, eighteen sailors, three soldiers, and fifty-eight French troops serving as international peacekeepers died when a terrorist bomb destroyed the Marine barracks in Beirut on 23 October 1983.[3] A terrorist bombing of the U.S. Embassy annex in Ankur, Lebanon, in September 1984 killed twenty-four more innocent people.[4] Hijackings, kidnappings, and murders of Americans by terrorists continued into the 1980s.

These attacks and others directed at U.S. service members highlighted the need for security forces capable of countering terrorist threats. President Ronald Reagan directed the military and other security agencies to enhance their capabilities in this area. The Marine Corps responded in

76

1987 by forming highly trained units called Fleet Antiterrorism Security Team companies dedicated to defending Navy, Marine Corps, and other assets and installations from terrorist attacks.

The FAST companies conducted special security missions as directed by the Chief of Naval Operations. They consisted of infantry Marines with specialized defensive, security, advanced-marksmanship, and close-quarters-battle skills. The companies temporarily augmented resident installation security forces when threat conditions were beyond the permanent organization's ability to address them adequately. FAST Marines turned lightly defended "soft targets" into "hard targets" by their presence and preparations. Their antiterrorism missions were defensive in nature and different from counterterrorism actions and activities, which are offensively oriented. The Marine Corps created two FAST companies, with one operating from the Mare Island Naval Shipyard in California on the West Coast and the other from the Naval Station, Norfolk, Virginia, on the East Coast.

The FAST companies quickly proved their worth. FAST Marines deployed to the Rodman Naval Station, Panama, in 1989 in anticipation of the expected sabotage of facilities by unknown intruders. There, they participated in Operation Just Cause to assist in the restoration of the democratically elected government and to arrest Manuel Noriega on drug trafficking charges.[5] FAST Marines provided security at U.S. naval installations in Bahrain during Operation Desert Storm and reinforced the U.S. embassy in Monrovia, Liberia, in 1991. Congressional approval of the findings of the Base Realignment and Closure report in 1993 led to the closure of Mare Island Naval Shipyard and disbandment of the West Coast FAST Company. I joined the remaining company in Norfolk in March 1994.

FAST Company was the largest infantry company in the Marine Corps when I joined it. Consisting of over 330 Marines, it was organized into six platoons of fifty Marines each and a headquarters platoon. A major with a first sergeant as a senior enlisted adviser commanded the company. First lieutenants or captains, with staff sergeants as platoon sergeants, commanded the platoons. The company initially operated from Marine Barracks Twenty-Eight (MB-28), the home for Marines in Norfolk since the early twentieth century. The company rotated two of its six platoons on a forty-eight-hour alert to respond to any crisis, at anytime, anywhere in the world.

I received assignment as the 5th Platoon commander. The 5th Platoon (FAST-5) had earned the name "Frog Family" while fighting in the jungles of Panama during Operation Just Cause. The Marines had discovered a small and colorful breed of poisonous frog in Panama that reportedly possessed enough venom to kill thousands. FAST-5 saw itself as a small but deadly unit just like these frogs. The platoon's motto was "Rock Hard and Watertight."

FAST Company was experiencing a high operational tempo when I arrived. Platoons deployed on a rotational basis to support the U.S. diplomatic mission in Somalia, and a platoon deployed to Haiti in October 1993. The 3rd Platoon received the task of reinforcing the U.S. embassy in Haiti after tensions increased following the military-controlled government's refusal to allow the popularly elected president to return to power. The platoon arrived in Haiti ready to fight its way from the airport to the embassy, but tensions quickly calmed. Third Platoon returned to the United States after a short stay but left its weapons and ammunition at the embassy to facilitate a rapid reinforcement if necessary. Two Marines remained in Haiti to maintain accountability of these items; one of the two rotated each month. I assumed this mission with 5th Platoon relieving 3rd Platoon shortly after joining the company.

The prospect of getting a "real-world" mission upon arriving at the company excited me. The 3rd Platoon commander, Capt. Will Randall, and I traveled to Port-Au-Prince to turn over weapons and equipment and to meet the key players at the embassy—Ambassador William Swing; David Ackerman, the regional security officer; and SSgt. Thomas Haughland, the Marine Security Guard (MSG) detachment commander. Ambassador Swing was a seasoned diplomat who had already served as the ambassador to the Republic of the Congo (1979–81), Liberia (1981–85), South Africa (1989–92), and Nigeria (1992–93). He was serving his second year as ambassador to Haiti when I arrived in 1994 and would continue in this post until 1998.[6] Ackerman was a former Army officer who was now in a successful career in the State Department Bureau of Diplomatic Security, and Haughland was a career Marine who later retired as a sergeant major.

Marine Security Guards have protected U.S. embassies since the beginning of the program in 1948.[7] The Haiti MSG detachment's primary task was to protect sensitive items inside the chancery building. FAST platoons, with their heavier firepower, received the task of providing exterior security for chanceries in crisis situations. FAST platoons possess pistols, rifles, shotguns, submachine guns, light mortars, rockets, and light, medium, and heavy machine guns. FAST-5 assumed responsibility for the embassy reinforcement mission in Haiti in March 1994 and began a rotation of the two Marines to maintain the weapons and equipment that 3rd Platoon had left at the embassy.

The first monthly rotation of Marines went well but changed for the worse, in June 1994, when I escorted Cpl. Kevin Butler to Port-au-Prince for the second rotation. We met Cpl. Ruggy Jones from FAST-5, Staff Sergeant Haughland from the MSG, and an expeditor at the airport. Butler and Jones were characteristic of most Marine noncommissioned officers—young but professional and able to accomplish any task you put before them. The expeditor was a local national working for the embassy who spoke Haitian Creole. His job was to get us through the customs checkpoint, manned by Haitian soldiers, without being searched. This was important, since Corporal Butler carried his military equipment concealed in his bag. This process had worked well in the past, but now the Haitian soldiers providing airport security had decided to exert their power.

Things did not go well as we walked into the airport terminal, and a heated conversation ensued between a group of soldiers and our expeditor. Staff Sergeant Haughland and Corporal Jones watched with concern from the other side of the customs checkpoint. Telling Corporal Butler to follow our normal procedure, he and I walked up to the customs table and attempted to make our way through but were stopped by the soldiers. I couldn't understand what was being said, but the soldiers clearly wanted Corporal Butler to open his bag. I waved them off and attempted to get the expeditor to see us through the checkpoint. Some Haitian soldiers were now yelling at the expeditor as others started to close in around us. Obviously fearing for his safety, the expeditor ran out of the airport, leaving us to work the situation out on our own.

The state of affairs escalated as soldiers grabbed Corporal Butler's bag and opened it up to reveal a helmet, flak jacket, and other combat gear. The soldiers went into a frenzy. They quickly grabbed the bag and directed the other three Marines and me into a back room where they dumped the contents of the bag on the floor. The twenty Haitian soldiers present were in a rage and continued to holler at us. I told Corporal Butler to shove the gear back in the bag because we were getting out of there. Soldiers blocked him from doing so.

Tensions increased, as different scenarios played through my mind. Because the de facto Haitian government had little control over the army, whose ranks were full of thugs, I had visions of being brought behind the terminal building and shot in the back of the head. The outcome uncertain, I quickly scanned the room and saw that all but one of the Haitian soldiers were armed with six-shot revolvers. The warrant officer in charge had a semiautomatic pistol that I hoped had a full magazine of nine or more rounds. I planned to jump this individual and grab his pistol to fight our way out and hoped the Marines would follow my lead and take similar action. Tensions continued to increase as the struggle with the gear continued. I had quickly approached the decision to act when the embassy regional security officer suddenly entered the room, yelled something in Creole to the soldiers, and marshaled us out of the room to a waiting vehicle. All of Corporal Butler's gear remained behind.

My heart pounded, but I took a deep breath as we drove to the embassy. The Marines and I talked about what just occurred and laughed when we learned that we all had had the same plan; all four of us had spotted the semiautomatic pistol and intended to jump the warrant officer. It's a good thing the situation did not come to that; it would have likely resembled a scene from the *Keystone Cops* as we banged our heads together attempting to jump the same soldier at the same time. The episode quickly hit the newspapers as an international incident.[8] It took months of diplomatic notes from the U.S. embassy to get some, but not all, of Corporal Butler's gear returned. This event was indicative of Haiti's troubled past.

Haiti

Like Somalia, Haiti has a rich but unstable and violent past. Christopher Columbus discovered the island during his search for the New World in 1492. He established the first Spanish settlement near modern-day Cap Haitian on the north side of the country when he landed his crew following the grounding of the *Santa Maria*. (This was also the site of an amphibious operation by U.S. Marines over five hundred years later in support of Operation Uphold Democracy.)[9] The settlement grew quickly, as the tropical weather and rich soil proved ideal for growing sugarcane, tobacco, and coffee. The French brought cocoa, indigo, and women to the island and established their first settlement in 1659, hoping to profit too.[10] Fighting over control of the rich lands soon ensued, and Haiti became a haven for pirates attacking merchant ships sailing between nearby Puerto Rico, Jamaica, and Cuba. France, Spain, and the British all vied for control of the island until Napoleon granted Haiti its independence in 1804 and, in doing so, established the first black republic in the world.

Haiti continued to struggle as an independent nation. Of its twenty-four rulers in the first hundred years of its existence, only eight served their full terms of office.[11] Only two of the eight retired peacefully. Privileged desserts of black and white freedmen who had inherited land and wealth replaced elite whites, keeping social inequality a contentious issue throughout the nineteenth century. U.S. business interests increased throughout the Caribbean at the start of the twentieth century, even as concerns about the instability in Haiti grew.

These concerns increased as World War I began in Europe. Thus, President Woodrow Wilson deployed Marines to occupy Haiti in 1915. The few ships' landing parties that were initially put ashore increased quickly to a full brigade of ten thousand men. The United States used humanitarian intervention and the protection of the Americas from foreign colonization under the Monroe Doctrine as legal justification for the occupation.[12] Haiti signed a treaty with the United States authorizing the Marines to remain in the country for ten years, but they remained for nineteen. The Marines established a military government and a national Haitian Constabulary, called the Garde d'Haiti.[13] They supervised Haitian financial affairs and many of the country's administrative and public services. However, their presence resulted in an insurgency led by a group called the *cacos* (guerrillas).[14] The Marines and Garde eventually defeated the cacos, but not before the shedding of much blood.

The Marines learned many lessons from this occupation and similar operations in Nicaragua and the Dominican Republic during the 1920s and 1930s. The Marine Corps in 1940 published a book, the *Small Wars Manual*, to capture these lessons. The Marines used the *Small Wars Manual* as a source document for creating the successful Combined Action Platoon Program during the Vietnam War. They would use it again in Iraq and Afghanistan during Operation Iraqi Freedom and Operation Enduring Freedom. The *Small Wars Manual* continues to prove its value today and is in the process of being updated as of the writing of this book.

Marines have found themselves having to employ all the elements of national power—diplomacy, information, military, and economics—throughout their history. Although not the preferred employment method of Marines, civilian subject-matter experts often cannot be sent to dangerous locations. Marines have had to adapt and develop a working knowledge of nonmilitary elements to set the conditions for more stable environments in which civilians can operate. Haiti was one such environment.

The end of the U.S. occupation in Haiti in 1934 did not result in peace. Power in the country continued to exchange hands. The Haitian military often injected itself into politics and controlled who became the president. This process continued until 1957, when François Duvalier, known as

"Papa Doc," became president. Duvalier was a student of voodoo and had previously worked on a U.S. medical aid project. He promised to end the rule of the mulatto elite and bring political and economic power to the black majority.[15]

There were several attempts to overthrow Duvalier, but he held power and created a paramilitary gang of thugs—called the "Tonton Macoute" by the Haitian people—to help solidify his hold on the country. *Tonton Macoute* translates to "Uncle Gunnysack"; Haitian Creole mythology believes the Tonton Macoute kidnaps and punishes unruly children by snaring them in a gunny sack and carrying them off to be consumed at breakfast. I grew to know the militia Tonton Macoute well during my time in Haiti.

In 1964 Duvalier declared himself president for life and kept power within his family. Prior to his death in 1971, Papa Doc named his son, Jean-Claude, as his heir apparent and called him "Baby Doc." Baby Doc was a poor leader and fled the country in 1986, with U.S. assistance. However, the Tonton Macoute maintained their brutal ways as interim military leaders once more controlled the countryside.

Jean-Bertrand Aristide, a leftist Roman Catholic priest, became the first freely elected president in Haiti's history in 1990. Aristide's rule was short-lived, however. The Haitian military, led by Brig. Gen. Raoul Cédras, executed a coup and exiled Aristide in September 1991. The United States countered this act by imposing a trade embargo on Haiti, but black-market smuggling with the Dominican Republic weakened the embargo's effect. Thousands of refugees attempted to flee to the United States in small boats, but most were returned to Haiti, and the United States increased economic and diplomatic pressure on Cédras. The United Nations voted to impose a ban on petroleum sales to Haiti in an attempt to get Cédras to the negotiating table.

The UN and Organization of American States sponsored the Governors Island Accord, which resulted in an agreement to allow Aristide to return to power by 30 October 1993.[16] The agreement granted amnesty to Cédras and the other coup leaders and promised assistance in modernizing the Haitian army. It also included provisions for a new Haitian police force. All UN sanctions would terminate once Aristide returned to office. The United States took steps to prepare for Aristide's return following the negotiations.

More than two hundred American and Canadian engineers and military police arrived on board the USS *Harlan County* (LST 1196) off the coast of Port-au-Prince on 11 October 1993 to assist with Aristide's return. However, Cédras changed his mind. A mob of angry Haitians led by the

Tonton Macoute blocked the ship's landing and threatened violence. The Clinton administration was unwilling to risk a landing in the face of this threat, particularly following the death of eighteen Americans in the Battle of Mogadishu the week prior. The ship returned to the United States, leaving Cédras with a perceived victory over the most powerful nation in the world. This action and the resulting tension it created were the original catalysts for deploying 3rd Platoon to reinforce the embassy.

Embassy Reinforcement Haiti

American embassies and their Foreign Service employees are essential to America's security, economy, and democracy. They are critical components of the whole-of-government approach required to tackle the complex security challenges confronting our nation. Although Marines deploy and operate in forward locations on a rotational basis, the Foreign Service represents the United States across the globe on a permanent basis. It does so by manning over 250 diplomatic and consular posts in foreign countries.[17] Each diplomatic post is led by an ambassador, or chief of mission.

The U.S. ambassador at each post is the personal representative of the President of the United States to the country of their assignment. They each lead a team of Foreign Service and Civil Service professionals generally organized into six sections—administrative, public diplomacy, political, economic, consular, and diplomatic security—to see to our country's interests.[18] The ambassador is supported by other agencies, such as the United States Agency for International Development (USAID), the Immigration and Nationalization Service (INS), the Drug Enforcement Agency (DEA), the Peace Corps, the Department of Defense (DoD), and many more.

Ambassadors normally have authority and control over all U.S. activities in their respective foreign countries. However, there are exceptions. They have no authority over anyone assigned to a combatant command, a U.S. government multilateral mission, or an intergovernmental organization during a crisis or contingency. They will, however, provide military commanders with recommendations and considerations for crisis action planning. Ambassadors, or acting chiefs of mission, also advise military commanders on U.S. foreign policy objectives to inform their military activities.

No U.S. military command existed in Haiti until FAST's initial deployment to reinforce the embassy. The FAST Marines remained under the operational control (OPCON) of the U.S. Atlantic Command (USACOM), a unified combatant command based in Norfolk, Virginia, and responsible for the region in 1993–94. The ambassador had tactical control (TACON) of the FAST Marines in Haiti. Tactical control authorizes the employment of a force, but the ability to reorganize a unit lies with those who have OPCON. Ambassador Swing further delegated TACON to his RSO, who had overall responsibility for the security of U.S. personnel and facilities in country.

RSOs advise ambassadors or chiefs of mission on all security issues concerning the diplomatic mission and coordinate all aspects of an embassy's security program. They are special agents from the State Department's Bureau of Diplomatic Security (DS). They receive assistance in their duties from other DS personnel, MSGs, FAST Marines, local and American guards, host government officials, and others. Ackerman's deputy in 1994 was Jack Barnhardt, with augmentation from a four-man Mobile Security Detachment (MSD) from DS to assist in providing personal protection to the ambassador during periods of increased threats.

My platoon and I received a warning order in June 1994 to reinforce once again the U.S. embassy in Haiti due to increased tensions. Our specified task was to provide external security to the embassy compound, while the MSG Marines provided internal security to the chancellery. Implied tasks included potentially securing the U.S. consulate, at a different location in Port-au-Prince, and possibly augmenting the MSD in protecting key embassy personnel throughout the city. We expected to deploy on 8 July.

FAST-5 received a deployment order on Friday, 1 July. This was an inopportune time. I was officer of the day for the Marine Corps Security Force Battalion on Friday, 1 July, watching as the masses departed Naval Station Norfolk to start a long Fourth-of-July weekend. FAST-5 received its deployment order just after most of the Marines had left for home. Regretfully, I recalled a number of people to complete the planning and make preparations to deploy a week earlier than expected. Planning proved difficult, as most government agencies and other organizations with which we needed to coordinate our travel had already secured for the weekend. This resulted in some less than optimal solutions.

FAST-5 received direction to enter Haiti covertly. No one wanted a repeat of the airport incident with Corporal Butler's gear. Guidance included traveling via commercial air and to shedding all appearance of being U.S. military personnel prior to entering the country. Diplomatic couriers from the State Department received the task of transporting our personal combat gear into Haiti using diplomatic pouches, which were immune from search. This did not sit well with me. Marines are taught never to separate themselves from their gear. My angst increased when I received the task of driving our gear from Norfolk to Washington, D.C., to rendezvous with "Bob" behind the State Department headquarters in Foggy Bottom. Bob met us with a rental moving truck and took possession of the Marines' gear. He looked puzzled when I asked for a receipt for the bags. I was a novice at this type of thing, but the Marine Corps had trained me well. I made Bob scratch out a handwritten receipt, and the gear was off to Haiti.

The problem of getting the Marines to Haiti remained. The United Nations had imposed an embargo on Haiti, which reduced the means available to enter the country; Air France was the only commercial airline still flying into Port-au-Prince. Unfortunately, the holiday weekend had also prevented the personnel responsible for making flight reservations from being available, and no one wanted to call them in. I was told to purchase my Marines' plane tickets using my personal government credit card.

Wiser heads prevailed when I pushed back on this plan. Unfortunately, several different organizations then acted simultaneously to schedule our reservations, which resulted in each Marine being triple-booked. The problem did not become apparent until our layover in Puerto Rico, and I was informed by Air France that they had canceled all our reservations due to the triple booking. A few frantic phone calls rectified the situation, and we continued on to Guadeloupe, our last stop before reaching Haiti.

Another Air France representative met me on arriving in Guadeloupe and informed me that our reservations were being canceled again. The representative stated we could not fly to Haiti without possessing return tickets. We did not have return tickets because we did not know the duration of our mission. This resulted in another chain of frantic phone calls. The issue was not resolved until twenty minutes before our scheduled departure the following day. The resolution required the intervention of the embassy and communication with the French chargé d'affaires in Haiti.

This was not the last of our problems. I still needed to cleanse the Marines of anything identifiable to the U.S. military. We planned to have a State Department courier meet us with additional diplomatic pouches in Pointe-à-Pitre, Guadeloupe. The courier was tasked to carry our identification tags, military identification cards, orders, and record books in a diplomatic pouch on a separate flight, while we made entry using civilian passports. It was a good plan. Unfortunately, the courier failed to bring any diplomatic pouches with him. I quickly shifted the plan and had the courier return to the United States with our tags and records, while I destroyed our orders and had our least conspicuous Marine carry all the identification cards hidden in his underwear.

Our final hurdle in getting to Haiti was passing through the Guadeloupe immigration checkpoint. The clerk behind the desk took my passport and asked me what my business was in Haiti. I looked him in the eye and said, "We are students, going to study in Haiti." He looked at me with a stern face and behind me at the group of muscular men with "high and tight" Marine haircuts. Our short notice for deployment had prevented us from letting our hair grow out. He asked again, "What is your business in Haiti?" I looked him in the eye again and said, "We are students." The gentleman laughed as he stamped my passport and waved us all through saying, "Yeah, yeah, yeah, students."

FAST-5 arrived in Haiti without further incident after those few stressful days and entered a world of which we had little knowledge. I knew how to lead an infantry platoon in combat, but I had no experience working with the Department of State (DoS) or other agencies outside DoD. Although similar in some ways, the organizations, cultures, and purposes of State and Defense are vastly different. Both share the same mission of serving our country. However, the DoD's 1.3 million active-duty and 742,000 civilian personnel vastly outnumber the DoS's 13,000 foreign- and 11,000 civil-service employees.[19] The DoD also possesses significantly more resources to accomplish its missions. Our mission was to employ these resources in protecting the embassy to allow the diplomatic mission to continue. This proved to be a learning experience for all.

The embassy personnel were as unfamiliar working with us as we were with them. They did a great job in providing the logistical support needed to sustain our mission in ways to which we were unaccustomed. The embassy provided us a house in the middle of Port-au-Prince that had been recently vacated by a USAID manager and his family. The house came fully equipped with a local cook, housekeeper, and gardener. This arrangement worked well until the cook tried to impress us by preparing a grand dinner one evening. Unfortunately, she used half of our monthly allocation of chow for that one meal. I politely let her go and assigned Corporal Butler as our mess noncommissioned officer. He drew cash from the embassy and purchased local food that we prepared ourselves. We kept the housekeeper and gardener, but required the Marines to clean their own rooms.

We also received a local driver and rental van to transport us to and from the embassy. Although my Marines were specially trained in defensive driving techniques, the RSO informed me that we could not drive in

Haiti. I adhered to this rule for a day, until our driver slammed the brakes when he thought a vehicle's backfire was gunfire directed at us. Marines are trained instead to speed out of potential ambush kill zones. In this case, we immediately threw the driver into the back seat and drove ourselves for the remainder of the deployment.

I worked with the RSO to address a number of other rules imposed on us. The RSO constrained our actions on arrival due to the dangerous security situation and potential for creating an international incident. I understood the guidance of Marines' only wearing uniforms while physically at the embassy, but I was uncomfortable with another important restriction. The Marines could not carry firearms while traveling outside the embassy compound or at our residence located over a mile from the embassy. This was a force protection issue, and I addressed my concern with the RSO and followed up with a number of "diplomatic notes" to the ambassador before finally receiving permission to arm ourselves. In the meantime, we staged nonlethal tear gas grenades at the residence, and I slept with a KA-BAR fighting knife under my pillow. The only option available if we came under attack was to employ the tear gas and cut and slash our way to the embassy or the MSG Marine House located about a half-mile away. Neither was a good option. This was not the last lesson learned about the differences between Marines and diplomats.

On arriving in country I quickly briefed the RSO and ambassador on my plan to defend the embassy. The 3rd Platoon had previously built two positions on the roof of the building, and I recommended they be expanded for use as both machine gun and designated marksman positions to engage targets outside the embassy compound. They would act as deterrents, and the Marines manning them could provide early warning of any danger approaching the embassy. I further recommended the construction of five ground positions to defend the interior of the compound should any adversaries breach the perimeter. These positions would be manned only during a crisis situation. A two-man reaction force would stage inside the embassy on a constant basis to respond rapidly to any threat. FAST-5 would coordinate all actions with the MSG, who maintained a Marine at Post-1, to control access to the chancery. FAST-5 also would work with the MSD to place razor wire along the top of the embassy compound wall. The RSO and ambassador approved the plan, and construction began immediately.

The Marines' hard work resulted in all positions being erected over a weekend when the embassy staff was away. We felt a sense of accomplishment that Monday morning, until Sergeant Mamayek, FAST-5's senior

FAST-5 on the roof of the U.S. embassy in Port-au-Prince, Haiti, July 1994. The DET guarded the embassy for three months prior to the start of Operation Uphold Democracy. *Author collection*

enlisted Marine in Haiti, informed me that we had a problem. Mamayek was a pro who later became a police officer, but he was clearly flustered that morning. The deputy chief of mission (DCM), the second in charge at the embassy, had ordered that we take down the fighting positions we just erected. I calmed Sergeant Mamayek down and told him not to worry.

Unfortunately, in my planning, I had looked at the problem through a Marine lens. I had thought of the ambassador as the commanding officer (CO), and therefore the one in charge, and had seen the DCM as the executive officer (XO), the one who carries out the orders of the CO. I was wrong. I walked outside to find the DCM ordering my Marines to take down the posts immediately. I explained to her that the ambassador had approved the construction of all posts, to which she responded, "Yes, but I did not approve it." I was perplexed. She went on to explain that Peter Arnett from the Cable News Network (CNN) was due to arrive in thirty minutes to interview the ambassador, and she did not want a perception that the embassy was under siege. She further directed that the razor wire that we and the MSD emplaced be taken down. We tore the positions down in record time, and I learned my lesson for the day, to ensure that all the stakeholders and decision makers at the embassy were informed prior to doing anything like erecting fighting positions. I was adjusting to this new environment.

FAST-5's mission to defend the embassy still remained. We just had to be more creative in how we accomplished it. We received permission to replace the razor wire, following a number of meetings with the RSO and DCM, but only along blind spots on the compound wall. We also received permission to reconstruct the ground positions, but at the same time we had to camouflage them so no one could tell they existed. This was done by digging them into the ground, reinforcing the positions with sandbags, and then covering the positions with large pieces of plywood. The plywood was covered with dirt and sod, and planters were placed around the positions to conceal them completely. If required, the Marines would toss the planters aside, throw off the plywood, and man the fighting positions.

A shortage in personnel posed another challenge to defending the embassy adequately. A FAST platoon consists of fifty Marines. However, I was only authorized twelve for this mission, due to an artificial cap placed by our government on the number of U.S. personnel permitted in country. (I would face a similar challenge in 2015 as a Marine Air Ground Task Force Commander engaging the Islamic State of Iraq and Levant in Iraq.) Having learned my lesson with the fighting positions, I asked to conduct a capabilities demonstration for the ambassador and DCM. I wanted to show how limited the ability of twelve Marines was to man the roof and ground positions and also detaining anyone making illegal entry into the embassy compound.

It was not uncommon for thousands of demonstrators to protest in front of the U.S. embassy in Haiti during 1994. I feared that demonstrators might get bold and attempt to storm the embassy, similar to what had occurred in Iran in 1979. In our demonstration for the ambassador and DCM, we simulated an illegal entry of the compound, using a role player to show that it took two Marines to detain a single infiltrator. Any nonlethal response to infiltrators would quickly exhaust our supply of men. I explained that we could defend the embassy indefinitely, if authorized to use deadly force, but risked creating a "CNN Moment," an image of dead bodies stacked up on the walls, if we did so. The ambassador got my point and asked what we needed. I told him I needed the remainder of my fifty-man platoon. He authorized only six more. FAST-5 would have to accomplish its mission with only eighteen Marines.

There were many threats confronting the embassy. The most dangerous were the Haitian armed forces, under the leadership of the military dictator who had ousted the freely elected president. Brigadier General Cédras had thousands of soldiers and policemen under his command in what they referred to as the Forces Armées d'Haiti (FAD). The FAD possessed

Thousands of Haitians, usually led by members of the Tonton Macoute, protest in front of the U.S. embassy in Port-au-Prince, Haiti, prior to the start of Operation Uphold Democracy. *Author collection*

small arms, 60-mm mortars, 75-mm and 105-mm howitzers, and 106-mm recoilless rifles.

The FAD's most lethal weapons were six Cadillac Gage V-150 commando armored personnel carriers.[20] Two of the V-150s possessed 90-mm main guns, while the other four had 20-mm cannons. All six vehicles also had 7.62-mm coaxial machine guns. The vehicles could have had devastating effects on the embassy if the FAD chose to employ them. Also they had five Monarch patrol boats with bow-mounted .50-caliber heavy machine guns that could be fired at the embassy from the bay located just across the road.

FAST-5 created fireteam-sized "hunter-killer" teams to deal with these threats. Each four-man team consisted of a leader armed with an M16/M203 40-mm grenade launcher, a rocket man armed with AT-4 rockets, a squad automatic rifleman with the M249 Squad Automatic Weapon, and an assistant automatic rifleman who carried extra rockets.

The FAD was supported by a paramilitary group called the Revolutionary Front for Haitian Advancement and Progress (FRAPH).[21] The FRAPH were thugs who terrorized the local population, death squads that operated in Haiti following Cédras' rise to power. Some believed the FRAPH were descendants of the Tonton Macoute. Regardless, this group was dangerous. They manned roadblocks across the city, beating and murdering their enemies, and reportedly had been behind the crowd that turned the USS *Harlan County* around when it attempted to dock.

Intelligence suggested the FAD had orders to fade into the hills and fight as guerrillas if the United States invaded, while the FRAPH would remain and fight. The FAD had more to lose in a foreign intervention. A Tonton Macoute headquarters was just across the street from the U.S. embassy, and there were indicators this group would attack it if the United States intervened. The fact that a pickup truck loaded with armed thugs drove past the embassy each night taunting the Marines gave credibility to this threat. Fortunately, this truck set a pattern we could exploit. We developed a plan to establish an "L-shaped ambush" outside the embassy compound if given the order to neutralize this threat. We also had the appropriate mix of weapons to engage the Tonton Macoute headquarters if authorized.

Other less-dangerous threats were just as concerning to us. The crowds of protestors who visited the embassy regularly were an eclectic group. There was no doubt plenty of Tonton Macoute, FRAPH, and FAD interspersed in the crowd but more disturbing were voodoo priests.[22] These elaborately dressed men and women would burst into chants and dance as they sacrificed live roosters by cutting off their heads and tossed the blood of the carcasses toward us. There were also rumors that the priests intended to blow "zombie dust" into the Marines' faces to put us into a comatose state. I was unwilling to risk the health and welfare of my Marines regardless of my lack of belief in zombies or zombie dust. We acquired plastic face shields for our helmets for protection whenever we engaged the crowds. The belief in zombies was real among the local population. I recall a newspaper article from Port-au-Prince that stated the Marines had two zombie battalions from the original intervention forces of 1915–34 buried beneath the Marine House and that we intended to bring them back to life to support an invasion. Voodoo priests and senior advisers aligned with Cédras also spread rumors that six battalions of friendly zombies would engage any foreign invaders.[23]

FAST Company was not the only unit making preparations for possible action in Haiti. Although the United States desired a diplomatic solution, the U.S. military was preparing for the use of force if required. At the same time FAST-5 prepared for deployment, Army Rangers rehearsed airfield seizures and Navy SEALS rehearsed port seizures.[24] The 24th Marine Expeditionary Unit (MEU), recently returned from a six-month deployment, received recall orders from leave. Marines and sailors at home enjoying a well-deserved vacation following operations in Somalia and other areas found themselves ordered to redeploy within ninety-six hours.[25] Their mission was unknown, but they made preparations for any contingency ranging from an invasion to a noncombatant evacuation operation (NEO).

Noncombatant Evacuation Operation

As American diplomats and military personnel watched the diverse threats in Haiti closely through the summer and fall of 1994, they took prudent steps to plan for a possible NEO. The United States wanted to find a peaceful resolution to the problems in Haiti, but also prepared for the eventuality that the danger to the diplomats might become too great to do so.

The DoD conducts NEOs to assist in evacuating American citizens, DoD civilians, and designated host-nation and third-country nationals whose lives are in danger.[26] U.S. forces transport evacuees from foreign nations to appropriate safe havens when directed by DoS. The chief of mission, and not the combatant commander or joint force commander, is the senior U.S. government authority for NEOs and is ultimately responsible for its successful execution and the safety of evacuees.[27]

NEOs can occur in permissive, semipermissive, or hostile environments. The level of threat in a given area determines the size and composition of the force conducting the operation. Detailed integrated planning occurs between DoD and DoS personnel using an embassy's Emergency Action Plan (EAP) as the basis. The EAP covers NEOs and other possible contingencies for specific countries. Geographic combatant commanders review and provide recommendations to the EAPs for the countries for which they are responsible.

Execution of a NEO is also a combined effort. The DoS has primary responsibility for notifying, marshalling, and processing those personnel to be evacuated. It also coordinates with the host nation for support and notification of pending actions. The DoD employs its security, transportation, and logistics assets to safeguard, assist in processing, and transport evacuees. Department of State and military personnel work side by side throughout the process.

Embassy staffs form Emergency Action Committees (EACs) to conduct the planning and coordination for NEOs and other contingencies. The EAC in Haiti consisted of two subcommittees. A Security Watch Committee (SWC), consisting of the DCM, RSO, defense attaché officer (DAO), military liaison officer (MLO), consular officer, and others, made determinations on the threat levels in the country. An Evacuation Committee planned the administrative and logistical requirements for a NEO. The DCM used the SWC to make a recommendation to the ambassador on whether we FAST Marines could be armed for our protection outside the embassy grounds. A split decision was sent to the ambassador, the RSO recommending approval and the DAO and consular officer recommending disapproval. It took more convincing before we received approval to arm ourselves outside the embassy compound.

The EAC worked the problem of how to notify and marshal potential evacuees. An estimated 3,300 U.S. citizens already had departed the country, leaving approximately 3,500 to evacuate. Estimates identified 50 percent of this group as minors, 20 percent of them under 10 years old. The large number was because of the many Haitian women who traveled to the United States to give birth and gain citizenship and healthcare benefits for their children, only to return to Haiti. This complicated the evacuation process. In addition to the Americans, over 1,300 French citizens, along with smaller numbers of other foreign nationals, remained in Haiti and might request American assistance in evacuating. Eighty percent of all possible evacuees lived in Port-au-Prince.

The embassy instituted a "warden" program to provide notification of all potential evacuees. The program consisted of designating wardens for different geographic areas who had responsibility for notifying the Americans in their areas on where to go for processing and extraction. FAST-5 assisted other embassy personnel in conducting route reconnaissance to the marshaling areas, while checking their suitability for use as extract points. Global positioning systems would confirm ten-digit grid coordinates to provide to military aircraft that might be used to extract personnel. A combination of ham radios, Voice of America radio transmissions, telephones, aircraft with loudspeakers, word of mouth, and handheld radios received tests for use in making notifications.

Unfortunately, few of these methods provided secured communication. This became evident when a Haitian broke into the MSD's radio net and threatened the ambassador while he was being transported from his residence to the embassy. A second incident occurred when another Haitian got on the embassy's radio net and claimed he was going to "blow the embassy up." This was not surprising. And, apparently, the embassy had issued General Cédras his own radio and the call sign, "Friend 7," prior to his leading the military coup against Aristide. I found this quite ironic.

The violence in Haiti increased as preparations for a possible NEO continued. Thugs killed eleven children just outside Port-au-Prince in one day; three decapitated bodies were found the next day. The Marines reported multiple incidents of small-arms and machine-gun fire in the vicinity of the embassy most days. We became so accustomed to the gunfire that we received a call from the MEU positioned on amphibious warships just over the horizon in which an excited voice asked if we were under attack. The MEU had assets conducting covert surveillance of the embassy and were concerned at the number of tracer rounds they saw flying over our positions. (Tracer rounds are illuminous bullets that provide shooters a view of the direction, or "trace," their fire is taking.) We told the MEU that we were fine and that it was just another day in Port-au-Prince. However, I did find reassurance in knowing other Marines were close by and ready for action.

Many remained hopeful that the violence would diminish and diplomacy would prevail. Rep. Bill Richardson (D-NM) met Cédras in Haiti on 19 July to inform him of the U.S. Congress' unified support of President Clinton in finding a resolution to the problem in Haiti.[28] Although Congress hoped for a peaceful solution, they would support the president if it required military force. The embassy spokesman, Stanley Schrager, went a step further when he stated the meeting with Richardson was not a negotiation or an ultimatum. He said, "The ultimatum is the fourteen U.S. naval ships outside Port-au-Prince and three-thousand Marines."[29] Time was running out for Cédras and his thugs. The United States continued preparations for an invasion.

★

Upholding Democracy

The situation in Haiti continued to unravel. Although General Cédras and the military controlled the government with the police subordinate to the army, the military was incapable of fully controlling the country. Cédras organized the country into seven military departments, with an army lieutenant colonel or colonel leading each department and in command of a tactical company of soldiers to control the area. Section chiefs appointed by the department heads led 565 subordinate communes. This organization facilitated control over the population rather than the defense of the country. It also divided loyalties.

Five main groups constituted the threat to U.S. forces in Haiti: the military, the police, Attachés, FRAPH, and Tonton Macoute. Overlapping affiliations and split loyalties existed among these diverse groups of potential adversaries. Divided loyalties diminished the Haitian army's ability to respond rapidly. For example, the leaders and crews who controlled the Haitian V-150 armored personnel carriers answered to three individuals. Cédras had the loyalty of some soldiers, while the army chief of staff, Brig. Gen. Phillipe Biamby, had the loyalty of others. The chief of police, Lt. Col. Michel François, had the loyalty of a third group. All three leaders had to give approval before the combined crews agreed to employ the vehicles, an inefficient chain of command American forces could exploit.

Nevertheless, it could also benefit the Haitians. Although Cédras sat in the seat of power for the time being, his removal did not guarantee an end to violence or set the conditions for Aristide's return. Just as with the mythological Hydra, if one head was cut off, two more were ready to take its place.[1] This increased the targeting problem for the Americans and threatened a prolonged operation if they failed to neutralize the right individuals and groups. U.S. forces would face similar challenges in engaging adversaries with decentralized organizations during future counterinsurgencies in places like Iraq and Afghanistan.

Black marketeering was rampant without strong government controls. Inflation had increased by 40 percent in the late summer and 75 percent since May 1994 as a result of a UN embargo and mismanagement of the economy under the military dictatorship. The cost of rice, sugar, flour, and cooking oil increased threefold. Gas prices increased to thirty-six Haitian gourde ($12 U.S.) per gallon, and criminals watered the fuel down with papaya, mango juice, or anything else that increased volume and their profits.[2] These hardships were only the start of the population's worries. Murder, intimidation, and atrocities became the norm during Cédras' military dictatorship. The loose control he held throughout the countryside fostered murders, kidnappings, arrests, and torture, which in turn resulted in thousands of refugees fleeing the country for a better life in the United States or elsewhere.

Thousands took to the open seas in inadequate and overloaded boats. The U.S. Coast Guard intercepted many and deposited them at the U.S. Naval Facility at Guantanamo Bay, Cuba, for processing. Others trying to flee Cuba joined the migrants, increasing the load on Coast Guard resources and requiring the construction of camps across the base. Tensions increased, causing breakouts from the camps and resulting in my platoon deploying to Cuba the following year to assist with the problem until the Coast Guard and U.S. Immigration Nationalization Service (INS) repatriated many of the migrants back to Haiti.

The United Nations and United States took major steps to mitigate human rights violations and the refugee problem in Haiti. Ambassador Swing identified these two issues as his top priorities upon FAST-5's arrival in country. First, the UN assigned personnel as human rights observers; and second, the United States brought in a number of representatives from the INS to work the refugee problem. To function sufficiently, these workers required a secure and stable environment. Unfortunately, Haiti was continuing its downward spiral.

Thugs and criminals working with—and without—their leaders' approval became bolder. They employed more roadblocks and searched the cars of Americans and other Westerners. They confiscated radios, and in one case weapons, from people who possessed diplomatic immunity. More anti-Western graffiti appeared throughout the city, and overt surveillance of U.S. personnel became commonplace. Nevertheless, the Haitians were unsophisticated in their approach. On one occasion a Marine manning a roof position called about a Haitian observing his position, who appeared to be taking notes. As I went to confront the man, I was amused to see him pretending to read a newspaper. However, the newspaper was upside down.

The ability to find a peaceful solution to the Haiti problem quickly diminished. The challenge became more pronounced when Air France announced its intent to suspend all flights to the country by 1 August 1994. The termination of commercial flights, combined with the seaborne quarantine imposed by the UN, promised to isolate Haiti from the rest of the world. It also necessitated that anyone needing to enter or exit the country do so quickly, before the borders closed. Air France's announcement initiated a "transportation trigger" requiring all nonessential personnel to depart the country. The UN human rights observers and INS personnel departed, just as more reporters arrived.

The crisis in Haiti was big news. Whether the United States conducted a NEO or invaded the country, the news agencies wanted to be on the scene, just as they had on the beaches of Somalia. We tracked 175 reporters in the Port-au-Prince area at the height of tensions. Most stayed at the Montana Hotel in the fairly affluent suburb of Pétion-Ville in the hills east of Port-au-Prince. Peter Jennings from ABC News arrived to interview Cédras. He joined Peter Arnett from CNN and many other reporters who sought a good story.

Some Haitians, including Cédras, held out hope for a peaceful solution to the crisis. Rumors suggested that Cédras was willing to step down peacefully if the United States recognized his de facto government. He also said, reportedly, that he did not want to close the door to negotiation, because the only way to open it again was to "kick it open."[3]

Those of us at the embassy knew the door was closing but had to maintain an appearance of normality. We accomplished this by going out to dinner occasionally. Pétion-Ville was a relatively safe place with some restaurants that offered decent service and items we believed were smuggled through the UN embargo using the black market.

While dining at Las Cascades restaurant one evening in Pétion-Ville, a group of FAST Marines and MSD members experienced a chance meeting. I noticed two Westerners sitting across the room who continually watched us. One of the gentlemen eventually came over and asked if we knew the other gentleman sitting at his table. We did not. He said, "That is Col. David

Hackworth, the most decorated American soldier alive. Would you like to meet him?"

David Hackworth was a veteran of the Korean and Vietnam Wars. He had enlisted at the age of fifteen, received a battlefield commission, and is reported to be the youngest colonel to serve in Vietnam. He gained notoriety for his exploits there and was reputedly the model for Colonel Kurtz in the movie *Apocalypse Now*. Hackworth had become disillusioned with the war and spoke out openly against the U.S. involvement in Vietnam. He had captured his story in an autobiography titled *About Face: The Odyssey of An American Warrior*, which I had read the previous year.[4]

Hackworth had lived in a self-imposed exile in Australia for several years before returning to the United States and becoming a reporter for *Newsweek*. He had a reputation for building trust with active-duty military personnel and getting them to divulge information. The gentleman with Hackworth that evening was Spencer Reese, *Newsweek*'s editor.

One of the MSD members and I approached Hackworth. I extended my hand and introduced myself as Lieutenant Bohm from the United States Marines. Mr. Reese asked if I wanted a drink. I responded, "No, thank you." Hackworth and I began the normal banter between people in the military who meet for the first time. We talked about where we've been, whom we knew, and what we've done. Hackworth jumped on the fact that I had been in Somalia and told me how impressed he was with the Marines he observed while reporting on Operation Restore Hope. He asked, "Can I get you a drink?" I politely declined.

The colonel asked what my mission was in Haiti, and I explained FAST-5 was there to reinforce the U.S. embassy. This was no secret and had been reported already in a number of news sources. Mr. Reese asked, "Are you sure we can't get you a drink?" I declined once more, now convinced they wanted to butter me up.

Mr. Reese leaned toward me and stated, "We are a little surprised to see you out tonight."

I said, "Oh, why is that?"

He responded, "You know, the invasion." He further went on to explain that "someone at the embassy was putting a heavy lean on them last night."

I replied, "What do you mean?"

Reese responded, "Our contact was told by the Pentagon that something is going down very soon."

I asked Reese who had shared this information with him. Reese looked at Hackworth, who nodded in response, and he told me his contact. Actually,

I was well aware of the preparations being made, but I replied that I was sorry and did not know anything about it.

The MSD agent and I excused ourselves and rejoined the Marines for dinner. I was later surprised to read about this encounter in another book written by Hackworth, *Hazardous Duty*.[5] He remembers the evening a little differently and claims he knew we were special operators in the country, setting the conditions for an expected invasion. I have nothing against Colonel Hackworth and appreciate his service to our country, but speaking with him at the restaurant, I was clear on who we were and what our role was. We did not divulge anything concerning pending operations.

Although FAST-5 was not part of the special operations community, its duties expanded beyond securing the embassy. The Clinton administration continued to impose a force cap on the DoS and DoD personnel in Haiti.[6] With the small number authorized, those of us on the ground expanded scope to provide the information and capabilities needed to plan and set the conditions for a potential NEO or invasion.

Because of the small number of intelligence "collectors" in country, those on the ground were required to work closely with each other. The Marine Corps has a saying, "Every Marine is a collector." This approach demands that Marines maintain a high situational awareness of their surroundings. Published information requirements that identify specific items that commanders, intelligence, and operations officers need to facilitate planning and decision making focus this awareness. Thus, Marines remain diligent in observing their surroundings to address these requirements during the conduct of their normal and diverse duties. This tenet held true in Haiti.

FAST-5 worked closely with the Defense Intelligence Agency (DIA) and other personnel to collect and report information required for the NEO and possible invasion. This included information on the disposition, composition, and strength of the Haitian military. There was particular interest in the V-150 APCs and in the Monarch patrol boats that moved to and from the port and Haitian naval base. The Marines watched both facilities from their positions on the roof of the embassy. FAST-5 conducted landing zone (LZ) surveys and route reconnaissance to verify previously collected data to support potential operations. The USACOM also tasked FAST-5 daily with collecting meteorological data to support airborne and air assault operations. Those of us on the ground in Haiti were not the only ones collecting information.

U.S. military preparations continued as efforts to build a coalition expanded. In addition to the data we collected in country, U.S. Army

OH-58D Kiowa Warrior armed reconnaissance helicopters, naval platforms, and other assets conducted surveillance.[7] The MEU and other forces
also continued to conduct rehearsals for a NEO or other operations, as
directed. Diplomats succeeded in getting Jamaica, Belize, Trinidad, the
Bahamas, and Argentina to agree to support UN efforts in and around
Haiti, although the two larger possible contributors, Canada and France,
had not yet committed any forces. We took other preparatory measures as
diplomatic discussions continued.

The uncertainty of what was to come required preparations for a possible
evacuation, defense, or siege of U.S. facilities. The tenets of Marine Corps
Doctrinal Publication 1, *Warfighting*, proved their worth once more. The
Marines were comfortable operating in this uncertain and chaotic environment and embraced their responsibility of being flexible and adaptable problem solvers. FAST-5 worked with the embassy staff and MSD to establish an
alternate command post at the ambassador's residence. We worked with the
Government Services officer to stockpile water, fuel, and food at the embassy
and other locations in case the security situation required us to "go firm."
FAST-5 also coordinated with the MSG and received permission to move
into the Marine House to strengthen our security posture in town.

FAST-5 worked with others to accomplish our unified mission. Our
detachment continued to improve our positions, run reaction and escalation-
of-force drills, brief rules of engagement (ROE), and work with the MSG,
MSD, RSO, and others to better coordinate our efforts. The MSD provided
FAST-5 and the MSG with training in personal protective details, motor-
cade operations, and other topics. We shared instruction and practical
application on defensive tactics and the employment of crew-served
weapons. The small number of personnel available meant that cross training
among all those involved with security operations was required in case we
sustained casualties and had to assist one another.

The off-shore MEU also planned for our employment in the case of
a NEO. TACON of FAST-5 would shift from the ambassador to the 3rd
Battalion, 6th Marines (3/6), the ground combat element (GCE) of the
24th MEU, if the Marines were to land in Port-au-Prince. The GCE tasked
its artillery battery, acting as a provisional rifle company, with assuming TACON of FAST-5 and augmenting security at the embassy. FAST-5
assumed TACON of any unit of platoon size or smaller tasked with reinforcing the embassy.

The 24th MEU concept of operations (CONOPS) assigned FAST-5 five
tasks in the event of a NEO:

1. Review the MEU CONOPS with the MEU forward command element (FCE).
2. Be prepared to provide security assistance to other nations' diplomatic missions.
3. Be prepared to provide personal protective services to designated "very important persons" (VIPs).
4. Be prepared to conduct surveillance missions.
5. Be prepared to assist the MEU GCE with processing American citizens and designated third-country nationals.

FAST-5 also assisted in developing the plan for the processing and transporting of evacuees.

The MEU anticipated needing two to five days to execute a NEO. The MEU identified the U.S. embassy, U.S. ambassador's residence, and the airport as the primary locations to gather evacuees for processing and holding. Planners anticipated requiring one to two days to marshal all evacuees and one to three days for further processing. The MEU intended to fly some evacuees directly to Charleston, South Carolina, for processing while transporting others to Guantanamo Bay for initial screening before flying them to Charleston. Each evacuee received permission to carry one suitcase for travel. The 24th MEU received the mission of securing all areas and travel corridors in Haiti to support the operation.

The MEU planned to employ all its assets in accomplishing these tasks. Two rifle companies of infantrymen, transported in a mix of CH-46 medium-lift and CH-53 heavy-lift helicopters, received the task to secure the airport. Another rifle company, mounted in armored amphibious vehicles with attached light armored reconnaissance (LAR) vehicles, brought ashore using Landing Craft Air Cushion (LCAC) hovercraft, received orders to secure the port.. The artillery battery's mission was to secure the area surrounding the embassy; it would be reinforced with a Combined Anti-Armor Team (CAAT) platoon equipped with missiles and heavy machine guns mounted on HMMWVs. Other CAAT and LAR units received the task of securing the corridors between these sites.

I continued to address the lack of personnel to accomplish our mission adequately as these plans developed. The ambassador's approval of six additional Marines was helpful but not sufficient if things went south. I worked with Staff Sergeant Haughland and received approval by the MSG Battalion in Quantico to employ the MSG Marines outside the chancery if required. I also worked with FAST Company in Norfolk on a plan to reinforce us rapidly—short of landing the MEU.

FAST Company worked with USACOM to develop a plan tasking twenty-five FAST Marines with deploying in mid-August with a SPMAGTF that was preparing to replace the 24th MEU currently off Haiti. The intent was to maintain the Marines on a one-hour alert to respond if called. The unit's mission involved using helicopters from the ships to "fast-rope" into the embassy compound to reinforce us on the ground.

Fast-roping is a technique for rapidly disembarking from helicopters without requiring the helicopter to land. The technique was first used by the British in the Falklands War. It consists of lowering a thick nylon rope to the ground from a hovering helicopter. Individuals use the ropes the way firemen use fire poles. They grab the rope firmly wearing gloves, and place the rope between their feet prior to sliding to the ground. The speed of descent is controlled by how tightly the individuals grab the ropes with their hands and feet. This technique is dangerous, because no safety harnesses are worn. The risks had become evident a year earlier during the battle for Mogadishu, when an Army Ranger lost his grip fast-roping during insertion and plummeted to the ground.

FAST-5 worked with other external organizations as well. The XO of the MEU, Lieutenant Colonel Preston, arrived in Haiti as a liaison to help coordinate the MEU's participation. Marines habitually deploy FCEs for just such occasions, and MEU XOs normally lead FCEs. A liaison from the Special Operations Forces (SOF) also arrived to coordinate SOF participation for potential operations. The SOF liaison informed me that a ship of a brand-new class was operating just over the horizon to support special operations.

Commissioned the year before, the USS *Cyclone* (PC 1) patrol craft was the first ship of its class to conduct close-to-shore and special operations missions.[8] The USS *Tempest* (PC 2) joined her sister ship to support Navy SEALs collecting hydrographic data on Haiti's beaches and port area. Unfortunately, one of these ships ran aground in the middle of the bay just off the coast of Port-au-Prince later in July. Fortunately, the Haitians chose not to engage the ship, despite the fact it was a sitting duck that could not escape even if it wanted to. (The ship eventually extracted itself during a high tide.)

The security situation continued to deteriorate as we grew closer to the transportation trigger of commercial flights to Haiti terminating on 1 August. The UN security chief departed the country. The French embassy brought additional guards in. Missionaries started departing in large

numbers. Adding to the tensions, an American citizen punched a Haitian soldier after the soldier slapped the American's wife. U.S. officials too
received overt threats during this time. The director of the U.S. Information
Services in Port-au-Prince received information that he was under surveillance and targeted for assassination if the United States invaded. Rumors
spread that Brigadier General Biamby had ordered the surveillance of all
official U.S. residences for use in conducting assassinations if the United
Stated invaded. Other threats emerged against U.S. personnel as well.

Growing tension among the local population exacerbated the threats
from the FRAPH and other organizations. The FRAPH organized a large
demonstration in front of the embassy on the seventy-ninth anniversary
of the original U.S. intervention of 1915. Protests against a possible intervention and the UN embargo resulted in a lot of yelling and unfriendly
gestures toward the Marines on post, and some demonstrators roughed up
Peter Arnett of CNN. Thousands also gathered on Rue Champs de Mar in
downtown Port-au-Prince, where numerous visible symbols of the original
1915 intervention still existed. These included the presidential palace, FAD
headquarters, and FAD barracks, all of which had been built under U.S.
control in the early twentieth century. I was amused to hear the FAD band
proudly playing the United States Marines' Hymn one day; the U.S. Marine
influence on Haiti was obviously still being felt seventy-nine years later
without the Haitians even realizing it.

Although there were humorous aspects, the danger was real. Émile Jon-
assaint, the puppet president put in place by Cédras, declared a state of
siege and outlawed any gatherings of three or more people. Thugs habitually slashed and spiked the tires of embassy personnel vehicles. Incidents of
rocks being thrown at the Marines on post increased. The embassy doctor
informed us that he had had dinner with a Haitian friend who had said,
"This can take care of the Marines"; he pulled out a high-power scoped
rifle and demonstrated his marksmanship by shooting out a lightbulb in
the distance. We canceled all liberty in town.

FAST-5 took measures to better meet the threats to the embassy. We
coordinated with the USAID and moved our billeting to their facility
located just down the road from the embassy, for a more rapid response
by off-duty Marines to defend the embassy, if required. We also exchanged
our rented van for a hardened Suburban. It did not appear that Cédras was
going to back down.

The United Nations had had enough. The UN Security Council passed
Resolution 940 on 31 July 1994.[9] It determined that the illegal de facto

regime in Haiti had failed to comply with the Governors Island Accord and was in breach of its obligations under the resolutions of the Security Council. It cited Chapter VII of the United Nations Charter and authorized the forming of a multinational force under unified command. It further authorized this force to use "all necessary means" to facilitate the departure from Haiti of the military leadership, the prompt return and restoration of the legitimately elected president, and the establishment and maintenance of a secure and stable environment to permit implementation of the Governors Island Accord. This was a game changer. It was the same language used to initiate Operation Desert Storm. It appeared we were going to war.

Planning continued as FAST-5 settled into a routine of guard rotations, react drills, and contingency meetings. I learned a valuable lesson during this period when I conducted a health-and-comfort inspection of my Marines' living spaces one day and was shocked to find a faded Haitian flag in a Marine's (who I will refer to as "X") dresser. The flag had clearly been flown outside for some time, and I asked Marine X where he got it. He chuckled under his breath and responded, "Sir, you really don't want to know." Troubling visions of what Marine X may have done to get this flag flashed through my head as I said, "I really want to know."

Marine X was not the best Marine in the platoon, but I knew I could rely on him in a fight. He reminded me, when I had recently come to the roof of the embassy to see how he was doing as he stood post, that I had mentioned we needed a Haitian flag to bring back home. (I recalled planning to give one of the locals some money to purchase a flag in town.) Unfortunately, my thinking out loud inadvertently planted a seed in Marine X's head. He interpreted my comments as "commander's intent." Marine Corps Doctrinal Publication 1, *Warfighting*, informs us that we achieve "harmonious initiative in large part through the use of commander's intent."[10] Its purpose is to allow subordinates to exercise judgment and initiative in the absence of orders to achieve the higher commander's intent. Based on my comments, Marine X decided he was going to demonstrate some initiative and "acquire" a Haitian flag.

Marine X's actions in acquiring this flag risked catalyzing the U.S. invasion of Haiti. I had a bad feeling in the pit of my stomach as he provided me the details of his caper. On the evening in question, Marine X shed his uniform blouse, stuck his 9-mm Beretta service pistol in his belt and his KA-BAR fighting knife in his teeth, and exfiltrated out of the embassy compound after being relieved. Moving through the shadows, he worked his way down the road to the Haitian Chamber of Commerce. Marine X hopped the fence, ran up to the flag pole, and cut the flag down with his KA-BAR. Hearing guard dogs barking, Marine X quickly exited the compound and safely made his way back to the U.S. embassy on foot. I felt sick thinking about the possible outcomes, like Marine X getting captured or having to fight his way back to the embassy that evening.

Marine X did not realize the gravity of his actions, but I certainly did. I learned to be very careful about what I said in front of the Marines from that point on. This lesson remains with me today. Taking some of the blame for Marine X's actions, I punished him by making him surrender the flag. It proudly hangs today on the wall of the FAST Company Command Post in Norfolk. To get it there, we had to return home safely first.

It was commonly known that an invasion was inevitable by mid-August. A newly formed SPMAGTF, called SPMAGTF Caribbean, under the command of Col. (later Maj. Gen.) T. S. Jones, relieved the 24th MEU. Jones was the commanding officer of the 2nd Marines, which formed the MAGTF base unit. Major Heseldon from the SPMAGTF replaced Lieutenant Colonel Preston from the MEU FCE.

Elements of the XVIII Airborne Corps also deployed on board the aircraft carrier USS *America* (CV 66). This was uncharacteristic but not unprecedented. Bohm's Bastards had tested the concept of employing ground forces from carriers a year earlier in Okinawa. Lt. Gen. Hugh Shelton, a future chairman of the Joint Chiefs of Staff and the current commanding general of the XVIII Airborne Corps at the time of the operation, assumed command of a combined joint task force (CJTF) responsible for all military operations in and around Haiti in what would become known as Operation Uphold Democracy.

The CJTF organized into two sub-CJTFs. The XVIII Airborne Corps became the base unit of CJTF-180, responsible for the initial invasion and securing of Haiti. The U.S. Army's 10th Mountain Division became the base unit for CJTF-190, responsible for establishing a secure environment and setting the conditions for transition of the mission to a UN-led operation to implement the Governors Island Accord. The initial focus for CJTF-180 and CJTF-190 was to secure Port-au-Prince before expanding to the interior of the country. The SPMAGTF Caribbean joined a third command, CJTF-120, and received the mission of landing in the vicinity of the city of Cap-Haïtien to secure the northern portion of the country.

Activity increased sharply in September. Ambassador Swing promoted me to the rank of captain on 1 September on the steps of the embassy. I had Sgt. Brian Mamayek, the senior enlisted Marine present from my platoon, and Sgt. Brian Matagaly, the deputy detachment commander of the MSG Marines, pin on my rank insignias. They nearly knocked me off my feet pounding them onto my collars. The J-3 from USACOM confirmed FAST-5's command relationships on that same day. This included remaining under the TACON of the ambassador and OPCON of USACOM in any future operation. This information was timely as Haitian demonstrations increased in intensity.

Five to six thousand demonstrators gathered in front of the embassy on 8 September. They continued to make threats and curse the Marines with voodoo rituals. A government official approached me on the roof of the embassy during this demonstration and discussed procedures for recalling my entire platoon if he asked me to do so. He intended to give me advanced noticed of the pending invasion but stated I could not share this information with anyone else. He further stated we "should come loaded for bear." I informed him that I did not agree with keeping information from the others responsible for security at the embassy. The anticipated operation was clearly nearing as coalition activity became more overt.

The CJTFs no longer tried to conceal their presence. The Army OH-58D helicopters continued their collection efforts. USS *Comte de Grasse* (DDG 974), a Navy destroyer, openly conducted collection operations in the vicinity of the cities of Saint-Marc and Gonaïves.[11] Army military information support teams (MIST) employed their assets.[12] They dropped three million leaflets on the cities of Port-au-Prince, Cap-Haïtien, and Les Cayes on 12 September. All of this activity excited the local people, who were ready to end the tyrannical rule of Cédras and his thugs.

Their haste to rid themselves of their oppressors caused more bloodshed. In one instance, the citizens of Cité Soleil, a suburb of Port-au-Prince, rioted against a local police station when they saw lights in the bay and thought it was the landing of the U.S. invasion fleet. The police brutally beat down the rioters once this proved false. In another case, Attachés beat and shot people retrieving coalition radios that had been parachuted to the ground for use by the population in listening to *Voice of America* broadcasts, which were part of an information operation plan.

I received word that the coalition task forces had set sail in mid-September on USS *America* (CV 66) and USS *Mount Whitney* (LCC 20) with the command element of CJTF-180 on 13 September and the amphibious warships USS *Wasp* (LHD 1) and USS *Nashville* (LPD 13) with the Marines of CJTF-120 and the SPMAGTF on that same day. Elements of CJTF-190 departed port the following day on board the USS *Dwight D. Eisenhower* (CVN 69). Many smaller vessels joined these capital ships as they steamed toward Haiti.

The plan shaped up nicely. I received a call from a captain serving as a staff officer with the 75th Ranger Regiment embarked on *America*. He informed me that the general scheme of maneuver on the planned night of the invasion was that a reinforced platoon of Rangers were to land with advanced elements of Lieutenant General Shelton's staff in the proximity of the embassy. This group's task was to establish a temporary command post from which the general could control the fight. A second group consisting of elements of the 82nd Airborne Division had the mission of landing near the ambassador's residence to secure the ambassador and the alternate command post we had established there. Spectra gunships would provide air cover, and reinforcements were expected within four to ten hours after initial inserts. I listened intently to the plan and was starting to explain how FAST-5 intended to support both inserts, when the captain dropped a bombshell on me.

The Rangers wanted FAST-5 to abandon its positions and hunker down inside the chancery when they inserted and assumed control of security of the embassy. I thought the captain must not have understood that we had occupied the ground for over three months defending the embassy, that we knew every nook and cranny of it, that we understood the patterns of life in the area and could tell good guys from bad, that we intended to mark and secure the LZ to ensure their safe arrival, that we were prepared to cut down the tree that obstructed the LZ and that they did not know was there, that we were prepared to cut the chain locking the gate they intended to pass through to get to the embassy. . . . I could go on. I tried to reason with my peer to no avail. We agreed to disagree, and he hung up.

The conversation did not end there. The next call I received was from a major. He tried to explain the situation to me and reiterated that FAST-5 was to hunker down in the embassy upon their insert, because the Rangers had concerns about fratricide. I explained that I too was concerned about fratricide, since we were the ones on the ground who would likely be on the receiving end of coalition firepower. I further explained our mission was to defend the embassy and that is exactly what we intended to do, unless otherwise directed by the ambassador. I attempted to convince the major that my Marines and his Rangers should establish concentric rings of security around the embassy with the MSG responsible for the chancery and FAST-5 responsible for the embassy compound, while the Rangers would assume defensive positions outside the compound to expand the security perimeter. I expected the discussion to end there, but I was wrong.

The next call I received was from a lieutenant colonel. This conversation got a little more spirited. The colonel voiced his frustration and informed me that I did not understand the severity of what was about to occur. I explained that I absolutely understood the gravity of the situation, because I lived it for the last couple of months. Although the Goldwater-Nichols Act was eight years old by the time of this operation, parochialism was still alive and well. It made no sense to me that the Rangers did not want to leverage the expertise and knowledge we possessed on the ground. They likely thought we wanted the glory of the moment at their expense. Arbitration of the issue rested with the USACOM J-3 Operations Directorate, because neither side was willing to back down. The ambassador backed me.

The USACOM J-3 decided on a ridiculous compromise. USACOM intended to create a joint FAST-Ranger security force commanded by a Ranger major with me serving as his executive officer. This ensured the Army enjoyed overall command of the operation. The Rangers informed me of their intent to employ machine guns on the roof of the embassy. I explained we already had machine guns on the roof providing 360-degree coverage with completed range cards, established principal directions of fire, and designated final protective fires. They also stated they wanted to employ snipers on the roof. I explained that our designated marksman had operated from the roof for months and had the place wired down. Each position and task the Rangers wanted to employ, we had taken care of upon our arrival. Regardless, the Rangers intended to employ their soldiers and weapons systems side by side with the Marines, just so they could say they had, while keeping all players happy. It was time for FAST-5 to consider heading home.

This was a lost opportunity for the staffs to properly coordinate their efforts prior to planning the operation. It also provided a lesson on how capable and specialized forces can become inwardly focused, not considering the capabilities and knowledge of what is already in place. Stovepiping and barriers like this were to be broken down following the tragic events of 11 September 2001, but much work still needed to be done in 1994.

Fortunately, we never had to execute this plan. On 16 September, former president Jimmy Carter, Sen. Sam Nunn, Gen. Colin Powell, four White House advisers, and a complement of diplomatic personnel arrived in Port-au-Prince to conduct final negotiations with General Cédras. The group met first with Ambassador Swing as FAST-5 continued final preparations for the invasion.

The evening of 17 September was particularly busy. Small-arms and automatic fire continued throughout the night with rounds impacting in the vicinity of our billeting. I tasked the off-duty Marines with sweeping through the compound four times throughout the night checking for Haitians infiltrating the wire. The Haitians were on edge and knew what was coming; rampant false reports of Americans landing were resulting in weapons firing wildly in all directions. For added safety, I pulled all the Marines into the embassy compound to sleep that night. The invasion was near.

September 18 was another busy day. I received word from the embassy military liaison officer (MLO) and defense attaché at 6:00 p.m. that "it's going!" At 6:45 p.m., one of my special operations friends provided me the invasion force's challenge and password. At 7:00 p.m., Major Heseldon informed me USACOM had set H-hour for one minute past midnight. At 8:00 p.m., I recalled all Marines to the embassy compound under the guise of conducting training. I informed them the invasion was on for that evening and issued final instructions. I tasked them with staging extra rockets, machine guns, and ammunition at all the positions and elevated our alert status. At 8:25 p.m., Major Heseldon informed me that he had received word of a twenty-four-hour postponement of the invasion.

President Carter's delegation had finally achieved success in its negotiations with Cédras. At 8:30 p.m., the MLO informed me that the invasion force had been told to stand down. Airborne forces from the 82nd Airborne already in the air heading to Haiti were turned around and returned home. The Rangers, Marines, and other elements of the CJTF-190 invasion force stood down; security forces under CJTF-180 would make unopposed landings the following day.

FAST-5 continued preparations due to the uncertainty of what was to occur. I watched a CNN report at 9:00 p.m. describing the negotiations going on just a few blocks away. At 9:10 p.m. I briefed the Marines on the changes. To say we were disappointed is an understatement. Marines are men and women of action. We had rehearsed for months in anticipation of this moment, but it was not meant to be.

General Cédras had agreed to step down. It was his desire to remain in Haiti, but the United States advised against it and assisted in securing for him and a select group of others exile in Panama. Some of the embassy personnel involved in the negotiations claimed that General Cédras agreed to step down only after General Powell reminded him of the effectiveness of American firepower. However, we also know that a number of the coup leaders received monetary compensation for stepping aside and allowing Aristide to return to power peacefully. The masses of FAD soldiers, FRAPH, Haitian police, and other thugs who saw their power snatched away received no deals.

Much of the Haitian population felt liberated when U.S. forces arrived in Port-au-Prince on 19 September 1994. The bonds of oppression had been severed, or so the people thought. The population started to lash out at the Haitian soldiers, police, and other thugs who had intimidated them for so long. The thugs struck back; the U.S. military had not disarmed or attempted to control them in any way. In fact, the majority of U.S. soldiers operating at the port during the first few days of Operation Uphold Democracy remained within the confines of the port facility as the situation disintegrated outside.

I stood on the roof of the embassy and observed what looked like a scene out of the 1968 Chicago race riots. Police and thugs chased and beat civilians with clubs and chains as U.S. soldiers remained behind the walls of the port. In their defense, the sudden shift in mission and need to reorganize had caught soldiers off guard. This same dynamic played out in Iraq nearly ten years later in the streets of Baghdad. One must plan for the transition from combat, for providing a sustained secure environment to allow a return to normality. Coalition forces did not initially achieve this in Port-au-Prince.

Rioting was rampant until more combat power was brought ashore and employed. Things began to quiet down somewhat after tanks and Bradley Fighting Vehicles landed on 20 September, but the atmosphere in Haiti continued to be one of violence and uncertainty.

A different example of how to operate was playing out with the Marines in the north. The Marines landed in Cap-Haïtien on 21 September and responded when they heard that Haitian police had fired into a group of Aristide supporters who were advancing toward a police station. A squad of Marines killed eight Haitian police in a firefight started, they claimed, by the police.[13] This action stifled further violence in Cap-Haïtien. The city was relatively peaceful from that day on. We can only speculate whether the population felt appeased by the Marines being in control, that the Haitians learned not to challenge the Marines' authority, or a combination of both. There was discussion about whether the Marines used excessive force in this case, but they clearly operated within published ROE, and their action proved effective. FAST-5 would experience a less violent but similar incident on a follow-on deployment back to Haiti in 1996.

The introduction of thousands of U.S. troops to Port-au-Prince provided a rationale for FAST-5's departure. The assistant operations and intelligence officers for the 2nd Battalion, 22nd Infantry, 10th Mountain Division visited the embassy on 22 September with word that their unit had received the mission of reinforcing the embassy, if needed. I walked them around and showed them our fighting positions, and like the Rangers, they wanted to occupy positions inside the compound too. I explained there was simply not enough room on the ground to do so, particularly since many of Lieutenant General Shelton's staff had established living and working spaces in the small compound. I agreed to allow them to place additional machine guns and a sniper team on the roof in anticipation of their assuming the mission.

All interested parties agreed that FAST-5 should remain in place for at least thirty days to ensure that a stable situation existed before redeploying. I was proud of what my young team had accomplished during this mission. Although my senior enlisted Marine was only a sergeant (E-5), because our platoon sergeant, SSgt. Reuben Pitts, was attending the Infantry Officer's Course in Quantico, the detachment had accomplished the important mission of allowing the diplomatic mission to work unhindered toward a peaceful resolution of the crisis. The Marines performed their duties while working beside military and civilian personnel much senior to them in rank and experience. Undeterred, they adapted to the environment, accomplished the mission, and learned valuable lessons along the way. This would not be FAST-5's last experience in Haiti. The platoon would redeploy to the country a year later to provide security to those tasked with rebuilding its dilapidated infrastructure, but we had other missions to accomplish first.

Migrants, Special Security Missions, and Stopping Terrorism

Operation Sea Signal

FAST-5 received the call to assist with another emerging crisis shortly after returning home. Deplorable conditions in Haiti following the military coup that had brought General Cédras to power had now resulted in an exodus of migrants. Many Haitians assumed the risks of a hazardous voyage across the sea for the benefits of living in the United States. Thousands took to the water in small boats without proper planning or preparation. Many lost their lives as the danger of uncontrolled illegal immigration into the United States increased. This set the conditions for another nontraditional mission for the military.

The Department of State and the Immigration and Naturalization Service (INS) of the Department of Justice administer immigration policy. Foreign Service Officers and INS agents operating from U.S. embassies and consulates process legal immigrants but have little control over illegal immigration. The U.S. Coast Guard, then under the Department of Transportation (now Homeland Security), is responsible for interdicting illegal migrants at sea before they enter the United States. National policy in 1994 directed the Coast Guard to immediately return Haitian migrants to Haiti before turning them over to INS agents there for release. However, a change in U.S. policy created a situation requiring military assistance.

Operation Sea Signal began in May 1994 to prevent the loss of life and stop the uncontrolled flow of illegal immigrants into the United States. The operation became necessary following a policy decision to screen migrants for refugee status on board ship rather than immediately returning them to Haiti.[1] This decision resulted in an increased processing load that quickly exceeded the Coast Guard's capacity to deal with the emergency. The U.S. Navy received the mission of assisting with interdiction efforts. Government officials initially screened migrants and provided them safe haven on board leased ships anchored off Kingston, Jamaica, but the numbers quickly overwhelmed capacity.[2] The Clinton administration decided to open the U.S. Naval Base in Guantanamo Bay, Cuba, as a temporary shelter. Thousands of additional Cuban migrants added to the problem in August 1994 when Fidel Castro changed his policy and allowed Cubans to leave their country.

During its previous deployment, FAST-5 was on the receiving end of migrants returning to Haiti. It had facilitated the embassy's immigration efforts but would now have to assist with migrant problems in other ways. Although not trained specifically for supporting such a task, the Marines looked to the tenets of their doctrinal publication, *Warfighting*, to prepare themselves for another nontraditional mission. Embracing their abilities as flexible, adaptable, problem solvers, the platoon's Marines embarked on a new mission into unchartered territory.

Frustrations and tensions grew as the U.S. government struggled with the number of migrants. Guantanamo Bay quickly ran out of capacity to house refugees. Panama agreed to accept thousands of refugees to assist with the problem, but only if they remained under American control. In December 1994, hundreds of the 8,600 Cubans waiting for processing in Panama rioted and broke out of their camps in protest of a recent decision that fueled uncertainty about their ability to gain entry into the United States.[3] They built barricades and threw rocks, bricks, and bottles injuring 236 American soldiers.[4] The Marine Corps Security Force Company, Panama, and others received the mission of reinforcing the Army and quickly regained control. Not surprisingly, the Panamanians wanted the protestors out of their country. This resulted in FAST Company receiving the mission of retrieving and returning the recalcitrants to Guantanamo Bay.

FAST Company deployed a headquarters element and two platoons on two amphibious warships in support of Operation Sea Signal. The mission called for transferring approximately five hundred of the protestors from Panama back to Cuba. FAST-5 was one of two platoons in the operation. We deployed on the amphibious transport dock ship USS *Nashville* (LPD 4).[5] The other platoon deployed on the amphibious tank landing ship USS

Lamoure County (LST 1194).[6] FAST Company worked with the Navy to transform the two amphibious ships into modern-day prison ships, because many of the Cubans we were to transport had already demonstrated violent and criminal behavior.

The FAST Marines and ships' crews worked together closely in preparing for the mission. Sailors and Marines transformed the well decks, which normally housed armored assault vehicles and landing craft, into cell blocks by welding together chain-link fences topped with razor wire. They established fire-hose teams to spray down any individual or group who caused problems. They established and rehearsed guard rotations, feeding plans, and riot-control and snatch teams. Preparations continued for a month. The ships stopped in Guantanamo Bay to coordinate the transfer of the Cubans at that end and conducted a liberty call at Key West, Florida, to rest before continuing to Panama.

Unfortunately, the mission was not meant to be. Senior leaders decided to fly the Cuban troublemakers back to Guantanamo Bay rather than transport them by ship. Although we were disappointed, the opportunity to work closely with the Navy, gain shipboard experience, become acquainted with Guantanamo Bay, and practice a nontraditional mission proved beneficial and rewarding. FAST-5 returned home, only to find itself assigned another special security mission.

Refuel/Defuel

The Marine Corps Security Force Battalion's mission in the mid-1990s was to augment naval installations, ships, and facilities where the organic security forces proved insufficient to address known or perceived threats. The battalion consisted of a number of ships' detachments and security-force companies. The Marine Corps Security Force Company Kings Bay, Georgia, and Marine Corps Security Force Company Bangor, Washington, provided fixed-site security at designated areas, and FAST Company augmented that security at specified naval shipyards during the transfer of nuclear fuel to and from nuclear-powered ships.[7]

In the summer of 1995, FAST-5 received the mission of conducting a refuel/defuel mission at Portsmouth Naval Shipyard in Virginia. Our task was to provide a security perimeter around the USS *Dallas* (SSN 700), a Los Angeles–class nuclear-powered attack submarine, while she underwent overhaul at the shipyard.[8] We maintained strict security in this area, granting access only to authorized personnel, regardless of rank or position.

FAST-5 leadership on the well deck of the USS *Austin* (LPD 4) that the Navy/Marine Corps team, in support of Operation Safe Passage/Sea Signal, February 1995, made into a prison ship to pick up Cuban recalcitrants who rioted in Panama. Note the chain-link fence and razor wire. *Author collection*

This did not sit well with one Navy captain who, in his dress white uniform adorned with medals, approached a FAST-5 Marine manning his post one day. The captain was on his way to a ceremony being held at a nearby pier. His intention was to take a shortcut through the secured perimeter around the *Dallas*, but our Marine politely informed the captain that this was not possible without the proper authority. The captain tried to use his rank and brush the Marine aside. The Marine blocked the captain's way and became sterner in his insistence that the captain could not enter the secure perimeter, whereupon the captain became agitated and tried to push his way through. The Marine, using the standard escalation-of-force procedure, issued a verbal warning to the captain, making clear his intent to use physical force to stop the captain if he failed to step back. The captain attempted to push through once again, and the Marine applied an armbar grip and forced him face down onto the dirty, oily ground.

Not surprisingly, the captain became extremely agitated and used some harsh words, but finally calmed down after further coaxing by the Marine. The Marine let the captain up to find the officer's pristine dress white uniform covered in dirt and grime. The captain's face turned red behind the smeared grease on his cheek, and he stormed off to the shipyard commanding officer's office to file a complaint. I hurried to the office after hearing what had occurred, but the shipyard CO informed me not to worry. He had told the captain that he was in the wrong and never to bother "his" Marines again. That was the last we heard about the incident. The Marines of FAST-5 were to establish a similar reputation on our second deployment to Haiti.

U.S. Support Group Haiti

Operations in Haiti had followed established plans while FAST-5 conducted its refuel/defuel mission. Multinational forces completed the first phase of the mission to return President Aristide to power peacefully and establish a stable environment. The United Nations assumed a peacekeeping role during phase two of the operation under the command of Maj. Gen. Joe Kinzer, U.S. Army. The operation began in April 1995 and continued into 1996. The United States established a new organization, separate from the UN mission, called United States Support Group Haiti, in March 1996. The Support Group received the mission of providing humanitarian assistance to rebuild Haiti's infrastructure.

Military engineer units from the U.S. armed forces provided the expertise needed for the rebuilding effort. Special security units provided protection for the engineers in their base camps and as they completed work projects within the local communities. The first units deployed as part of the support group were the Air Force's 820th Red Horse (construction and logistics) Squadron and an Air Force Security Police (SP) unit to protect the Red Horse.[9] Navy Seabees from Naval Mobile Construction Battalion Five (NMCB-5) received the mission of relieving the Red Horse, while FAST-5 received the task of protecting the Seabees.

The Navy had created naval construction battalions following the entry of the United States into World War II. Civilian construction workers actively supported military efforts at the start of the war, but the need for men to perform construction work and fight too became apparent with the capture of Wake Island by the Japanese in 1941. Japanese soldiers killed or captured over a thousand civilian construction workers during that battle. The result was the creation of the Seabees. Over 325,000 Seabees would serve honorably during the war and live up to their motto of "We Build, We Fight."[10] Although the Seabees were trained to fight, FAST-5's presence ensured they did not have to do so on this operation.

FAST-5 returned to Haiti in March 1996 in support of U.S. Support Group Haiti during Operation Fairwinds. Fifth Squad (*above*) provided security to Navy Seabees helping rebuild the infrastructure of the troubled country. *Author collection*

FAST-5 was under the TACON of U.S. Support Group Haiti, commanded by Col. David Patton, U.S. Army, but remained under the operational control of the Marine Corps Security Force Battalion in Norfolk, Virginia. Colonel Patton was an Army Military Police officer, who had just completed a tour as the UN Executive for Haitian Security, which provided overwatch for the program to rebuild the Haitian criminal justice system. Not surprisingly, he understood the security mission well and proved to be knowledgeable, fair, and supportive.[11]

The scope of FAST-5's security mission in Haiti continued to develop as we prepared for deployment. Policy discussions, funding issues, and political considerations all impacted the number and type of work projects for which the Seabees received authorization. FAST-5 completed preparations as these discussions continued. We renewed our efforts to learn Haitian Creole, started taking malaria pills again, conducted threat assessments, and gave operational security briefings.

The security situation in Haiti during this deployment was less dangerous than during our last visit. Criminal activity was the new primary security threat. Reports indicated that thirty to forty criminal gangs existed in the country at the time, with ten to twenty of them well organized. Elements of the Tonton Macoute and Attachés likely made up some of these gangs. Criminals operated near six main road intersections in Port-au-Prince, where vehicle traffic slowed and provided prime targets. Gang members operated in groups of three. One individual usually drew the attention of local security personnel, another distracted the driver of a vehicle, while the third stole from the vehicle anything he could grab. Some bold thieves grabbed the sunglasses right off the faces of U.S. soldiers, as they drove by.

The ROE were ambiguous on dealing with this threat. Senior leaders wanted to demonstrate that Haitians did not have to expect the normal brutality. To provide a less threatening posture, they released guidance that soldiers and Marines could not load weapons and could not mount machine guns. They hoped to portray a safe and stable environment so as to attract business investors to Haiti. I did not disagree with that rationale. However, the enemy gets a vote. In some cultures, "might means right," and people do respond to power and authority.

I trained my Marines on this new ROE as I struggled with another issue. Maj. Rayburn Griffith, our commanding officer in FAST Company, was everything a Marine wants in a commander. He was tough, fair, and caring, with a presence that exuded confidence and put us all at ease. Unfortunately, Major Griffith had had a run-in with a senior officer from higher headquarters during a previous tour, and this officer still held a grudge. The word was out that Major Griffith's performance was under scrutiny, and that the offended officer was seeking justification to recommend his relief. The sergeant major of the battalion informed me that Major Griffith's future rode on the success of FAST-5's pending mission.

Major Griffith was completely within his right to scrutinize the preparations for and execution of our mission. I met with him to brief him on the progress of preparations and expected a lot of questions, considering his burden. At the conclusion of my brief, I looked toward him and stood by for the barrage. Instead he looked up with a big smile and said, "Jason, like Napoleon said to his generals, don't f— it up!" That was the best commander's intent I had ever received. His comment broke the tension and conveyed his trust and confidence in our ability to accomplish the mission without close supervision. It also said a great deal about the character of a man who cared more for his Marines preparing to deploy than for his own well-being. I have remained close to Ray Griffith, who retired years later as a colonel, and to his son Ben, now serving as a Marine infantry officer.

FAST-5 had just enough time at home to enjoy Thanksgiving dinner with family before deploying back to Haiti at the end of November 1995. Unlike our first deployment, which had focused on the fixed site of the U.S. embassy, this mission required a number of HMMWVs to support operations across the country. The company possessed only a few vehicles, so we borrowed a number from the 2nd Marine Division at Camp Lejeune, North Carolina. (Our mission had a high enough priority to receive the 6th Marine Regimental commander's personal HMMWV.) We loaded twelve vehicles into a single C-5 Galaxy cargo aircraft and flew into Port-au-Prince International Airport.

Colonel Patton and the U.S. Support Group Haiti Command sergeant major, Sgt. Maj. Joe Stanley, met us. I watched as the HMMWVs drove off the aircraft and my platoon sergeant, SSgt. Mark Irish, formed the platoon to report to Colonel Patton. As I reported, I observed the sergeant major looking past our fifty-man platoon formation. I asked what he was looking for; he responded, "Where is your sergeant major?" I laughed at the thought of having a sergeant major for such a small unit, but the sergeant major was serious.

This demonstrates a difference between the Army and the Marine Corps. The Marines push greater responsibility down to lower levels. For example, an Army squad is led by a staff sergeant (E-6) and consists of two fireteams of four soldiers each, for a total of nine men per squad. A sergeant (E-5) leads a Marine squad, and it consists of three fireteams of four men each, for a total of thirteen per squad. Army platoon sergeants are sergeants first class (E-7). Marine platoon sergeants are staff sergeants (E-6), one rank lower. Marine E-7s are company gunnery sergeants who lead companies of approximately two hundred Marines instead of a platoon of only fifty. Marine sergeants major lead battalions of nearly a thousand men, certainly not fifty-man platoons.

This new mission received the title of Operation Fairwinds. FAST-5 assumed responsibility for security of its expeditionary base camp located within the perimeter fence of the airport, called Camp Fairwinds, the base camp had been built by the 820th Red Horse. Colonel Patton, his staff, and his higher headquarters, and the Combined Joint Task Force (CJTF) itself, which was based on the 101st Airborne Division (Air Assault), were located across the road in an industrial park referred to as the Light Industrial Complex (LIC).

In addition to guarding the base camp, FAST-5 provided security at a second base camp and eight separate worksites. The Seabees of NMCB-5, under the capable leadership of Lt. Chris Collins and Master Chief Garside, were professionals who did some extraordinary work. A detachment from NMCB-7, led by Lt. John Stone, later relieved the detachment from NMCB-5. The Seabees repaired large portions of Harry S. Truman Boulevard, a main road through Port-au-Prince. They fixed schools and hospitals, operated a cement batch plant, and dug wells to provide fresh water to the community. FAST-5 provided security at each of these sites and for over a thousand convoys to allow the Seabees to remain focused on their construction work.

The construction work performed by the Seabees required materials that had to be shipped into the port facility some miles away from Camp Fairwinds. We learned very quickly, the hard way, that these materials were like gold to the Haitian population. They would go to great lengths to steal whatever items they could get their hands on. On our first convoy, the trucks carrying these materials had to make slow turns to navigate the crowded Haitian roads—even though we only moved at night, to avoid the heavier traffic of the day—while exiting the port facility. The local gangs took advantage of this and immediately swarmed the trucks, cut the straps holding the materials, and tossed as many items off as they could before the Marines moved in to stop them. We had to change our tactics or risk losing more material.

The second convoy from the port proved more successful as the Marines adapted to a new environment and threat. We maneuvered the HMMWVs closer in on the flanks of the trucks and used defensive driving tactics usually employed for personal protective details like those performed by the Secret Service. We also learned that speed, when possible, provided security in this environment. Unfortunately, we were to lose too many Marines in Iraq in later years thinking this adage was equally true against improvised explosive devices (IEDs); we quickly learned in Iraq that you cannot outrun IEDs, no matter how fast you drive. However, these new tactics worked in Haiti. We confused the gang members, but a few still got to the trucks. We needed to do better.

The third convoy from the port was the most successful. Continuing to adjust tactics, we now added deception to our plans. It was dark, so I had two trucks and a HMMWV pull up toward the main gate from which we had previously departed and turn on their headlights. I had their crews run their engines and appear to be making preparations for departure, all to draw the attention of the gang members forming on the other side of the gate. The remainder of the vehicles, with their headlights off, quietly moved farther down the port facility to a side gate.

The gang members never saw the actual convoy coming. They all screamed and ran toward the road when the convoy seemed to appear from nowhere, and it sped right past them before they realized what had happened. The gang made a feeble attempt to stop the convoy a few miles down the road, by blocking the way with what appeared to be a wall of pig feces, but I ordered our lead vehicle to ram through it. That vehicle smelled terrible for the remainder of the deployment, but the convoy got through with no losses.

The Haitians tested us again on 28 December 1995. I arrived at the FAST-5 combat operations center to find a female Seabee petty officer crying and a male petty officer with a scared look on his face. They informed me that they had left our base camp in a dump truck full of wood without a Marine escort. Gang members had stopped their truck at gunpoint and stolen the wood.

FAST-5 devised a plan to prevent this from occurring again. We had another dump truck loaded with wood depart the following day using the same road. However, this time I had our counterintelligence (CI) Marines film the event from a tower while a hidden squad of Marines mounted in HMMWVs stood ready to pounce. The CI Marines waited until the gang members swarmed the truck before calling the squad to action. Within two minutes the Marines had dispersed the crowd and detained two gang members. This show of force, and the professionalism and tactics displayed in our convoy operations generally, convinced the Haitians to stop challenging the Marines. They spread the word about the "white sleeves," which was the nickname given to the Marines, because of the way in which we roll up our uniform sleeves inside out. (Soldiers roll up their sleeves with the dark side facing out.)

Some soldiers who observed our operations claimed we had used excessive force in handling the gang members we detained. Colonel Patton appointed an investigating officer to conduct a commander's inquiry on the matter. One of the gang members had alleged that Marines had injured his leg; the investigating officer confirmed that he had hurt it himself when jumping off the moving truck. The investigating officer substantiated a claim that the Marines had used pepper spray on the second detainee but determined this did not constitute excessive force. We Marines believed we had done our duty; allegations from people who we had believed were on the same team disappointed us. However, Colonel Patton was fair and took prudent steps in investigating the matter.

FAST-5 faced other challenges that required creative solutions. The Haitian presidential election occurred on 17 December 1995. Its successful

Lance Corporal Box detains a Haitian gang member who attempted to hijack a
Navy Seabee truck. The word quickly got out not to mess with the "White Sleeves."
Author collection

execution showed measurable progress for the U.S. and UN missions in Haiti.
However, we had faced a challenge in one local community that needed a
solution before the people would vote. The Seabees had established a water
well in one village, taking possession of a Haitian open-air structure. They
used it as a storage area and workshop and could not move their gear without
disrupting the project and delaying delivery of fresh water. Unfortunately, the

building the Seabees occupied was the area's historical voting place. The village elders refused to allow anyone to vote unless the Seabees moved out of it. The Seabees and village elders all stood firm. The Marines intervened with a workable solution after a discussion with the villagers. The Haitians were not as concerned about the specific facility used as they were with having protection against rain on election day. FAST-5 offered them one of our large general-purpose tents, and the Haitians quickly accepted. With the problem solved, the elections concluded without further incident, and the Seabees completed their project on time.

This incident provided a valuable lesson in communications. First, one must ask those one intends to help what their real needs are before acting. The failure to follow this rule in later years during Operations Iraqi Freedom and Enduring Freedom in Afghanistan wasted time, effort, and resources as American forces built what they thought our partners wanted instead of what they actually needed.

The arrival of the holiday season provided some relief for the Marines and sailors. A Club Med beach resort on Haiti's southwestern shore that had closed in 1987, following the violent overthrow of Duvalier, reopened on 21 December.[12] Marines, soldiers, and sailors joined tourists from Europe and Canada for relaxation on the beach. American service men and women received free passes from their commands as part of a rest-and-relaxation program. It proved to be a surreal environment where military personnel and civilians partied together. This was not how Marines envisioned service in the infantry, but there were no complaints.

FAST-5 also benefitted from a United Services Organization (USO) show immediately before Christmas. The USO had begun entertaining American troops in the early days of World War II, and they did us the honor of providing a show in Port-au-Prince in 1995.[13] A dance troupe and singers put on a wonderful show. Many Marines and sailors joined the troupe on stage to share their own musical talents. The troupe also pulled Command Master Chief Garside from the Seabees and me on stage to sing "My Girl," by the Temptations, but I think we scared many listeners away. The dancers used my room to change costumes between acts; a lingering reminder of this great event remained in the form of the pleasant smell of their perfume. This certainly beat the standard smell of sweating bodies, burning trash, and raw sewage one often experienced in Haiti.

The U.S. Support Group received a visit from the chairman of the Joint Chiefs of Staff, Gen. John Shalikashvili, U.S. Army.[14] Colonel Patton accompanied him in a visit to Camp Fairwinds, where the chairman shook hands, took pictures, and engaged in conversation with many Marines and sailors. A Marine general, John Sheehan, the commander in chief of the U.S. Atlantic Command at that time, also visited the Support Group. Being a Marine, General Sheehan agreed to address FAST-5 separately. Interestingly, he informed us that he had a great-uncle who had served as a Marine in Haiti as part of the original occupation forces in 1915.

FAST-5 was nearing the end of its mission in Haiti, but it continued to support the Seabees at a number of worksites in January 1996. FAST-3 received the mission of relieving us in late spring, and preparations began for the transition. However, the Army was not going to let us leave without first testing our pride. Soldiers challenged FAST-5 to a boxing "smoker" before we departed. The challenge fired up my Marines. They were scrappers and loved a good fight. Marine training emphasizes combined-arms expertise. We employ the synergistic effects of all available firepower to achieve the mission and are trained to use anything available as a weapon in life-or-death situations. Fighting by the rules in a boxing ring is something else. The talent pool of fifty Marines from which we had to choose our fighters was a little smaller than the thousands of soldiers the Army had in country. However, there was no holding my Marines back. They were still sore about the allegation of excessive force leveled at us by soldiers in the convoy incident. Unfortunately, the Army exploited that pride and suckered us in.

The smoker was a disaster for the Marines. I knew we were in trouble when I walked up to the ring on the night of the fights to see numerous Army generals, colonels, and other field-grade officers sitting in the front rows and took my seat as a lowly captain and the only officer representing the Corps. It was ugly. The Army won eight of the nine matches. Corporal Jacobs won our only bout, out of sheer determination and an unorthodox style of flailing at his opponent, who was used to fighting experienced boxers. I later found out the Army had a number of "ringers" that evening; many of the soldiers our Marines faced were Army Golden Glove boxers. We had failed in our intelligence collection before entering that battle.

Although the Marines lost this battle, we like to think we won the war. An indication of the importance of our mission became evident when I received an order to send one of our Marines back to the United States to participate in the 1995 presidential State of the Union address. Cpl. Gregory Depestre was a member of FAST-5 and of Haitian descent. President Clinton had him sit in the balcony beside the First Lady, Hillary Clinton,

FAST-5 on board the USS *Intrepid* (CV 11), a World War II aircraft carrier now serving as a floating museum in New York City, during Fleet Week 1996. FAST-5 received the task to be the ceremonial guard for President Bill Clinton at a function on the ship. *Author collection*

and pointed him out by name during his speech. This was a fitting conclusion to FAST-5's time in Haiti. General Krulak's description of the "strategic corporal" proved true. Our Marines' tactical actions on the ground had strategic implications.

Antiterrorism Mission Bahrain

On 25 June 1996, a truck loaded with five thousand pounds of explosives exploded outside Khobar Towers, killing nineteen airmen of the U.S. Air Force's 4404th Wing and wounding 498 others.[15] Khobar Towers was a high-rise apartment building in Dhahran, Saudi Arabia, that U.S. forces had used for billeting personnel since Operation Desert Storm in 1990. Investigations identified Iran or Hezbollah as the likely perpetrator of the attack.[16] That raised concerns for the safety of other U.S. military personnel and facilities located in the Middle East. FAST-5 was about to miss its second Fourth of July weekend at home in two years.

FAST Company received its notification order on 29 June 1996 to deploy a force to the Kingdom of Bahrain, a small island nation in the Persian Gulf connected to Saudi Arabia by a causeway. Bahrain was the home of U.S. Naval Forces Central Command and the Navy's Fifth Fleet.[17] A continuous American naval presence had begun in Bahrain in 1948 with the establishment of a small shore facility shared with Britain's Royal Navy.[18] What was originally known as the U.S. Middle East Force provided logistical and communications support to Navy vessels with embarked Marines. American forces assumed control of the ten-acre base in 1971 when the Royal Navy departed and renamed the facility the Administrative Support Unit Bahrain in 1979. The base received the title of Administrative Support Unit (ASU) Southwest Asia in 1992 to depict more accurately its role. The limited space afforded by the base required naval personnel to live off base in downtown Manama, Bahrain's capital. The Navy leased a ten-story apartment building, the Mannai Plaza, for this purpose.

FAST Company received the mission of securing the ASU and Mannai Plaza from terrorist attack. The company deployed a headquarters element and two platoons to accomplish it. FAST-5 received the mission to secure the Mannai Plaza, while its sister platoon, FAST-4, secured the ASU. Administrators, logisticians, communicators, medical personnel, bomb-sniffing military working dogs (MWDs), a Marine CI sub-team, and a Navy explosive ordnance disposal (EOD) team augmented the company. FAST Company's commanding officer, Major Griffith, deployed with the headquarters element to provide command and control. Col. William Parrish, commanding officer of the Marine Corps Security Force Battalion, accompanied him to coordinate a more permanent security force for the ASU.

Our unit received the initial order to deploy on 6 July, but intelligence reports precipitated a more rapid move. FAST-5 departed Norfolk on 2 July and arrived in Bahrain on the evening of 3 July. We quickly surveyed the ground, issued orders and ammunition, and began manning positions by 8:00 a.m. the next day. The commander of U.S. Naval Forces Central Command (COMNAVCENT) wanted us in place by the Fourth of July to deter any terrorist activities as Americans celebrated.

The Americans in Bahrain served important roles in the Middle East. At the time of the Khobar Towers bombing, nearly five thousand Air Force personnel operated from Kuwait and Saudi Arabia enforcing a United Nations–sanctioned no-fly zone over Iraq. Army Patriot missile batteries protected American and coalition forces throughout the area, while four brigades' worth of prepositioned Army armor assets, strategically located throughout the region, provided a deterrent force. U.S. forces conducted military exercises with partner nations, and U.S. naval forces expanded

The Mannai Plaza in downtown Manama, Bahrain, that housed hundreds of U.S. service personnel and was guarded by FAST-5 following the deadly bombing of Khobar Towers in Saudi Arabia that killed fourteen airmen in 1996. *Author collection*

to include a carrier battle group and amphibious ready group with an embarked MEU throughout most of the year. The command element and support establishment for these naval forces operated from Bahrain.

Although friendly to the United States, Bahrain was a dangerous place. The country is predominately Muslim, with both Shia and Sunni populations. The Shiites controlled much of the wealth and power in the island, which did not sit well with the majority Sunni population and often resulted in civil disturbances. Over five hundred nonviolent demonstrations and approximately 1,700 attacks occurred in Bahrain around the time of FAST's deployment.[19] These attacks usually consisted of improvised explosive and incendiary devices. They did not specifically target Americans, but nevertheless, we had concerns that terrorists in the area would use the confusion created by civil unrest to attack our personnel and positions.

FAST-4 augmented a ninety-man Naval Security Force (NSF) to secure the ASU. The ASU consisted of a number of buildings and facilities supporting the U.S. Naval Forces Central Command and Fifth Fleet command groups. It also contained administrative, logistical, and recreational activities for the region's naval forces. The base itself formed a secured compound, surrounded by a twelve-foot-high chain-link fence, motion detectors, and security cameras. FAST-4 lived on the base in the only American barracks available in the country and augmented the NSF with machine gun and designated marksmanship positions, security patrols, and a reaction force. Approximately a thousand meters and a Sunni neighborhood surrounding the ASU separated it from the Mannai Plaza.

FAST-5 lived in and secured the Mannai Plaza. It was a Bahraini-owned, American-leased property that housed over four hundred American service men and women. The NSF provided two sailors armed with pistols to guard the entrance, while Bahraini security police manned outposts covering the four approaches to the building. FAST-5 augmented these positions with additional ground positions, entry control points, designated marksman and machine-gun positions, and a reaction force. The Fleet Marine Officer assigned to the Fifth Fleet also took the initiative to position fifty-five-gallon drums filled with sand approximately 100–150 feet from the base of the Mannai, the start of a barrier that would-be suicide bombers could not pass.

Establishing a secured perimeter in the middle of a Sunni city is a daunting task. Although the initial actions taken to secure the Mannai following the Khobar Towers bombing were helpful, they were also insufficient. Analysis of the Khobar Towers bombing indicated requirements for a perimeter two to three times farther out than the one initiated at the Mannai to provide adequate standoff from a bomb detonation. Estimates showed that 80–90 percent of the casualties at the Khobar Towers had resulted from glass fragmentation.[20] FAST-5 lowered this risk by pushing the perimeter out as far as terrain and neighborhood would allow and backing it up with a tank ditch. The Mannai Plaza lies on landfill created to provide the congested city with more space for construction. This resulted in a high water table, which we exploited by digging ditches that quickly filled with water, creating a natural moat to block high-speed avenues of approach to the plaza.

FAST-5 conducted its own civil affairs operation to ensure that the security preparations of the landfill did not degrade relations with the Sunni neighbors. Locals had used the fields we used as a security zone to play soccer. FAST-5 worked with Commander Naval Forces Central Command to provide the funds, engineering equipment, and personnel needed to create a professional soccer field out of what had been an open sandlot. We used an Arab linguist from our counterintelligence team to coordinate this effort with local leaders, who were receptive and helped in the planning. The project was a success. It helped to build rapport with the local population and proved invaluable in gaining information on activities in the local community.

Unfortunately, we did not always maintain the same rapport with the sailors living in the Mannai Plaza. Some sailors felt inconvenienced by the all-hands evacuation drills we periodically held. We conducted these drills at random times, at a minimum of once per week, to keep residents rehearsed in the proper procedures for evacuating the building and marshaling personnel for accountability purposes. We established a standard of three and a half minutes to have the entire building of over four hundred personnel evacuated, based on lessons learned from Khobar Towers. It had taken three minutes and thirty-seven seconds from the time an airman had spotted terrorists running away from a truck in front of the Khobar Towers before it exploded.

During a security sweep one of our bomb-sniffing military working dogs hit on what he thought were explosives in the Mannai. The dog handler and dog had just completed a tour of the building and entered our combat operations center (COC) located on the first floor when, to our surprise, the dog quickly sat in the manner that meant he smelled explosives. We all froze, and everyone stopped talking. I looked at the dog handler and asked if the dog's action was a fluke. He responded, "No, sir, he does not do that unless he has a good hit." I immediately gave the order to evacuate the building and called out our EOD team. After conducting a thorough search of the COC, EOD determined that the dog had hit on a link of five previously fired 5.56-mm machine-gun rounds used to practice the safe loading and unloading of the squad automatic weapon. I found myself surprised by how sensitive the dog's senses were, that he could pick up a small amount of gunpowder residue on spent brass, secured in a watertight ammunition can, and stored in a wooden box. I was glad the dogs were on our side.

I had little sympathy for the sailors who felt inconvenienced. The Marines and sailors of FAST were standing posts in some tough conditions. It was not uncommon for temperatures to rise to well above a hundred degrees with high humidity during our deployment. It is difficult to remain alert when suffering from the heat. We employed ice vests worn under flak jackets for Marines on post. The weather also affected our dogs. We had special "booties" made for them, because the ground was so hot it could burn the bottoms of their feet. Men and dogs both had to minimize their exposure outdoors. We restricted Marines to standing post for no more than four hours at a time, while we held the dogs to no more than twenty minutes outside before being brought back into an air-conditioned space.

We took seriously the responsibility for protecting the lives of those under our charge. The tragic event at Khobar Towers was a constant reminder of the cost of lowering one's guard. Our senior defense officials took the safety of our service men and women seriously as well. The secretary of defense appointed a retired U.S. Army general, Wayne Downing, to lead a team to examine the circumstances surrounding the bombing and assess the security posture of all American forces in the region.[21] Downing was a legend from the Army Special Forces. He had two Silver Stars, five Bronze Stars, and the Purple Heart for combat in Vietnam and Operation Desert Storm. In 2001, Downing would come out of retirement to accept appointment as the National Director and Deputy National Security Advisor for combating terrorism, to coordinate the national campaign "to detect, disrupt and destroy global terrorist organizations and those who support them."[22] On this occasion, Downing and his team interviewed over four hundred service men and women and assessed thirty-six sites throughout the Middle East. FAST Company was one of the units inspected by the task force.

Our performance encouraged General Downing, who stated, "The U.S. Marine FAST security teams were the most impressive security forces observed in the theater. They are superbly trained, well equipped, and well led. They provide a useful model for development of service training programs."[23] Downing's report listed every action FAST took in preparing for, training for, and executing our mission as recommendations for others to follow. The secretary of defense tasked the Army and Air Force with creating similar antiterrorism security units after reflecting on Downing's report.

A tragic event was averted by the professionalism demonstrated by the Marines of FAST-4 just as Downing was completing his report. I was traveling between the Mannai Plaza and the ASU one day and waiting in a line of vehicles attempting to enter the base. There were six cars in front of my vehicle being systematically searched for weapons and explosives by FAST-4's Marines. Additional Marines from FAST-4 manned an ominous-looking .50-caliber heavy machine gun positioned to destroy any vehicles attempting to make unauthorized entry. I watched in amazement as a civilian jeep jumped the curb behind me and sped toward the front gate at high speed. My first thought was that it was a suicide bomber trying to take out the Marines.

The Marines would have been completely within their rights, and within the rules of engagement, to fire at the vehicle. All indicators pointed toward a threat. However, they held their fire. The split seconds they took to make a determination to shoot or not seemed like an eternity, but their training served them well. They remained calm and demonstrated the tactical patience needed to assess the situation properly. They made the right decision. This was no suicide bomber but a sailor who had a choking child in his car and had made a seemingly threatening move with his vehicle in his haste to seek medical aid. I thank God that this event did not end differently.

After FAST proved their expertise on the ground, Commander Naval Forces Central Command tasked FAST Marines with assisting the NSF in conducting harbor patrols. Warships often came into Bahrain to replenish supplies and provide crews with shore liberty. The ships berthed at the pier facility located approximately 1,500 meters from the ASU. Their crews and embarked Marines provided security on the pier, while the FAST Marines and NSF protected the seaward side from waterborne threats. We used thirty-foot Boston Whalers, with M-60 medium machine guns mounted in their bows, to accomplish this task. Our success in presenting "hard targets" to the terrorists only made them look for "soft" targets elsewhere.

In a similar situation in Yemen a few short years later, terrorists bombed the Navy destroyer USS *Cole* (DDG 67).[24] In October 2000, two suicide bombers manning a small motorboat full of explosives detonated against the side of the *Cole*, killing seventeen crew members and wounding thirty-nine others. The bombers were al-Qaeda operatives who had received their orders from a terrorist, little-known at the time, named Osama bin Laden. This was not bin Laden's first attack though, and I would find myself called to respond in another capacity to what had been some of his earlier dirty work.

8

★

Terrorist Attacks, Company Command, and Recruiting the Force

Terrorist Attacks

n 1996, Secretary of Defense William Perry argued that "we must gird ourselves for a relentless struggle in which there will be many silent victories and some noisy defeats."[1] FAST Company's antiterrorism mission in Bahrain was a silent victory. Unfortunately, the United States also experienced some serious defeats. The most notable occurred on 11 September 2001, when nineteen terrorists hijacked four U.S. commercial airliners and killed nearly three thousand people in attacks against the World Trade Center in New York and the Pentagon in Washington, DC, and in Shanksville, Pennsylvania. Osama bin Laden, leader of the terrorist group al-Qaeda, orchestrated these attacks. His hatred for America had begun long before 9/11. Bin Laden and his followers had sought out and attacked soft targets with devastating effects on the world stage to raise awareness of their call for jihad, using terrorism, information, and symbolism as weapons.

Two of their most deadly attacks occurred eight years to the day after U.S. troops had deployed to Saudi Arabia following Iraq's invasion of Kuwait. On 7 August 1998, bombs exploded nearly simultaneously at the U.S. embassies in Nairobi, Kenya, killing 213 and injuring 4,500, and Dar-es-Salaam, Tanzania, killing 11 and injuring 85.[2] Bin Laden and al-Qaeda were lashing out in response to the offense they perceived in American troops occupying Saudi Arabia, home to the Muslim holy cities of Mecca and Medina.

FAST Company was part of the U.S. response, rapidly deploying Marines to provide security following these attacks. Unfortunately, the company's limited size prevented it from having a presence in all areas experiencing heightened threats. The Marine Corps recognized this limitation and eventually took steps to establish two additional FAST companies to raise the number of available platoons from six to eighteen. However, that expansion was still in progress, and the FAST platoon in Kenya needed relief.

Company Command

I believe the rank of captain and the corresponding billet of company commander represent the best situation that any officer can have in the Marine Corps. The formative years of being a platoon commander are rewarding and fun, but they pale in comparison to the honor and privilege of commanding Marines in the way a company commander does. The responsibility commanders have in leading and developing their Marines is not one they take lightly.

The young men and women of our country are living currently in difficult times. The divorce rate in America is over 50 percent, which can result in many children being raised in single-parent homes, where the sole parent must work to support the family. This can often result in the young learning more from friends, TV shows, and social media than their parents. In addition, too many Americans now have a sense of "entitlement": they believe society owes them something and that everyone gets a "soccer trophy." Those who live in the real world know this is not true. One must earn what one gets out of life. Unfortunately, thirteen weeks of Marine Corps boot camp cannot unravel the poor lessons society teaches young people.

Graduating from boot camp is for Marines the beginning of a transformation process that continues until the day they terminate active service. Marines never stop growing, whether they serve a single four-year tour or a forty-year career. It is every leader's responsibility in the Marine Corps to coach, train, and mentor their people to grow both personally and professionally. Marines accept their responsibility for developing ethical warriors, who serve honorably while in uniform and ultimately return to society as better citizens. The billet of platoon commander is the closest an officer will get to direct leadership of enlisted Marines. Company commanders occupy the "sweet spot" where they can still shape the development of their enlisted Marines but also, for the first time, lead and mentor officers.

Infantry Officer Advanced Course (IOAC)

As I completed my tour with FAST Company, the prospect of becoming a company commander excited me, but I first had to go back to school. Marine officers follow a career progression that starts with The Basic School (TBS) and follow-on military-occupational-specialty school before they join their first operational, or "fleet," unit. One's first fleet tour normally lasts three years and is followed by a nonoperational, or "B" billet, tour with the supporting establishment. Many officers prefer to remain in the fleet, but Marine Corps wisdom prevails. History demonstrates that broader experience and a break from deployments and other operational requirements produce better leaders able to sustain their performance longer. My tour with FAST Company was an uncharacteristic "B" billet in that I deployed more in that job than my first fleet tour.

The Marine Corps selects many officers to attend resident schools following completion of a "B" billet. Each of the military services has its own professional military education (PME) institutions. Lieutenants attend basic officer courses (BOCs). The BOC for the Marine Corps is TBS. Captains attend career-level schools (CLS). The CLS for the Marine Corps is the Expeditionary Warfare School (EWS). Majors attend intermediate-level schools (ILSs). The ILS for the Marine Corps is the Marine Corps Command and Staff College (MCCSC). Lieutenant colonels attend top-level schools (TLSs). The TLS for the Marine Corps is the Marine Corps War College (MCWC). EWS, MCCSC, and MCWC are all part of the Marine Corps University, located at Quantico, Virginia. Each of the service schools is open to members of the other services. This fosters relationships and knowledge that facilitate future joint operations. In 1997, for my CLS, I had the pleasure of attending the Army's Infantry Officer Advanced Course (IOAC), at Fort Benning, Georgia.

Army schools are outstanding. The IOAC curriculum consisted of twenty weeks of studying and planning infantry tactics at the company, battalion, and brigade levels. The Army in 1997 organized its infantry into five categories: light (foot mobile), mechanized (armored personnel carriers), airborne (parachute), air assault (helicopter), and Ranger (special skills). The Army introduced Stryker brigade combat teams in 2002, providing a middle-weight force more deployable than mechanized units, but with more firepower than light units.[3] Marine Corps infantry does not specialize like the Army; Marine infantry units do it all. It is not uncommon for a single Marine infantry unit to operate on foot, from vehicles, and

from helicopters. Marine infantry also has separate light armored reconnaissance units that operate from LAVs (light armored vehicles, similar to
the Army's Strykers).[4] Marines do not habitually conduct airborne operations, although some specialized units employ airborne capabilities.

The IOAC consisted of approximately 220 students, including approximately twenty international students and four U.S. Marines. I was one of the
four Marines. My wife Sonja and I sponsored Major Mansur Khan and his
family from Bangladesh for the school year. International military students
often attend American schools to build relationships and establish common operating concepts among partner nations. Instructors used lectures,
small group discussions, and practical exercises to teach the curriculum.

Students organized into squad-sized seminar groups led by seasoned captains. Capt. John Norris led my seminar. Norris was a former Marine corporal
who had won a Bronze Star during Operation Desert Storm before attending
college and being commissioned in the Army. He eased my transition into
the Army school, because Captain Norris and I spoke some of the same
language. This language was shaped not only by our common experiences in
the Marine Corps but also by our voracious reading of military history.

Many military officers and staff noncommissioned officers are amateur
historians. We learn from the past to ensure we don't repeat the mistakes
of those who came before us. The cost and sacrifice of not doing so are too
high. Professional reading of military history, both classics and contem-
porary works, assist leaders in visualizing the patterns of past events and
placing their current situations into context. Attendance at resident PME
schools helps to fill in the gaps and take one's level of understanding from
that of self-study to new heights. I received an excellent education at IOAC.
It prepared me well for my pending assignment as a company commander.

Golf Company

I checked into 2nd Battalion, 1st Marines (2/1) in September 1997 and
received the assignment of assistant operations officer. My responsibilities
included planning and coordinating the operations of the battalion, but
this billet also allowed me to observe each of the rifle companies in action.
It gave me a sense of which company I might want to command. Although
Marine infantrymen are generalists in their employment, units assigned
to MEUs normally focus their training on one of three means of mobility: helicopters (helos), amphibious vehicles, or small boats. In the 1990s,
MEUs had responsibility for conducting any one of eighteen separate

mission-essential tasks. Each MEU received certification as "Special Operations Capable" (SOC) once it demonstrated mastery of these tasks. Each task required one, or a combination, of the means of mobility assigned to the rifle companies. I hoped to receive command of Golf Company, which was the designated helo company. I got my wish.

I took over command of G/2/1 in October 1997. One of the most important decisions a new company commander can make, if given the chance, is to choose a company first sergeant to serve as his senior enlisted adviser. Battalion sergeants major usually manage assignments of senior enlisted personnel within a battalion. I was fortunate to have Sgt. Maj. John Estrada as the battalion sergeant major. Sergeant Major Estrada was a professional, who later served as the fifteenth Sergeant Major of the Marine Corps from 2003 to 2007 and as the U.S. ambassador to Trinidad and Tobago from 17 March 2016 to 20 January 2017. I observed the senior enlisted Marines of the battalion for some time, and although we were an infantry battalion, I was most impressed with the gunnery sergeant running our chow hall.

GySgt. Ed Sax was a Marine cook. However, Gunnery Sergeant Sax lived by the Corps' ethos that every Marine is first and foremost a rifleman. His background as a cook did not matter to me as much as his leadership ability, professionalism, and passion for leading Marines. I asked Sergeant Major Estrada to assign Gunnery Sergeant Sax to Golf Company after his selection for promotion to first sergeant. The company command team rounded out with 1st Lt. Jason Perry as the company executive officer, and GySgt. Dennis Bowden as the company gunnery sergeant. Sax was later promoted to sergeant major and led his Marines in the battle of Fallujah before retiring. Perry is today a colonel, in command of an infantry regiment. Bowden was selected for the coveted title of Marine Gunner. Gunners are chief warrant officers and the weapons subject-matter experts of the Marine Corps. These exceptional men enabled Golf Company's success.

Golf Company implemented an aggressive training schedule in anticipation of deployment. Our battalion received orders to form as a battalion landing team (BLT) and deploy as the ground combat element of the 13th Marine Expeditionary Unit (Special Operations Capable). A BLT is a reinforced infantry battalion that is augmented with additional combat power to include tanks, amphibious vehicles, artillery, engineers, reconnaissance, and light armored reconnaissance units. Golf Company spent as much time training with the air combat element (ACE) as it did with the ground combat element (GCE), since it was the designated helo company.

Our ACE consisted of a composite squadron centered on the "Purple Foxes" of Medium Helicopter Squadron (HMM) 364. The squadron flew

The best billet for a captain in the Marine Corps—company command. Golf Company, 2nd Battalion, 1st Marines at Camp Horno, Camp Pendleton, California. October 1998. *USMC Photo*

CH-46 medium-lift helicopters, reinforced with detachments of CH-53 heavy-lift helicopters, UH-1 Huey and AH-1 Cobra attack helicopters, and AV-8B Harrier attack jets. The 13th MEU (SOC) also possessed a logistics combat element (LCE) formed around MEU Service Support Group 13.

Our workup for deployment consisted of a plethora of training events. We started by focusing on our core mission–essential tasks as an infantry unit. These included individual skills like weapons handling and first aid; progressed to collective skills training at the fireteam, squad, and platoon levels; and concluded with a complex practical exercise referred to as the Combined Arms Exercise (CAX), held at the premier Marine Corps training center in Twentynine Palms, California. The CAX integrated all the combat power available to a reinforced infantry battalion maneuvering forces across the desert floor to achieve synergistic effects on notional enemy forces in a live-fire evolution.

The GCE follows this training by joining the rest of the MEU in conducting assigned mission essential–task training to develop the special skills required for deployment. This training includes integrating with the Navy and operating from shipboard in the execution of the eighteen potential missions the MEU might have to perform when deployed, such as raids, evacuations of noncombatants, and humanitarian assistance.

Operation Resolute Response

Golf Company received the call to execute one of these missions sooner than anyone expected. Two platoons from FAST Company deployed to Kenya and Tanzania within forty-eight hours of the al-Qaeda bombings of the American embassies in those countries. Responsibility for U.S.

military operations in Africa lay across three unified commands in 1998. The European Command (EUCOM) had responsibility for West Africa; Pacific Command (PACOM) had responsibility for the waters of the Indian Ocean and islands off the east coast of Africa; Central Command (CENTCOM) had responsibility for East Africa. In 2007, the Department of Defense established Africa Command (AFRICOM), which assumed responsibility for the entire continent. However, forces from CENTCOM responded to the bombings in 1998 in Operation Resolute Response.

Gen. Anthony Zinni, USMC, the CENTCOM commander, tasked Naval Forces Central Command with establishing a joint task force (JTF) to support Operation Resolute Response. A Marine brigadier general, Stephen Johnson, commanded the JTF, which included Navy Seabees and Marines from FAST Company. Its priorities in both countries were to locate people trapped in the damaged embassies and care for the wounded. The FAST Marines provided security to protect the Seabees and State Department personnel as they cleared the areas and rummaged through the debris to collect property and documents for transfer to new facilities.

Both embassies were located in the middle of major cities in neighborhoods that offered little standoff from bomb threats. The State Department consequently identified more rural areas for constructing new embassies, there would be greater protection there for the diplomatic mission, but they would take months to complete. Diplomats established temporary operations at the USAID facility in Nairobi in the meantime. Golf Company's mission was to relieve the FAST platoon and provide security at this site, three weeks prior to our scheduled deployment with the 13th MEU (SOC).

I chose Lt. Chris Ruwe, Golf Company's 3rd Platoon commander, to lead the mission. Chris and his platoon sergeant, SSgt. Kevin Oxner, ran a tight ship. (Ruwe later became a staff judge advocate for the Marine Corps and remains on active duty as a lieutenant colonel today, while Oxner would continue to rise in the staff noncommissioned officer ranks.) I was confident they possessed the maturity and leadership abilities needed to lead their Marines on an independent mission. The relief of the FAST platoon required only a single platoon, rather than the entire company, to complete the task. Lieutenant Ruwe led his platoon, while I deployed the remaining three platoons of the company on board the USS *Boxer* (LHD 4), an amphibious warship known as a "landing helicopter deck," as part of the scheduled deployment.[5] Our BLT commander, Lt. Col. Robert Wagner, and I accompanied Lieutenant Ruwe on a site visit to Nairobi to conduct a final coordination prior to his departure in November 1998. Wagner was an old-school, former enlisted Marine and one of the few remaining Vietnam veterans still on active duty at the time. He later retired as a colonel.

The FAST and Marine Security Guard Marines had done well in enhancing security measures at the temporary embassy. I reminisced about my own embassy-reinforcement mission in Haiti as I walked the grounds, inspected positions, and met with key embassy personnel. The MSG Detachment had included only six Marines at the time of the terrorist attack. Unfortunately, one of the detachment's Marines, Sgt. Jesse Aligana, died in the bombing.[6] Capt. Brian Tosh, the FAST platoon commander, took us to the original embassy to inspect the damage caused by the bombing. The tour of the destroyed embassy was eerie. Two terrorists had approached the rear of the American embassy in a truck filled with explosives on the morning of 7 August 1998. A local guard had attempted to stop the truck and received return fire. The terrorists threw a stun grenade in his direction. The explosion of the grenade caused bystanders in nearby buildings to come toward the windows to see what had caused it, as the guard called the Marine at Post One for assistance. The truck bomb exploded as this call was occurring. The resulting blast severally damaged the embassy, collapsed a nearby building, and destroyed a bus full of people in the street. I visualized it all in my head.

The scene was devastating. It reinforced to me why we Marines do what we do. The senseless killing of over two hundred and wounding of thousands of innocent bystanders was incomprehensible. The remnants of human remains were still visible on the walls as we walked through a destroyed office. I followed the bloody handprints along a long hallway— clearly made by someone blinded by the dust and smoke as he or she tried to find a way out of the building following the blast. We stopped for a moment of silence at the elevator shaft where Sergeant Aligana had fallen to his death while doing his duty. Lieutenant Ruwe and I needed no further convincing of the importance of the lieutenant's mission and of the cost of failing at it. Our thoughts were heavy as we returned to the FAST Marines' billeting for a final meal before returning home to join our Marines.

Our final day in Nairobi was 10 November. This day is important to every Marine, whether on active duty or long retired. It is the birthday of our Corps, celebrated by Marines across the world regardless of location or circumstances. Maj. Gen. Commandant John Lejeune declared 10 November as the official birthday of the Corps in 1921. Lejeune chose this date because it was the day the second Continental Congress first authorized the raising of two battalions of Marines in 1775. Lejeune issued Marine

Corps Order No. 47, Series 1921, which laid out the history, mission, and tradition of the Corps and directed that it be read to every command on 10 November each year.

The reading of the order normally occurs with the cutting of a birthday cake. It is a Marine tradition that any guests of honor receive the first pieces of cake, followed by the oldest Marine. The oldest Marine then passes a piece to the youngest Marine to symbolize the passing of the Corps' knowledge, history, and tradition from one generation to the next. The FAST Marines too held a cake-cutting ceremony and recognized our battalion commander, Lieutenant Colonel Wagner, as the oldest Marine. Lieutenant Colonel Wagner, Lieutenant Ruwe, and I continued celebrating the birthday with beer and hot dogs as we waited at the airport in Amsterdam for our flight home.

Final preparations for deployment continued as we returned to Camp Pendleton. Lieutenant Ruwe and the 3rd Platoon deployed two days before Thanksgiving, ahead of the rest of the MEU, from March Air Force Base, in California's Riverside County, in a C-141 Starlifter that stopped in Charleston, South Carolina, the Ascension Islands, and the African nation of Zambia before arriving in Kenya. The remainder of the MEU deployed on the three amphibious warships of the Navy's Amphibious Squadron Seven (PHIBRON 7). The squadron consisted of the landing ship dock USS *Harpers Ferry* (LSD 49), landing platform dock USS *Cleveland* (LPD 4), and the USS *Boxer*.[7] Golf Company deployed on the *Boxer*.

Marines run to the sound of the guns in war, but during times of peace they at least want to be in a position to be the first called on to a fight when a crisis occurs. This requires Marines to be forward deployed, like Golf Company was in December 1998. The MEUs are best poised to respond rapidly as the nation's premier crisis-response forces.

Deploying with a MEU guarantees Marines will see the world, whether they are engaged in combat operations or not. The 13th MEU (SOC)'s deployment in the western Pacific during 1999 (WESTPAC 99-1) was no exception. We departed San Diego on 5 December 1998, trained in Hawaii during the second half of the month, and enjoyed New Year's Eve in Hong Kong, before further training in Singapore. After liberty in Thailand and before training in Kenya, we spent a month in Kuwait honing our combined-arms capabilities. Golf Company then prepared for conducting a noncombatant evacuation of U.S. personnel in Eritrea as that country continued its border war with Ethiopia. We stopped in the United Arab

USS *Boxer* (LHD 4), home away from home. Marines can't wait to get off ship during deployments, but look forward to returning to the warm showers, chow, and clean beds ships offer after being in the field for long periods of time. *Author collection*

Emirates before enjoying liberty in Bali, Australia, and Hawaii; we arrived back home in California on 4 June 1999. It was a great deployment, with a great group of men and women, of whom many are still dear friends today. However, upon our return, it was time for me to grow in other ways.

Operations Officer

Company commanders want to keep command of their companies for as long as possible. Unfortunately, a command tour normally lasts only two years, which allows the commander time to build a team, train it, and conduct a single deployment with it. One of the five company commanders of the battalion is normally permitted to remain in the battalion following a deployment to assume the post of battalion operations officer. This is a key billet in the development of an officer and essential for those who want to command battalions one day. I hoped to remain in 2/1 following our return from WESTPAC 99-1, but the regimental commander, Col. Jay Paxton, had other plans. (Paxton was a Cornell University grad who later became the thirty-third Assistant Commandant of the Marine Corps.) I received assignment as the operations officer for our sister battalion, the "Thundering Third" 3rd Battalion, 1st Marines (3/1), under the command of Lt. Col. Doug Stillwell who was later promoted and commanded his own MEU. The battalion was preparing to deploy and needed help in getting ready. I was thankful for the opportunity but was torn because I also found out that I had been selected to attend the Marine Corps Command and Staff College and would not be deploying with the battalion.

We worked hard in the 3/1 Operations Section, starting from scratch and working with the other staff sections in developing a comprehensive Standard Operating Procedure (SOP) to guide our actions in combat or in the execution of the other missions the battalion would receive during its upcoming deployment with a MEU. The fruition of our efforts became evident in our successful completion of a combined-arms exercise at Twentynine Palms, before the battalion transferred to the MEU. I turned the reins over to my good friend Capt. James McArthur, with whom I had served in 3/9 when we were both lieutenants, and transferred to the 1st Marine Division staff as the assistant training officer, pending my transfer to Quantico to attend school. However, I first had another mission.

Operation Skilled Anvil

The collapse of the Soviet Union in 1989 had created a power vacuum in Eastern Europe that had resulted in increased tensions, ethnic fighting, and mass migrations. Power struggles commenced as former Soviet states declared independence and fought for identity. Tensions came to a head in Kosovo, where ethnic Albanians opposed ethnic Serbs and the government of the former Yugoslavia. The North Atlantic Treaty Organization (NATO) intervened, as fighting between opposing factions produced a growing refugee problem and talks of ethnic cleansing and genocide appeared in the press. The United States initiated a major planning effort in response to this growing conflict—Operation Skilled Anvil.

Operation Skilled Anvil was established to develop a comprehensive and executable war plan for potential crisis areas in Eastern Europe.[8] EUCOM established a JTF in October 1999 using, as the base unit the Southern European Task Force (SETAF), under the command of Maj. Gen. Paul T. Mikolashek, U.S. Army (who later retired as a lieutenant general). SETAF had its headquarters at the Caserma Carlo Ederle in Vicenza, Italy, but the JTF headquarters originally operated in Heidelberg, Germany. As a newly promoted major, I received individual augmentation orders to join the Skilled Anvil staff in Germany.

My orders assigned me to work in the J-3 Operations Section, but things changed on my arrival in Germany. The Marine lieutenant colonel, Louis Rachel, who welcomed me as I walked into the command post seemed a little too happy to see me. Rachel informed me that he was trying to return to the United States to assume command of the Marine Corps Officer Candidate School but that the JTF had refused to let him go without a replacement. He did some wrangling, and before I knew it, I went from working in the J-3 as a newly promoted major to becoming a J-5 planner filling a lieutenant colonel's position. Having just left 3/1, I was confident I could command a thousand-man battalion, but the smallest unit I would work with on this assignment was an entire 50,000-man Marine expeditionary force, not to mention elements from across the entire joint force. I had just graduated to the operational level of war.

Although I had proven my abilities at the tactical level of war, where battles are fought, I knew nothing about the operational level, where campaigns are designed. The Infantry Officer Advanced Course prepared one well to command a company and serve as a battalion operations officer. MCCSC would teach me operational art, but I had not yet attended it. I had to learn the hard way, through on-the-job training and an aggressive self-study program. This was a "heavy row" at first. I was initially lost but quickly assessed my environment, identified the smart people in the room, and attached myself to them to learn. I befriended an Army Airborne major from the SETAF staff and a Green Beret major who also augmented the staff as my mentors. I learned my lessons well and began to lead my own operational planning teams (OPT) and soon was briefing the commanding general on our work.

The JTF continued planning as we approached Christmas 1999. It shifted its headquarters from Germany to Vicenza so the staff from SETAF could be closer to their families. We established a new command post at an old missile facility built on the side of a mountain, a throwback to the Cold War, when Italy and the United States had partnered to defend against Soviet aggression. Although the facility no longer served its original role, Vicenza was a good location for planning a major operation. The JTF completed the plan and was disestablished in February 2000. This gave me time to return home, close out my duties with the 1st Marine Division, and move back to Quantico to attend intermediate-level school.

Marine Corps Command and Staff College

Command and Staff College proved refreshing and rewarding. I finally got to formally learn the fine art of operational warfare that I had had to learn the hard way as part of the JTF. Command and Staff's organization was similar to IOAC, in that some classes were lectures to the whole student body of approximately two hundred students, but most learning occurred at the conference-group level. Each conference group consisted of joint military officers, midlevel managers from other agencies, and a mix of international officers. My family and I sponsored a colonel and his family from the Philippine Marine Corps. Another difference from IOAC was that each conference group had a civilian PhD instructor in addition to the military faculty adviser. This facilitated our study of military history and challenged students to think through problems in new and innovative ways that a military-only faculty may not have stimulated.

The school also offered a master's degree program, in which I gladly participated. It was a great year of learning, one that whetted my appetite for more. I intended to submit for admission to the School of Advanced Warfighting (SAW), a follow-on year of higher learning, but my adviser told me not to bother. The Marine Corps had other plans for me.

Recruiting Duty

The manpower branch of Headquarters Marine Corps contacted me at Command and Staff College to suggest that I volunteer for recruiting duty. I respectfully declined, as my mentors in the Marine Corps had always warned me to stay as far away from recruiting as possible. The duty had a reputation for being tough and as far away from the infantry as one can get. Manpower contacted me again; this time its message came in loud and clear, "Congratulations! You were just selected to command a recruiting station." They tasked me with prioritizing eight available recruiting stations to which I might be assigned. There were some wonderful choices, such as San Diego, Dallas, and other high-population centers. The list also included Charleston, West Virginia, currently ranked dead last—forty-eighth out of the forty-eight stations in the nation—and I listed Charleston as my last choice also. Manpower contacted me again. "Congratulations, you're heading to Charleston!" The wisdom of sending a New Yorker to recruit in the mountains of West Virginia was lost on me, but I was up for the challenge.

Recruiting Station (RS) Charleston was actually headquartered in a small town called Hurricane (pronounced "Hurricun") thirty miles west of Charleston, the capital of West Virginia. The original RS comprised twenty-seven recruiters spread across most of the state. However, it had recently combined with RS Cincinnati to become a single station and expanded to include sixty-five recruiters operating across the southern half of Ohio, eastern Kentucky, northeast Tennessee, southwest Virginia, and about 80 percent of West Virginia. The RS organized the recruiters into thirteen recruiting substations (RSSs), each led by a staff noncommissioned officer and responsible for finding mentally, morally, and physically qualified men and women and persuading them to volunteer to serve as Marines.

The American all-volunteer force is a great success, but it comes at a cost. The United States spends between sixty-three to sixty-eight cents of every defense dollar on manpower alone. This pales in comparison to investments in research and development and the procurement of military gear and equipment needed to maintain an advantage against future adversaries. President Richard Nixon had made the decision to transition from a draft to an all-volunteer force during the Vietnam War. A number of factors led to his decision. The climate in the 1970s was ripe for disestablishing the draft.[9] Growing unpopularity with the Vietnam War and the poor quality of draftees entering the military resulted in both a society and military ready for change. Nixon established a commission to advise him on establishing an all-volunteer force. It determined that demographics, costs, and thinking in the country would support a change. Thus, the active draft ended in January 1973, and the all-volunteer force began. Young men are still required to register for the draft with the Selective Service when they turn eighteen, but no one has been drafted into the military since 1973. The 2016 decision to open the ground-combat-arms military occupational specialties to females resulted in some debate about whether they too should be required to register for the draft, but there appears to be no appetite in the country for that now. Regardless, the establishment of the all-volunteer force magnified the importance of the recruiting service.

Recruiters now had to work harder to find, screen, and convince young men and women to join the services. This required countless hours of prospecting in which recruiters have to make phone calls, knock on doors, participate in local events, and visit high schools to make contacts with potential applicants. RS Charleston had responsibility for 463 high schools in its area. I will never forget my first visit to one.

Grundy High School is located in beautiful Grundy, Virginia. The population of Grundy was just over a thousand in 2001.[10] Grundy is the county seat of Buchanan County. It lies in the heart of Appalachia, sixteen miles from the Kentucky border, where the Hatfields and McCoys had feuded in the late nineteenth century. Not surprisingly, the area supported the Confederate cause during the American Civil War, when the state of Virginia seceded.

I was excited to visit my first high school with one of my recruiters. We entered the front lobby of the school wearing our dress blue uniforms and feeling good. The school principal was waiting for us. After my recruiter introduced me, I stuck out my hand and said, "Good morning, sir, Major Bohm. It's good to meet you." The principal took a step back, looked at me with a frown, and with his deep southern accent asked, "Are you a Yankee?" I thought, *Oh crap, how do I answer this one?* Never one to back down, I looked him square in the eyes and replied, "Yes, sir, true blue and damn proud of it." The principal's face twitched in anger, and he said, "We don't like Yankees around here."

I responded, "Yes, sir," looked at my recruiter, and said, "Let's go." That was the shortest high school visit I made during my command of RS Charleston.

I attended a mandatory recruiting leaders course shortly after assuming command. The course was held at the Xerox Document University near Leesburg, Virginia. (I never determined why the Marine Corps felt it necessary to run this course at a civilian facility rather than on a Marine Corps base.) I yearned for the excitement of the fleet as I walked the halls of the university. The realization that this was a three-year tour was setting in as I looked up at a TV monitor hanging from the ceiling.

Something was going on in New York City. It all became clear as I watched the second airliner crash into the Twin Towers. Sadly I was not surprised by what I saw. My years of studying, and preparing to defeat, terrorism led me to believe it was only a matter of time before a catastrophic event occurred in the U.S. homeland. This was a game changer. I knew the military was going to be busy. Apparently, the leaders of the Marine Corps Recruiting Command knew this too. They quickly sent word out to the recruiting force that it would deny any requests for transfer back to the fleet to join the fight.

I was not happy. I had just missed Desert Storm and now I was going to miss another big fight. However, I had my own—more local—fight to worry about. Confirmation that I would not be permitted to return to the fleet allowed me to focus on our recruiting mission. Mission is everything on recruiting duty, of which there are two parts. The first is contracting, in which a recruiter convinces someone to join the Marine Corps if they are found to be fully qualified at a Military Entrance Processing Station (MEPS). Enlistees are considered "poolees" once they enlist, because they are now part of a "pool" of people waiting to ship out to boot camp. The second mission is "shipping," which consists of getting a poolee to boot camp. Recruiting stations receive both contracting and shipping missions each month. Recruiters refer to recruiting duty as "thirty-six one-month tours," since they receive a new mission every month. You can be happy at making mission one month, just to feel like a failure by missing mission the next—or as recruiters say, "Hero to Zero."

There are advantages to this duty though. One can't help but feel satisfied finding, molding, and sustaining future generations of Marines. The Marine Corps possesses the youngest members of all the services and experiences the largest per capita turnover of personnel each year. Approximately 35,000 Marines enlist in the Corps and go through boot camp every year. Living in local communities across the country also connects Marines with those they selflessly serve. Lt. Gen. Brute Krulak's assertion that "the Nation does not need a Marine Corps, the Nation wants a Marine Corps" holds true. Each RS has a marketing and public affairs (MPA) representative to assist with fostering the relationship between the Corps and community. My MPA did not serve me well when I checked in. He committed me to participating in a "Toys for Tots" and Christmas-tree lighting ceremony at the West Virginia state capitol shortly after my arrival. The Marine Corps Reserve established the Toys for Tots Program in 1947 to collect toys for less fortunate children.[11] Our local reserve unit had responsibility for this program and got West Virginia governor Bob Wise to agree to kick off the annual campaign to raise toys when he officially lit the state Christmas tree.

My MPA signed me up to "observe" the ceremony as the senior Marine in the state. I specifically asked whether I had a speaking role in the ceremony and was told emphatically no, that the commanding officer of the local reserve unit would take care of any speaking, since this was a reserve program. I arrived at the state capitol approximately ten minutes before the ceremony was to begin and was surprised to see the governor's personal assistant waiting for me as I pulled up. He quickly ushered me into the capitol through a side door, with my MPA in tow. He asked if I was ready. I looked at my MPA and asked, "For what?" The governor stepped out of a side room and greeted me before my MPA could answer the question. The governor shook my hand and said, "Thanks very much for doing this." I responded, "My pleasure, sir," as the governor's assistant opened a door to a room filled with hundreds of people, news cameras and reporters, and a tall Christmas tree with gifts under it.

People cheered as we entered, and the governor stepped up to the podium. He greeted everyone and informed them how grateful he was that the Marines were taking care of West Virginia's citizens in need. He then turned to me and said, "Ladies and gentlemen, Major Jason Bohm." By that time I was not happy with my MPA or the commanding officer of the reserve unit. I had no prepared comments, but I adapted and overcame, as any good Marine would do.

Although that event had a humorous side, my tour of duty was not a humorous one. In fact, recruiting was the hardest thing I ever had to do in my life. The stress of taking the RS from being dead last in the nation, combined with the constant pressure of making mission, was difficult. Exacerbating the problem was the fact that I had to "clean out" some substandard Marines before the RS could grow in a positive direction. The duty included long days, long weeks, and long months. I was on the road often, trying to influence and implement positive change in our Marines spread across five states. To make matters worse, my commanding officer was an old-school authoritarian who believed in leading by threats and fear. I was cursed at constantly and threatened with relief five times on recruiting duty.

Things worsened when the Marine Corps dropped the staffing for recruiting duty in order to push more Marines out to the operating forces to engage in what became known as Operation Iraqi Freedom. RS Charleston took the brunt of this hit for the 4th Marine Corps District, since we had a lower-quality pool of prospects from which to recruit. This resulted in a number of areas and schools not being covered by Marine recruiters, even though our mission was never lowered. We still had the task of achieving 100 percent of our mission, even though we were only being manned at 85 percent strength. The district commander's intent was to fully man stations in better markets at our expense to help the district succeed in its mission. RS Charleston was the economy-of-force station for the 4th District, which did not help morale.

I did all I could to keep my recruiters focused on mission. This required me to use every trick in my leadership bag that I had developed over my twelve years in the Marine Corps. The pressure was huge. I had three young children at the time and never got to see them. They were asleep when I went to work, and they were asleep when I got home. My wife started letting them stay up later so I could spend some time with them, but this meant I had even less time to decompress, eat dinner, prep my uniforms for the next day, and get to bed to begin the whole process again. There were no vacations to recharge one's batteries. We got Thanksgiving Day and Christmas Day off, and that was pretty much it, as directed by our district commander. I started getting angry.

I kept my frustration and anger inside to buffer my Marines from the stressors, so they could focus on accomplishing our mission, but started releasing it at home. This resulted in outbursts, rarely warranted, at my wife and kids. Things came to a head one evening when my wife looked me in the eye and said, "We don't know how to act around you anymore. Whether things are good or bad, you are always angry. It has to stop." Sonja walked out of the room and left me to my thoughts. I felt like I had a thousand-pound block of ice sitting on my shoulders and the world was coming down around me. This was a life-changing moment. I realized I could not face these challenges alone. I had to rely on someone, or something, to help me through these tough times. I looked up to the ceiling and said, "God, I cannot do this on my own. I am putting my life in your hands," and I meant it. I immediately felt as though that hunk of ice melted off my shoulders.

I went to church the next day and was enlightened. I looked down as I took a seat in a pew and found a small book titled *The Book of Hope* beside me. I picked it up and arbitrarily opened it to a passage titled "Perseverance." The passage described how God places us in challenging times and situations during life and explains that we can handle these challenges in one of two ways: we can become embittered, or we can become better. The choice was ours to make. It was our opportunity for spiritual growth. It was like a lightbulb had turned on in my head. I finally understood that all that I had experienced in life up to that point was preparing me to take this leap of faith—to fully believe in God and to put my life in His hands. This liberating moment made my entire recruiting tour worthwhile, and my life has never been the same since. I no longer succumbed to the stresses of life, and I have kept things in perspective ever since.

This realization assisted me as I prepared for a sad task. On 21 March 2003, 1st Lt. Therrell Shane Childers, U.S. Marine Corps, became the first American casualty of Operation Iraqi Freedom while serving as a platoon commander with Alpha Company, 1st Battalion, 5th Marines (1/5). The Marine Corps is a small place. The 1/5 was commanded by my former company commander and mentor in 3/9, Capt. Fred Padilla. Captain Padilla was now a lieutenant colonel and had led 1/5 in the attack across the Iraqi border to capture the Rumaila oil fields twenty miles north of the Kuwaiti border. Childers' mission had been to capture Pumping Station No. 2. He was leading from the front when he was shot in the stomach by Iraqi soldiers fleeing the area. His parents lived in Wyoming, but his grandmother and extended family lived in West Virginia, in my area of responsibility. I received the mission to preside over a memorial service held for Childers.

The outpouring of love and support for the Childers family was over-whelming. Hundreds of people attended the ceremony in a local park in Huntington, West Virginia. It was a crisp spring day with a gentle breeze that caused a giant American flag, which was hanging between two extended ladders on fire trucks, to flutter. A local pastor prayed, and the community showed its support. We all understood this was the first but likely not the last casualty in this war.

I approached Lieutenant Childers' grandmother in my dress blues, hold-ing a folded American flag. I knelt down beside her, and presented the flag, stating, "On behalf of the President of the United States, the Commandant of the Marine Corps, and a grateful nation, please accept this flag as a sym-bol of our appreciation for your loved one's service to country and Corps." The war was no longer some mystic event far away or on one's TV screen. It was now real for those on the home front. This event only increased my frustration with missing the fight.

My three years with RS Charleston were some of the hardest for me pro-fessionally, but also the most personally rewarding. Not only did my life gain perspective, but my family and I also made some very dear friends. It was now time to move on, though, and finally contribute to the fight in Iraq.

9

---- ★ ----

Battalion Landing Team XO, the Tsunami, and Operation Iraqi Freedom

What President George W. Bush designated the "Global War on Terrorism" (GWOT) did not wait for me to complete my recruiting tour. President Bush took immediate action following the events of 9/11, as I continued to enlist the young men and women preparing to engage our enemies. The National Security Council informed Bush that Osama bin Laden and al-Qaeda had perpetrated the attacks against America, and the president declared to the world, "Make no mistake: The United States will hunt down and punish those responsible for these cowardly attacks."[1]

The events of 9/11 constituted a game changer for the United States. America would no longer maintain a predominately defensive posture against terrorism. The president made it clear that the country would assume the offensive against those who challenged its national security. The United States launched missile and bombing attacks, coordinated with the insertion of special operations forces and CIA operatives into Afghanistan to assist Afghan Northern Alliance forces fighting against the Taliban and al-Qaeda. Special-operations task forces began working with Afghan opposition forces and temporarily secured a 6,400-foot runway, referred to as Objective Rhino, in southern Afghanistan.

President Bush wanted an even more robust response to the 9/11 attacks and found a solution in the Marines. The 15th MEU, under the command of Col. Thomas Wauldhauser, was already supporting operations in the area, and the 1st MEB, under Brig. Gen. James Mattis, was forward deployed conducting Exercise Bright Star in Egypt. Mattis received the task to create and employ a task force to conduct small raids into southern Afghanistan. The 26th MEU, commanded by Col. Andrew Frick, later joined with the 15th MEU, elements of the 1st MEB, and Marine Forces Central Command (Forward) to create Task Force-58 under Mattis' command. Mattis led Task Force-58 in conducting a four-hundred-mile attack inland from naval amphibious warships to secure Forward Operating Base (FOB) Rhino in November 2001.

The seizure of FOB Rhino was the first of many accomplishments of Task Force-58. Mattis led his force in interdicting lines of communications along the main highway in southern Afghanistan. The task force occupied Kandahar International Airport and secured the American embassy in Kabul while detaining several hundred prisoners of war. The Marines also supported numerous sensitive site-exploitation and reconnaissance missions.[2] The Marine contribution to what became known as Operation Enduring Freedom continued to expand as the United Nations sanctioned the establishment of the International Security Assistance Force (ISAF) to lead operations in Afghanistan. Marine operations in Afghanistan would ebb and flow in scope and size over the following years and still do today. Wauldhauser would continue to rise in the ranks and is currently the commander of the U.S. Africa Command. Mattis' star also continued to rise, and after serving as the Commander, U.S. Central Command, he was secretary of defense until December 2018. Meanwhile, the Marines contributed to the GWOT in other ways as well.

In February 2003, Lt. Gen. James Conway led the 1st Marine Expeditionary Force (I MEF) in an attack across the Kuwaiti border to help seize Baghdad and defeat the Iraqi army in what became Operation Iraqi Freedom. The I MEF was part of a larger campaign that included the U.S. Army's V Corps; U.S. air, naval, and special forces; and British forces. This combined force swiftly defeated the Iraqi army, but then confronted a new adversary in the ill-trained, but dedicated, paramilitary forces, the fedayeen.

The term "fedayeen" comes from the Arab word *fida'i*, (suicidal assassin) and originally referred to Arab commandos fighting against Israel in the 1950s.[3] The title resurfaced in 2003 to describe unconventional forces loyal to Saddam Hussein; they first appeared on the battlefield in Nasiriyah during I MEF's march to Baghdad. The fedayeen represented a mix of sons of former Iraqi Ba'ath Party officials and poor teenagers attracted by pay twice that of regular soldiers.[4] They wore civilian clothing and traveled in civilian cars, buses, and motorcycles. Distinguishing these fighters from among innocent civilians proved difficult—until they presented a weapon or fired on friendly forces. Although the coalition quickly defeated the conventional Iraqi army, disposing of the fedayeen and other unconventional forces proved tougher.

Unconventional forces have employed nontraditional methods against regular armies since the beginning of time. Smaller, weaker, and poorly equipped forces often have used a combination of conventional warfare and unconventional methods. American colonists skillfully employed them in defeating the British army during the American Revolution. However, American forces in their turn bore the brunt of these tactics once American ambitions expanded west and across the seas. American Indians employed guerrilla tactics against the American army in Florida and across the western frontier. Philippine insurgents tangled with the Americans following the Spanish-American War. Rebels in Haiti, Nicaragua, and Santo Domingo employed unconventional tactics against American forces during the Banana Wars in the early twentieth century. Chinese and Korean forces dressed as civilians and mixed with refugees to attack American forces during the Korean War, while the Vietcong fought among the people during the Vietnam War. Although "irregular" is not a new concept, Americans have had to relearn the many lessons about it that their forces had learned the hard way in previous wars.

U.S. armed forces must prepare to execute any mission across a wide range of military operations. These missions span from humanitarian efforts at the low end of conflict to conventional warfare at the high end, with everything in between. Military leaders debate whether to prepare for the most dangerous enemy in conventional warfare, or for the most likely scenario, operations short of war. My experiences in Somalia and Haiti had led me to believe the Marine Corps was not doing enough to prepare for what I learned now had the title of "Military Operations Other than War" (MOOTW) as I attended MCCSC immediately prior to the attacks of 9/11.

I had completed a master's degree in military studies in that school, with a thesis titled "Complacency Kills: The Need for Improvement in How the Marine Corps Prepares for Future Conflict."[5] In it I asserted that although the Marine Corps prepares well for war, it needed to improve in preparing for MOOTW. I described the enormous challenges the Marines faced in responding to crises across a wide spectrum of conflict where the usually clear lines separating the levels of war fade and where it was increasingly difficult to distinguish combatants from noncombatants, in environments like the Three Block Wars described by General Krulak. I also cited the joint publication *Joint Vision 2020,* which described a force needing to be "dominant across the full spectrum of military operations—persuasive in peace, decisive in war, preeminent in any form of conflict."[6]

I suggested a number of steps by which the Marine Corps could improve at the low end of conflict. These included initiating standardized cultural and language training, improving simulation training, and an updated edition of the *Small Wars Manual* first published in 1940 following the Banana Wars. I recommended publishing a MOOTW training and readiness manual and a quarterly MOOTW magazine focused on noncommissioned officers. I also called for MOOTW instructor and staff training courses. My thesis also recommended implementing a MOOTW combat-readiness evaluation and improvements to existing urban-training facilities.

Although I like to think of myself as a visionary, the reality is that the Marine Corps was already well aware of its need to prepare for MOOTW. However, having Marines prepare for all possible missions risks making them experts in many skills but the masters of none, by spreading training time and resources too thin. Leaders must prioritize different kinds of training by analyzing missions for the core essentials in which their units must remain proficient, while identifying assigned tasks for which they must also train. Ultimately, Marines must be prepared to do whatever the nation needs them to do. This fact became evident as I transferred back to the operating forces.

Battalion Landing Team Executive Officer

I received orders to assume duties as the executive officer of the 1st Battalion, 1st Marine Regiment (1/1). The battalion was part of the 1st Marine Division, stationed at Camp Horno, the home of the 1st Marines, at Camp Pendleton, California. Things had been moving fast since my last tour in the operating forces. The war against terror was in its third year, and infantry battalions like 1/1 were rotating in and out of Iraq for temporary assignment to Multinational Force West (MNF-W), one of the coalition headquarters established under Multi-National Force-Iraq (MNF-I), which was responsible for prosecuting Operation Iraqi Freedom (OIF).

The MNF-W had responsibility for conducting combat operations in the Al Anbar Province of western Iraq. Command of the unit rotated every twelve months between I and II MEFs, beginning in March 2004 with I MEF commanded by Lt. Gen. James Conway, who later became the thirty-fourth Commandant of the Marine Corps. The command consisted of over

30,000 Marines, sailors, soldiers, and airmen operating across the expansive Euphrates River valley, spanning from the Syrian border to Baghdad. Regimental combat teams (RCT), Marine air groups (MAG), logistics elements commanded by colonels, and select Army units constituted the MNF-W. Battalions like 1/1, rotating approximately every six months, sourced the RCTs.

The Marine Corps had a valuable lesson about unit rotations during the Vietnam War. The practice during that conflict was to rotate individuals, rather than units. Individual rotations in Vietnam occurred on a thirteen-month basis. The result was reduced unit cohesion and combat readiness. Fresh replacements were constantly rotating into units without having trained or built relationships with them. It was not uncommon for veteran Marines to distance themselves from the "new guys" who had not yet learned how to contribute and survive in the dangerous jungles and villages of Vietnam. Many were liabilities to their units until they gained experience. This dynamic changed during OIF. Units now formed, trained, and deployed together. I had the good fortune of joining 1/1 as it conducted its premier training event prior to its deployment.

Exercise Mojave Viper (EMV) was a newly crafted event that combined the traditional warfighting skills conducted during the Marine Corps' old Combined Arms Exercises (CAX) with a security and stability operation (SASO) element to prepare units for the special kind of fighting being experienced in Iraq.[7] The CAX portion of EMV consisted of a fourteen-day live-fire training cycle, progressing from the fireteam to battalion levels. Skills developed during this phase included combined-arms integration techniques, fire and movement, and the integration of large-scale maneuver with direct, indirect, and aviation fires involving all elements of the MAGTF.

The SASO phase of training commenced with the exercise force conducting a notional "relief in place" at an FOB established in a mock city inhabited by live role-players. Small units conducted specified training events covering urban patrolling, IED training, tank and infantry integration, and various other skills necessary for operations in an urban environment. The exercise culminated with a three-day, twenty-four-hour-a-day, battalion-level operation performing the type of missions conducted in Iraq.

Although 1/1 was preparing for deployment to Iraq, its employment there was uncertain. Our battalion was designated as a battalion landing team (BLT) and the ground combat element for the 15th MEU. As such, the BLT also would have to execute any one of the special missions performed by MEUs, including amphibious raids, evacuations of noncombatants, humanitarian assistance missions, and more. The 15th MEU successfully completed a certification exercise and gained the Special Operations Capable (SOC) designation prior to deploying in December 2004.

The 15th MEU (SOC), commanded by Col. Thomas Greenwood, was a traditional MAGTF with command, ground combat, air combat, and logistics combat elements. Greenwood was a "legacy" Marine who had joined his father and brothers in serving in the Corps and later went on to work in the National Security Agency. Artillery, reconnaissance (Recon), light armored reconnaissance (LAR), AAVs, tanks, and combat engineers reinforced our battalion to equip the BLT as the GCE, under the command of Lt. Col. David Furness. AV-8B Harriers, CH-53 heavy-lift helicopters, UH-1 utility helicopters, and AH-1 Cobra Gunships reinforced the White Knights of HMM-165, flying CH-46 medium-lift helicopters, to establish the ACE under the command of Lt. Col. Eric Steidl. MEU Service Support Group-15 (MSSG-15) was under the command of Lt. Col. Jay Hatton, and formed the LCE. (All three commanders went on to distinguished careers: Hatton working at the Marine Corps University, Steidl commanding his own MEU, and Furness becoming a general officer and assuming command of the 2nd Marine Division.)

The 15th MEU (SOC) deployed with a standard three-ship amphibious ready group (ARG). The BLT headquarters, the majority of Weapons Company, Charlie Company—comprising our designated helicopter company, the artillery battery, LAR Platoon, Recon Platoon, and a Maritime Special Purpose Force platoon—embarked on the USS *Bonhomme Richard* (LHD 6).[8] Alpha Company—our designated mechanized company, an AAV platoon, and one combined anti-armor team (CAAT) platoon—deployed on the USS *Rushmore* (LSD 47).[9] Bravo Company—our designated small-boat company, a combat engineer platoon, and a tank platoon—deployed on the USS *Duluth* (LPD 6), on what would be her final cruise before decommissioning.[10]

The MEU and the ARG both fell under Expeditionary Strike Group Five (ESG-5), commanded by Rear Adm. Christopher Ames. The Navy had introduced the "Expeditionary Strike Group" concept in the early 1990s; it consisted of combining the capabilities of surface-action groups of destroyers and cruisers with submarines, maritime patrol aircraft, the MEU, and the amphibious warships of the ARG to provide greater combat capabilities to theater combatant commanders. Expeditionary strike groups can be combined with aircraft carrier strike groups (CSG) and Maritime Prepositioning Force (MPF) ships to create expeditionary strike forces (ESFs) that provide even more lethal and sustainable capabilities.

Deploying surface combatant ships in support of amphibious operations was not a new concept. The Navy/Marine Corps team expertly employed this concept throughout World War II and has done so, with varying levels of success in other operations since then. It was not uncommon for ARG/MEUs to deploy independent of surface combatants and submarines during the Cold War years of the 1980s and early 1990s, when the Navy's focus was on employing submarines and CSGs to deter and, if necessary, defeat Soviet aggression.

The removal of the Soviets from the strategic landscape permitted the Navy to consider once again combining all the elements of naval power into a single naval-battle concept. The Navy and Marine Corps continue today to assess the ability to maximize naval capabilities, as shown in their capstone documents *A Cooperative Strategy for 21st Century Seapower* and *The Marine Corps Operating Concept: How an Expeditionary Force Operates in the 21st Century.*[11]

Marines and sailors stood side by side, while manning the railings of the amphibious warships as the 15th MEU (SOC) departed Naval Base San Diego. While the MEU settled into what they believed would be a routine deployment, the Marines tried to gain their sea legs and find their ways through the labyrinths below decks. Ships ran man-overboard drills, and leaders worked to find space to train their Marines, as the MEU continued to prepare for possible employment in Iraq.

Although the 15th MEU expected to remain on board ship as a strategic reserve on arriving in the Central Command area of operations, the chances of operating ashore were good. The last three MEUs deployed to the region had conducted ground operations in Iraq. The 11th MEU from I MEF had operated in Najaf, the 24th MEU from II MEF in northern Babil, and the 31st MEU from III MEF in Al Anbar Province. The I and II MEFs planned a transfer of responsibility (TOR) for Anbar Province, and Iraq scheduled its first freely held election during our deployment. The 15th MEU prudently continued preparations for possible employment.

Although scheduled to make stops and train across the Pacific, the 15th MEU maintained its focus on Iraq. Members of the Marine Corps Intelligence Activity, the Naval Postgraduate School, and the Naval War College embarked with us for our transit to Hawaii to provide needed training. Arabic language and cultural training augmented the combat skills acquired by the Marines. Special-skills training such as survival, evasion, resistance, and escape (SERE) also reinforced daily operations and intelligence briefings on Iraq.[12] Study of *Lawrence of Arabia* and other works assisted Marines in understanding the Arab mind.[13]

Thoughts of Iraq quickly dissipated as the MEU/ARG pulled into Pearl Harbor for a liberty call. Ships deploying from the West Coast use Hawaii as a way station to refuel and an opportunity for their personnel to enjoy time ashore prior to the long transit across the vast Pacific Ocean. The bars and beaches of Waikiki Beach are a strong draw for Marines and sailors looking to cut loose after a long hard workup.

On our way in, the ships rendered passing honors to the sunken hulk of the USS *Arizona* (BB 39), destroyed in the surprise attack by Japanese forces on 7 December 1941. Although it was a somber moment, our chests swelled with pride as we passed the huge and historic battleship USS *Missouri* (BB 63), knowing that America had turned the tides of war in four short years and forced the Japanese to sign the terms of surrender on board the *Missouri* in Tokyo Bay. Many wondered how long the current war against terror would last as their ships pulled pierside.

Hawaii was just the first stop in the MEU's expected cruise across the Pacific. The MEU planned to train in Singapore, Malaysia, and Guam, prior to departing the Pacific Command's area of operations for the Persian Gulf in Central Command's area. The BLT also planned to conduct needed maintenance on its vehicles while in Guam. The fedayeen in Iraq were increasing their employment of IEDs against coalition forces, as operations shifted to counterinsurgency (COIN). Marines had quickly adapted by welding scrap metal to their soft-skinned vehicles for additional armor protection. This temporary "hillbilly armor," as it became known, had proven insufficient. Defense contractors had then developed "up-armor" kits to strap onto the sides of Marine vehicles. Unfortunately, the vehicles' existing suspensions could not support the added weight. Our battalion acquired upgraded suspension systems to install in Guam, they arrived immediately prior to deploying.

Operation Unified Assistance

The MEU/ARG arrived in Guam on 28 December 2004, after celebrating Christmas at sea, and immediately began unloading. Only a single utility landing craft and air cushion landing craft (LCAC) had got ashore when the order to cease all landing operations immediately arrived. We had just received word that a 9.0 magnitude underwater earthquake had occurred in the Indian Ocean west of Indonesia, causing an enormous tsunami that impacted across southern Asia, killing thousands. The U.S. Geological Survey (USGS) determined that the earthquake had caused a six-hundred-mile-long rupture across the ocean floor and generated in a giant wave, reaching fifty feet in height, that traveled as far as three thousand miles from its epicenter and struck eleven countries.[14] The tsunami reportedly released the energy of 23,000 Hiroshima-type atomic bombs.[15]

The Pacific Command directed Commander Marine Forces Pacific to establish a joint task force for humanitarian assistance and disaster relief (HA/DR) in support of the governments of Sri Lanka, Thailand, and Indonesia. Lt. Gen. Robert Blackman, USMC, assumed command of a coalition force he designated Combined Support Force 536 (CSF-536). General Blackman established a headquarters in Utapao, Thailand, with a combined coordination center to orchestrate the efforts of over 12,000 U.S. military personnel and thousands more from other nations. Blackman later retired and became president and chief executive officer of the Marine Corps Heritage Foundation.

The plan was still developing as the 15th MEU received a deployment order from the III MEF Command Center to position itself on the eastern side of Sri Lanka to facilitate HA/DR operations. Our MEU commander, Colonel Greenwood, provided planning guidance for the MEU to be prepared to conduct the following missions:

1. Insert an initial response team.
2. Provide food, water, limited medical aid, and shelter for displaced personnel.
3. Provide limited infrastructure repairs.
4. Plan for multiple humanitarian assistance sites.
5. Plan for combined air and surface transportation options.
6. Plan for security at airfields and forward operating bases.
7. Be prepared to clear obstacles, beach landing sites, and landing zones.
8. Conduct intelligence, surveillance, and reconnaissance of beaches, landing zones, and infrastructure.
9. Coordinate with host nation government and military forces, nongovernment organizations, and privately owned organizations.
10. Maintain a Tactical Recovery of Aircraft and Personnel (TRAP) capability.
11. Maintain a "Sparrow hawk" (platoon-sized) reinforcement capability.

Colonel Greenwood designated Lt. Col. Jay Hatton, the MSSG-15 commander, as mission commander for this operation and tasked him with
developing three courses of action: one light, using afloat forces only; one
employing a single ground lodgment from which to conduct operations;
and one including multiple lodgments.

As the MEU/ARG sailed through the Straits of Malacca on 1 January
2005, the crisis continued. CSF-536 designated Indonesia as the main effort,
as estimations of over 150,000 dead and millions of displaced there arrived.
Carrier Strike Group Nine (CSG-9), led by the aircraft carrier USS *Abraham Lincoln* (CVN 72), received responsibility for the area surrounding
Thailand. The 3rd Marine Division was assigned Indonesia, and CSF-536
tasked Expeditionary Strike Group Five with Sri Lanka.

The scope of the crisis in Indonesia required our MEU/ARG to split
its forces to provide relief simultaneously in different locations. The USS
Bonhomme Richard and USS *Rushmore* operated in the waters west of the
Aceh Province of Sumatra, Indonesia. We prepared to employ the whole
MEU to relieve the suffering in that country, but the Indonesian government directed a minimal American presence ashore. Regardless of the
absence of orders to do so, the BLT prepared for possible missions ashore:
a TRAP force; mass casualty response; platoon and company reinforcements; light-, medium-, and heavy-warehouse working parties; convoy
escort and route security; fixed site security; and ground support teams
(GSTs) to assist the ACE in delivering humanitarian supplies. The GSTs
consisted of a team leader, assistant team leader, seven security Marines,
two helicopter support-team Marines, and a corpsman. Although the
BLT had thousands of capable Marines itching to lend assistance, it was
not to be. The BLT's primary role was only to provide a few squad-sized
GSTs each day.

The 15th MEU received orders to conduct operations under the direction of the 3rd Marine Division, commanded by Brig. Gen. Christian
Cowdrey, and redesignated Combined Support Group-Indonesia (CSG-I).
The MEU assumed responsibility for an area of operations spanning from
Banda Aceh in northern Sumatra a hundred nautical miles south to the
town of Meulaboh. Elements of the MEU spent two weeks delivering over
a million pounds of humanitarian aid, using LCACs and flying 275 helicopter missions.[16] Humanitarian supplies included rice, other food rations,
bottled water, water containers, plastic sheeting, lumber, shovels, canvas
sheets, hand sanitizer, fuel cans, generators, and body bags.

The USS *Duluth* and embarked Marines proceeded to Galle, Sri Lanka, where they conducted the first-ever U.S. Marine amphibious landing in that country. Elements of the BLT, MSSG, and ACE combined in efforts to aid local residents.

Although it was a good mission, the Marines on the *Bonhomme Richard* and *Rushmore* remained frustrated knowing they had so much to offer the Indonesian people but could not since their government was apparently unwilling to accept a full commitment. The Marines did not understand why it would not, and as BLT executive officer I had a difficult time explaining it. A rumor spread that Indonesia did not trust the United States following the implementation of the Leahy Amendment to the fiscal year 2000 Foreign Operations Appropriation bill of the U.S. Congress.[17] The amendment had banned U.S. military assistance to Indonesia in the form of foreign military sales, exercises, and participation of Indonesian officers in U.S. military schools associated with the International Military Education and Training (IMET) program. Senator Leahy had initiated the amendment in response to alleged human rights violations previously perpetrated by Indonesian officers in East Timor.

The law had been in place for over a decade at the time the tsunami and had had a chilling effect on relations between the United States and Indonesia. A generation of senior Indonesian officers had arisen who knew little about the Americans and trusted them less. In fact, word spread that the Indonesia staff college had conducted a scenario-based exercise in which the United States had used the cover of a natural disaster to invade their country. Apparently, some found the parallels between that notional exercise and the American response to the tsunami too close for coincidence.

Another rumor was that the Indonesian government wanted all American personnel out of their territory within ninety days. I never determined the validity of these rumors, but I was aware that the Indonesian government had concerns about an ongoing insurgency and that an Islamic extremist group with alleged ties to al-Qaeda had established a relief camp in the area designated for Marine operations.

The Indonesians' lack of trust manifested itself in other ways. Marines received orders to hide any weapons in packs and seabags, rather than carry them at the ready as trained. The *Bonhomme Richard* also had to leave Indonesian territorial waters to conduct proficiency training for its AV-8B Harrier pilots. Indonesia refused to allow this training in its waters. This did not sit well with the MEU when it lost one of its six Harriers on a training mission. The pilot safely ejected, but the aircraft remains at the bottom of the Indian Ocean.

Regardless of the real reason for minimizing a Marine presence in Indonesia, Marines and sailors were stymied just off the coast of a country where thousands suffered. The goodwill demonstrated by the Americans in what became known as Operation Unified Assistance did much to build bridges between the two countries, but this was little consolation for the men and women who wanted to help but were not allowed.

Although there was plenty of work to be done in the Pacific Command region, the Central Command commander was asking for the 15th MEU to "chop into" (report to the commander of) the Middle East region, as planned. This was made possible by tasking the USS *Essex* (LHD 2), which had delivered the 31st MEU to Iraq, to the Pacific Ocean to relieve the *Bonhomme Richard*. The 15th MEU departed the Pacific region on 19 January 2005 and prepared to conduct sustainment training in Kuwait during February and March, while remaining the strategic reserve for employment in Iraq.

Operation Iraqi Freedom III

Our arrival in the Central Command area of operations was surrounded by as much uncertainty as we had faced in the Pacific Command. The BLT planned to go ashore in Kuwait to conduct a month of live-fire sustainment training at the Udairi Range Complex, located at Camp Buehring, northwest of Kuwait City and twenty-five miles from the Iraqi border.

The U.S. Army established Camp Buehring in January 2003 as a staging base for units moving in and out of Iraq. Its name honored Army lieutenant colonel Charles H. Buehring, who died in a rocket attack in Iraq in October 2003.[18] Camp Buehring offered training in everything from battle-sight-zeroing personal weapons to the specialized training in IEDs and escape-and-evasion training needed to operate in Iraq. The camp supported 15,000–20,000 personnel but was full when we attempted to train there. The Army's 3rd Infantry Division was staging for movement to Iraq, elements of I and II MEF were in the process of turning over, and the 11th, 24th, and 31st MEUs were transitioning back to their ships.

Colonel Greenwood actively solicited an opportunity for the MEU to get into the fight, and we eventually worked our way into Buehring and commenced training. Several possibilities existed; it was just a matter of what the combatant commander was willing to free up. We developed plans to assist British forces in the Basra area in conducting what they referred

A scene of the devastation caused by the 2004 tsunami that hit Indonesia. The 15th MEU (SOC) was among the first to respond, but Marines were frustrated by the limited role they were permitted to play in the relief efforts. *Author collection*

to as sector security recovery (SSR). The British SSR was similar to our sustainability and support operations (SASO). Another possibility was for the MEU to serve as a possible quick reaction force (QRF) to back up the 155th Brigade Combat Team of the U.S. Army National Guard, which had just relieved the 11th MEU in the Karbala and Najaf areas. The general in charge of Afghanistan wanted a two-thousand-man unit to augment his forces during upcoming elections in that country. The BLT also received the task of providing Marines to protect vessels being harassed by pirates near Al Faw, Iraq. The Marines would have jumped at the opportunity to conduct any one of these missions, but they were only concepts until approved for execution.

The BLT continued to hone its warfighting skills as we awaited a decision on our future. The rifle companies conducted Military Operations in Urban Terrain (MOUT) training. Our tanks, LAR, and mechanized company conducted a live-fire convoy course, and the artillery battery practiced the art of indirect fires. I had an opportunity to visit with Tango Battery, 5th Battalion, 11th Marines and got to fire an M198 155-mm howitzer during my visit. Tradition dictated that I bite the bullet (or primer) used to ignite the charges and drink a ladle full of dirty and oily water used for the swab that cleans the inside of the howitzer barrel. I happily complied on both counts to honor the "King of Battle" in training that day.

I also got to train with my vehicle crew. Although primarily on foot, Marine Corps infantry in Iraq often operated from vehicles due to the vast distances. I put together a handpicked crew to operate our HMMWV. Sergeant O'Bryant was our driver and motor transport expert. He could fix anything. Sergeant Flores was our communications expert. He maintained and operated one high-powered and one low-powered PRC-119 very-high-frequency (VHF) radio and a PRC-113 ultra-high-frequency (UHF) radio. Corporal Lang was our machine gunner. He maintained and operated an M240G medium machinegun. To cover different scenarios, our HMMWV also carried special-mission kits, such as landing zone marking kits, enemy prisoner of war/detainee kits, communication pack-outs, medical kits, tow kits, and others.

Although each crew member was a subject-matter expert in his occupational field, we cross-trained each member of our crew to perform the duties of the others if necessary. We also conducted numerous immediate-action drills to include identifying threats, taking fire from all sides, breaking contact, countering ambush, emergency-towing procedures, and more. We repeated these drills continually until they became second nature and "muscle memory" guided us through our actions with no conscious thought.

One's fellow crew members become family in such situations. The crew eats, sleeps, and operates as one. My crew made my day when they painted "Bohm's Bastards" on the side of our vehicle. It had been twelve years since I had served in Somalia with the original "Bohm's Bastards," but I was just as proud of this small team of warriors.

The future employment of the MEU was still in doubt when I joined the MEU commander in a flight to Basrah, to coordinate our expected mission with the British army. We met with the British 4th Armored Brigade staff and a British major general Jonathon Riley, who was commander of Multinational Division-Southeast (MND-SE), a regional coalition command established to control the southeast region of Iraq. It was a subordinate command under the Multinational Corps-Iraq (MNC-I), headquartered in Baghdad. Our two staffs were preparing for introducing the 15th MEU to Basrah when we received word that the U.S. Army's 1st Calvary Division had requested the 15th MEU to backfill a battalion from the 1/7 Calvary, which was departing before its relief arrived.

Battalion Landing Team (BLT 1/1) executive officer and his crew on the road to Baghdad. BLT 1/1 responded to the deadly tsunami that hit Asia, fought in southern Baghdad, and prepared to defeat Somali pirates on this one deployment with the 15th MEU(SOC) 2004/2005. *Author collection*

Any doubt as to our future was cast aside on 26 February 2005, when the 15th MEU received orders to detach from Expeditionary Strike Group Five and Naval Forces Central Command and come under the OPCON of Marine Forces Central Command and TACON of MNC-I, commanded by Lt. Gen. George Casey, who later became the thirty-sixth Chief of Staff of the Army. There were four possible courses of action for our employment: assist Army units fighting in Mosul, relieve the 1/7 Calvary in southern Baghdad, join the Marines in Ramadi, or remain in Kuwait until needed. We expected to remain in country for approximately forty days to backload the ships of the ARG and still make our out-chop date from the Central Command area, as originally scheduled.

MNC-I made the final decision to employ the MEU in northern Babil/southern Baghdad under the tactical control of the 256th Brigade Combat Team (BCT) of the Louisiana National Guard, part of the 3rd Infantry Division serving as Multi-National Division-Baghdad. MNC-I assigned the MEU its own area of operations (AO) that extended south to the town of Mahmudiyah, and east to west from the Tigris River to Route 8, designated "main supply route (MSR) Tampa."

The area was a hotbed of insurgent activity, referred to as the Throat of Baghdad. The Iraqi army's Medina and Republican Guard Divisions had operated here during the original invasion, Operation Iraqi Freedom I (OIF-I). The area also had the nickname of "Rocket Alley," because insurgents used it to fire 120-mm and 122-mm rockets into Baghdad and at the Baghdad International Airport.

The BLT organized the area of operation into four sectors and assigned a company to each. The BLT also assumed responsibility for two "tactical control points" (TCP) along Route Tampa, a six-lane highway, through the area of operations, three lanes moving north and the other three moving south.

The BLT's Tango Battery assumed responsibility for Checkpoint (CP) 22A. Second Lt. Anthony Delacosta commanded a platoon from Tango and an eight-man radio retransmission team in defending CP-22A. (Delacosta remains on active duty today as a major.) The retransmission team operated radios to cover the BLT Tactical Net One for primary command and control, BLT Tactical Net Two for administration and logistics, and the Artillery Conduct of Fire Net for calling in fire support, if needed.

Second Lt. John Price of the BLT Headquarters and Service Company (H&S) Security Platoon commanded his Marines in the defense of CP-26A. (Price transitioned to civilian life following this tour in the Marine Corps.) Having headquarters Marines performing tactical tasks was possible thanks to the Marine Corps' ethos of training "every Marine as a rifleman" before learning their primary occupational specialties.

The BLT headquarters element established its command post at FOB Falcon, as the companies established their headquarters in their sectors. Our Marines conducted reliefs in place, with left-seat, right-seat orientation "drive-alongs" with Marines from 2nd Battalion, 24th Marines (2/24) and soldiers from the 6th Squadron, 4th Brigade, 3rd Infantry Division. The 2/24 was a Marine reserve unit, and the 6th Squadron was the reconnaissance, surveillance, and target-acquisition unit for the 4th Brigade, operating in the area. The intent of these actions was to shift primary responsibility for the area gradually from those currently operating there to our Marines. The concept had our Marines begin the turnover by literally riding along in the right seat of vehicles controlled by those already operating in the area, until their situational awareness allowed them to assume control from the left seat.

The battalion prepared different force-package options consisting of headquarters Marines to reinforce and support our Marines in the sectors rapidly, if needed. We established five force-package options that could move by either ground or air assets: command and control (C2), operational, logistics, medical, and recovery options.

The C2 option included a "jump" command post consisting of the BLT commanding officer traveling with his intelligence and operations officers in a single vehicle, a forward command post formed by taking the "Alpha" command group forward in six vehicles, or a "C7/P7" option to move the forward command post using mechanized assets (C7-command variant AAVs and P7-personnel variant AAVs).

We created light-, medium-, and heavy-reinforcement options. The light option consisted of a single Motorized Assault Platoon (MAP), the medium option included reinforcing a MAP with a section of two M1A1 main battle tanks, and the heavy option consisted of a reinforced infantry platoon transported in AAVs joined by a tank platoon of four tanks.

The logistics package consisted of prestaged chow, water, and ammunition, all rapidly deployable using seven-ton trucks, and medical and recovery teams. The medical package involved employing either a casualty-evacuation helicopter or transporting one of our two battalion surgeons and two corpsmen in AAVs to the site of a mass casualty. The recovery team consisted of sending out a motor-transport contact team from the BLT, MEU Service Support Group (MSSG) wrecker, or M88 tank retriever, depending on what type of vehicle needed recovery. These force packages provided maximum flexibility to address any issues our companies might confront. Their establishment proved to be prudent.

Insurgent rocket and mortar attacks on Baghdad originating from the BLT's area disrupted political and economic progress. Insurgents established a pattern of firing rockets and mortars from two known areas against the Baghdad International Airport and the Green Zone, the location of many government facilities. These rocket/mortar locations, or "boxes," received the designations of objectives "Arizona" and "Texas" in an operation developed by the BLT called Operation Warning Track.

The BLT devised Operation Warning Track to disrupt insurgent activities and deny the insurgents the ability to harass and intimidate the newly elected Iraqi government. The operation consisted of inserting four force reconnaissance and three battalion reconnaissance teams into the BLT's northern sectors to find suitable landing zones for inserting two rifle companies via helicopters. The companies received the task of conducting search-and-attack missions against insurgent forces at objectives Arizona and Texas, as mobile assault platoons patrolled main supply routes and established "snap" vehicle checkpoints along roads to disrupt insurgent movement. The BLT leveraged national intelligence, surveillance, and reconnaissance assets to identify enemy targets and established Tango Battery in position to provide fire support. The BLT also scheduled fixed- and rotary-wing close air support to support operations.

Operation Warning Track proved successful; Baghdad experienced no indirect enemy fire from the BLT area of operations for the duration of the two-week operation. It also provided the BLT with valuable experience in the tactics, techniques, and procedures being used by the insurgents. The insurgents had learned in the past three years not to engage coalition forces directly, preferring hit-and-run tactics, indirect fire, IEDs, and the extensive use of weapons caches to hide weapons and munitions. An example of the items found in one cache located by Charlie Company during the operation included thirty mortar rounds, two antitank mines, sixty hand grenades, four pounds of TNT, a suicide vest loaded with C4 explosives, blasting caps, detonation cord, circuit breakers, fuses, batteries, and other devices used to build IEDs. Although hesitant to engage us directly, the enemy still inflicted casualties.

The insurgents directed sporadic small-arms and indirect fire against our Marines throughout Operation Warning Track. Checkpoint 22A received three mortar rounds on 17 March 2005, one of our communications Marines sustained a shrapnel wound to his leg. The prior planning and rehearsals conducted by the BLT proved beneficial, as we deployed a "dust off" casualty evacuation helicopter and retrieved the Marine from the point of injury within ten minutes. U.S. forces came to take the "golden hour"—which referred to the first hour after a traumatic injury—very seriously. Marines understood that their chances of survival increased dramatically if they received medical treatment within that hour.

The BLT became increasingly familiar with the area of operations by living among the people. Critical intelligence about IEDs, caches, and other insurgent activity began to flow in from civilians whose trust we earned. Valuable information about the terrain throughout our area of operations was also gathered during this operation. There were many canals, narrow dirt roads, and dikes throughout the area to channel precious water to farmers' fields. Many of the roads could not sustain the weight of our military vehicles. One of our LAR vehicles rolled into a canal after the ground collapsed under it.

A seven-ton truck loaded with supplies for the rifle companies also rolled into a canal during a night resupply run I was leading. I was convinced we needed to destroy the truck in place. I didn't think it possible to pull it out of its deep and narrow position. I called for the MSSG-15 recovery team and was astonished by their ability to retrieve the truck. The accident had crushed the cab and mud and reeds covered the vehicle, so we nicknamed it "the Swamp Thing" and employed it as a mobile roadblock against vehicle-born IEDs at FOB Falcon.

The insurgents' knowledge of the ground led to another BLT operation. The fedayeen employed civilian vehicles to transport contraband, weapons, and IEDs throughout the BLT area over its intricate road network. The BLT responded by executing Operation Double Trouble, which consisted of multiple unannounced "snap" vehicle checkpoints (VCPs) throughout the area of operations. VCP teams equipped with portable speed bumps, spike strips, cones, alert and stop signs written in Arabic, and search and detainee gear established temporary roadblocks along roads and trails to search vehicles and disrupt insurgent activity on the roads. Insurgents employed false floors, hidden compartments, and removable panels on vehicles in attempts to smuggle their wares. This operation proved so successful that it became an enduring task, renamed Operation Hardball.

The BLT conducted several other operations to accomplish specific tasks during its time in Iraq. Operation River Sweep focused on disrupting insurgent use of the Tigris River and identifying weapons caches. Operation Iron Fist was a joint operation to interdict insurgents attempting to escape west across the Tigris River from the town of Salman Pak, where a combined U.S. Army special operations and Iraqi Security Forces (ISF) team had conducted a clearing operation. The ISF/SOF team detained fifty insurgents on this operation. Operation Strong Will safeguarded Islamic pilgrims traveling through the BLT area of operations to the holy cities of Najaf and Karbala. Operation Bear Trap focused on killing or capturing insurgents operating on MSR Tampa.

The MEU accomplished a great deal during its time on the ground in country. It conducted 413 cordon-and-search operations, 339 patrols, and 180 VCPs, inspecting 578 vehicles. Moreover, it conducted thirteen raids, discovered twenty-seven IEDs, fifteen caches, and detained sixty-four insurgents. The Marines ran into two IEDs and received sporadic indirect and direct fire, but luckily only sustained minor injuries. Iraq was still a dangerous place, but our tactics and attention to detail helped to mitigate the threat. One must guard against becoming complacent though. This became evident on one of our final days in country.

Our headquarters and service platoon guarding CP26A had just completed turning over its position to a relieving Army unit and its members were sitting on their packs awaiting transportation out of the area when insurgents attacked the position. Two carloads of insurgents drove to the vicinity of the checkpoint and offloaded attackers. The Marine platoon commander heard shooting, but he thought it was partner Iraqi forces being dropped off and shooting rounds into the air, as they habitually did. His opinion changed when the volume increased, and an Iraqi soldier walked up to them with a head wound.

The Marines immediately jumped into action and assaulted the insurgents. They riddled the two vehicles with fire, killing some insurgents, and wounding others, and chasing those who tried to retreat. The platoon corpsman administered first aid to the injured Iraqi soldier, yelled for the Army medic to take over, grabbed his rifle, and joined his Marines in the attack. The Marines aggressively pursued the insurgents for 1,500 meters before capturing all six who tried to escape, none of whom had anticipated the aggressive fighting spirit of United States Marines. Significantly, these were headquarters and service Marines and not infantrymen, once again validating the combat training of all Marines.

The MEU learned many lessons on this mission. We reinforced the value of remaining on the offensive and taking the initiative away from the enemy. We reinforced the importance of avoiding patterns that the enemy can exploit. The value of employing helicopters to avoid IEDs on the ground and for resupply to reduce ground convoy requirements was another lesson. We learned that the enemy's ability to interdict air assets lagged behind his ability to disrupt ground operations. We learned to overwhelm the enemy with simultaneous operations from multiple avenues of approach. We learned that in this environment fighting dismounted was more effective than fighting mounted. The enemy's fear of our attack helicopters and his preference for dispersed cache operations was evident. We also learned that although technology is useful in a counterinsurgency environment, "human intelligence," information supplied by local people, is essential.

These lessons augmented other enduring lessons we learned. We confirmed that fixed-site security missions reduce the availability of forces needed for offensive operations. We learned that twenty-four-hour-per-day operations are a prerequisite for success on today's battlefield. We validated that speed of execution helps generate operational tempo. We learned that raids planned and executed on actionable intelligence are less intrusive to the local population than random cordon-and-searches. We learned to employ snipers and explosive-ordnance disposal technicians as combined-arms assets. We learned the value of providing company commanders with "solatia" funds (for compensating injuries and damage) in dealing with the civilian population. We learned to treat humanitarian and civil-affairs efforts as decisive operations in a counterinsurgency. We learned to use to our advantage the fact that the Iraqis fear insurgents more than they dislike U.S. and coalition forces.

One of the most important lessons learned during our time in country was the need to get off the FOB and out of our vehicles to operate among the people. This tactic built trust and helped to detect threats before they struck. Our Marines became very effective in sweeping dismounted in front of vehicles and in conducting "5 and 25" checks. Any time a vehicle stopped, Marines dismounted and did a quick five-meter check around the immediate vicinity of the vehicle to find any close threats. The search extended to a twenty-five-meter radius beyond the vehicle if none were found. These actions resulted in our finding all but two IEDs laid against our force. We shared this lesson with the Army cavalry unit that replaced us, but they remained too tied to their vehicles and sustained six IED attacks in their first seventy-two hours on the ground.

Our time in Iraq was short as the MEU had to return to its ships and continue its deployment. Although there was plenty to do in Iraq, there was also more to be done at sea. Many units across the joint force possessed the skills to operate on the ground, but only the Marines and our Navy and Coast Guard partners had the skills required to perform missions on the oceans. One of these missions is vertical board search and seizure (VBSS).

The VBSS mission consists of taking down ships at sea to combat terrorism, piracy, and smuggling. Navy and Marine VBSS teams send a surface force in small boats to secure a targeted vessel from the waterline up, and an air mobile force inserted by either landing or FAST-roping from helicopters.

The 15th MEU received the mission to prepare for a VBSS, before we even departed Iraq, to address an age-old but reemerging threat—piracy. Somali pirates had hijacked a foreign-flagged vessel and demanded $200,000 in ransom. The MEU developed a plan to conduct a VBSS using our Maritime Special Purpose Force (MSPF) and with raids against two suspected pirate camps on the Somali coast using rifle companies. This was a ready-made mission for the MEU.

The MEU loaded back on board and transited the Straits of Hormuz on 18 April 2005. The schedule had us proceeding to Australia, but the plan changed, and the ships made full steam toward the waters off Somalia to await an execute order for the VBSS and raids. We received conflicting word over the next couple of days on whether the ship's owners had paid the ransom and secured the release of the crew of the hijacked vessel, but preparations and rehearsals continued. This mission like many others was not to be. We received the order to stand down, and the ships continued to Australia for liberty. Such is the life of a Marine. The nation expects us to be the most ready when the nation itself is least ready. This often means planning, rehearsing, and preparing for missions that never occur. Although the Marines were frustrated, a week of liberty in Brisbane helped to quell the disappointment.

Our deployment was ending, and the MEU followed the stay in Australia with three days in Hawaii for liberty, refueling, and linking with family members who joined us for the transit home to San Diego on what is referred to as a tiger cruise. This is a Navy and Marine Corps tradition where select family members are authorized to travel on ships for limited periods to experience the shipboard life of Marines and sailors. Lieutenant Colonel Furness, my commanding officer, and I both had our sons meet us in Hawaii and stay in our joint stateroom for the transit home. The "tiger" days consisted of tours, static displays, hands-on practical application with the tools of our trade, video-game competitions, and more, as the Marines and sailors made final preparations for concluding the deployment.

The Marines and sailors manned the railings of our ships once more as we pulled into Naval Base San Diego. Loved ones reunited after six long months of separation. Family and friends longing to embrace once again the people most important in their lives packed the piers. Some Marines and sailors saw their newborn children for the first time. Families settled back into routines of having mothers and fathers back at home and sharing the responsibilities of raising a family. Many Marines received orders to other units on return, and I was no exception. I received word that I was selected for promotion to lieutenant colonel and had orders sending me back to the 1st Marine Division staff.

1st Marine Division, I MEF (Forward), and Iraq Again

1st Marine Division Current Operations Officer

I was not home for long following my deployment with the 15th Marine Expeditionary Unit (MEU), when I received orders to Headquarters Battalion, 1st Marine Division at Camp Pendleton to assume duties as the division current operations officer. Happy with the assignment, I did not have to move my family, and I got to remain in the operating forces serving in the 1st Marine Division, known as the Blue Diamond.

I worked for the assistant chief of staff for operations (G-3), Col. Joel Schwankl. Schwankl was another old-school Marine, and he had a knack for building teams. The G-3 orchestrated the planning, coordination, and execution of exercises, training, and operations for the division, which followed a constant cycle of preparing units for deployment to either Iraq in support of Operation Iraqi Freedom, or on ship as part of the GCE of a MEU. The work was busy, but enjoyable.

Colonel Schwankl and others of us from the G-3 soon received orders to transfer to the First Marine Expeditionary Force to augment its G-3 Operations Section for deployment to Iraq in support of Operation Iraqi Freedom 05–07 (2005–7). It and Camp Lejeune's II MEF rotated in assuming responsibility for the Al Anbar Province of Iraq as Multinational Force West (MNF-W), it was I MEF's turn. The MEF intended to send a forward element to conduct these duties under Maj. Gen. Richard Zilmer, while the MEF commander stayed in Camp Pendleton with the remainder of the unit to fulfill its other responsibilities. (Zilmer later earned a third star before retiring and remains active as a senior mentor in the Marine Corps today.) Colonel Schwankl assumed duties as the current operations officer for what became known as I MEF (Forward), and I assumed duties as the ground combat operations officer.

I MEF (Forward)

I MEF (Forward) formed at Camp Del Mar, in Camp Pendleton, and prepared for deployment. We drafted SOPs, ran command-post exercises, and conducted mandatory training for I MEF's deployment. I received orders to deploy early as part of the advanced party with a group of talented officers and senior staff noncommissioned officers to set the conditions for the transfer of responsibility from II MEF to I MEF. We flew through Bangor (Maine), Shannon (Ireland), and Budapest (Hungary) prior to landing in Kuwait, where we joined elements of the 3rd Battalion, 5th Marines for a KC-130 flight from Ali Al Salem Air Base in Kuwait to Al Taqaddum Air Base in Habbaniyah, Iraq. A short hop in a CH-46 helicopter took us to our destination, Camp Fallujah. Camp Fallujah was a former Iraqi armored brigade headquarters located just outside the city of Fallujah, approximately thirty miles west of Baghdad. Elements of the U.S. Army 82nd Airborne Division during Operation Iraqi Freedom I occupied the base and in 2004 turned it over to I MEF.

Marines fought two battles in Fallujah. They first attacked the city in April 2004 during Operation Vigilant Resolve to defeat extremists and apprehend those who had killed four American contractors. Elements of the 1st Marine Division made good progress before turning the operation over to a newly formed Iraqi Security Force unit designated the Fallujah Brigade. This brigade did not perform well, and insurgents returned to take over the city, thus the need for a second operation to secure it later that year. I MEF executed the second Battle of Fallujah, known as Operation Al-Fajr/Phantom Fury, in November 2004. Although the Marines defeated the four- to five-thousand insurgents who chose to oppose them openly in combat, many more returned to conduct an insurgency after the battle.

By then, Operation Iraqi Freedom had transitioned from a conventional war to a counterinsurgency. Operation Phantom Fury proved to America's adversaries once more the folly of engaging American forces in a conventional fight. The fedayeen and other insurgent forces now relied primarily on unconventional warfare to delegitimize the nascent Iraqi government, while imposing casualties on coalition forces to attempt to break their will in a protracted war. Although conventional wisdom demonstrates that the stronger of two opposing forces will prevail, history also demonstrates that this rule is no longer valid when one is confronted by a more resolute force. Will and determination add strength and endurance to an otherwise weak force.

Many factors can influence and shape one's will. Author David Galula lists political, social, economic, racial, religious, and cultural differences as causes for insurgencies.[1] He identifies the need for a "cause" stemming from one or more of these factors as necessary for an insurgency. Combining the will, means, and ability to fight for a cause can drive change and lead to victory. As will is a human dimension, winning over the local population in any insurgency must be a primary objective. This understanding changed the way in which we planned for conducting operations in Al Anbar Province in 2004.

Operations in Iraq up to this point had focused primarily on "kinetic" combat operations. The hard-learned lessons of Operation Desert Storm and more recently of Operation Phantom Fury convinced the insurgents they needed to shift tactics if they were to survive. They looked to the Vietnam War and the Battle of Mogadishu to determine how a smaller and weaker force could potentially defeat the United States. Small, agile forces hiding among the people and continually inflicting casualties on American service members can mitigate the technological and firepower advantages of American forces. But the insurgents were not the only ones who needed to change tactics.

Coalition forces had to shift their approach if they hoped to win over the local population and deny support to the insurgents. Many Marines had a difficult time adapting to this new approach. Marines train to be fierce warfighters. But in fighting an insurgency they must also train to be compassionate partners, when required. The situation in Iraq required such an approach. Heavy-handed action that risked killing innocents and destroying property had the potential of feeding enemy propaganda and creating more enemies in this new stage of the operation.

Winning the support of locals requires a wide and diverse strategy that protects the people, sees to their needs, and builds confidence in the local and national governments. Traditional military plans that seek out the enemy to destroy them with fire and maneuver were no longer sufficient. What was now demanded was a plan consisting of several lines of operation (LOOs). Such LOOs included first providing a secure environment by defeating the insurgents, while establishing security forces to maintain the peace. Armies have the responsibility to guard against external threats and to defend borders. Police protect the population internally. Galula refers to police as "the eye and the arm of government in all matters pertaining to internal order."[2] Leadership and governance provide a representative voice for the people and direct essential services. A healthy economy is a requirement to provide jobs, so citizens can take care of their families. Information becomes a powerful tool in building legitimacy for local officials while mitigating the enemy's ability to do the same.

Developing these LOOs required a mental shift on the part of the Marines. Our strategy went from one of "clear and hold," to one of "clear, hold, build, and transition." The Marines did not have any current doctrine to guide them in determining how to fight a counterinsurgency. The *Small Wars Manual* and David Galula's *Counterinsurgency Warfare: Theory and Practice*, published in 1964, became primary sources for developing plans to defeat the insurgency and transition control of Iraq back to the Iraqis.[3]

One of the primary principles of COIN is to live and operate among the people to win their support. Marines began clearing enemy strongholds with their Iraqi partners while establishing small forward operating bases within local communities for units of squad to platoon size. This practice achieved its desired effect of establishing and strengthening relationships with the local population but had the unintended consequence of developing a generation of Marines who lost touch with the tenets of maneuver warfare and *Warfighting*.

Vehicles weighed down by armor to protect against the blast effects of IEDs and Marines forced to wear heavy bulletproof vests and protective plates to protect against enemy fire exacerbated this dynamic. The judgment and decisions of leaders on what gear their Marines should wear changed to appease government leaders and an American public looking to reduce casualties.

These thoughts weighed heavily on my mind as the other members of the I MEF advanced party and I settled into Camp Fallujah. The camp was a small city surrounded by a six-mile-long wall. In addition to the II MEF Command Element and Headquarters Battalion, Regimental Combat Team Eight (RCT-8), 1st Battalion, 1st Marines (1/1, my old battalion), 3/5, the 8th Communications Battalion, the artillerymen of Bravo Battery 1/11, the scout platoon of the 1st Tank Battalion, a detachment from the 6th Civil Affairs Group, Marine reserve artillerymen being employed to run a detention center, and U.S. Army engineers from the 54th Engineers who conducted route clearing operations, all formed up in the camp.

Camp Fallujah had all the amenities of home. Marines could shop at a post exchange or Iraqi bazaar. The camp provided laundry facilities, a barber shop, two chow halls, and numerous gyms. A base chapel provided a sanctuary for the Marines. They lived in numerous large tents or trailers affectionately referred to as "cans" spread throughout the camp. The camp also provided numerous showers and bathrooms, what Marines call "heads." Numerous plastic portable toilets rounded out the camp's ambiance.

I moved into an area located in the center known as the "Battle Square." The Battle Square housed the MEF Combat Operations Center (COC), from which the MEF provided the command and control for all of MNF-W spread across western Iraq. Lt. Col. Mark Tull, who also came from the 1st Marine Division, and I moved into a hard-stand building that had once housed Iraqi army officers. Tull was a Philadelphia boy whose company and dry humor I enjoyed. (He was later promoted to colonel and served as the chief of staff for the Marine Corps Recruit Depot San Diego.)

Enemy mortar and rocket fire landing within Camp Fallujah provided a reminder that Iraq was still a dangerous place. This danger posed a challenge for General Casey, commander of Multinational Force-Iraq. Casey saw the securing of Iraq's international border with Jordan and Syria as a strategic imperative. To him stopping the flow of foreign fighters was more important than gaining control of the population centers to win over the people. ISF established thirty-two forts and two combat outposts to guard the borders. Four ports-of-entry (POEs) also controlled access to the country. POEs Waleed and Trebil allowed access through Jordan, POE Ar Ar remained open with Saudi Arabia, while POE Al Qa'im along the Syrian border remained closed.

Casey laid down three top priorities for Iraq: first, the maintenance of a persistent presence in controlled areas. He called for robust partnering between coalition and Iraqi forces to assist in reestablishing and professionalizing the ISF. Second, he called for establishment of a strong police force to provide security for the population and a stable environment for economic growth. In fact, Casey declared 2006 "The Year of the Police." Finally, he gave reconstruction efforts priority over military operations, because he wanted to drive a wedge between the insurgents and the population.

Commanders hoped to achieve the goals of our counterinsurgency strategy in a clean and sequential manner. However, insurgencies are not clean; the enemy gets a vote. Coalition operations called for advances across all the lines of operation: governance, security, information and commu-nications, and economics, simultaneously. At times, it felt like we took two steps backward for every one step forward, as enemy activity or friendly actions disrupted progress. This posed a challenge to determining metrics of success.

Measuring success in an insurgency is difficult. How does one measure the support of the local community or the effectiveness of an information campaign? Measuring the wrong metrics can lead to inaccurate assump-tions and poor decisions. For example, some commanders strove to build as many schools as possible in their areas of responsibility. On the sur-face, building schools seems like a good thing, until one realizes there is no money for furniture, books, or teachers. An empty building does not help a community, especially when its people have no clean running water and would prefer to have invested in a well. Conducting a thorough intelligence analysis prior to developing operations orders is as essential in a counter-insurgency as it is in combat. Failure to do so in either situation will lead to mission failure.

My partners and I from I MEF weighed these considerations as we pre-pared for the rest of our team to arrive. The I MEF (Forward) main body planned to arrive on 28 January 2006, with the transfer of responsibility (TOR) between I MEF (Forward) and II MEF set for 28 February. II MEF intended to transfer responsibility for MNF-W to the 2nd Marine Division, one of its major subordinate commands, and have it conduct the TOR with I MEF (Forward) as it redeployed home. This was problematic since the 2nd Marine Division Staff operated from Camp Blue Diamond in Ramadi and would not arrive in Fallujah until after the arrival of the I MEF main body. We made it work by systematically replacing II MEF staff positions with members of the 2nd Marine Division and the I MEF advanced party.

The operational tempo remained high throughout the transfer of responsibility. In addition to enemy activity, friendly requirements ensured an influx of tasks. Large numbers of VIPs visited the MEF and required support. I sat in a confirmation brief for an upcoming congressional del-egation (CODEL) of four members of Congress, and found myself sur-prised to hear that II MEF hosted 273 visits throughout the year. Although important, each visit bled off needed security forces, fire support, vehicles, and other assets. Little did I know that I would be escorting members of Congress in other CODELs in a future job. The development of the ISF was a primary point of interest for many of the VIPs.

The Marines and soldiers in MNF-W made good progress in building the capacity and skills of the ISF. At the time I arrived, two Iraqi division

(1st and 7th) headquarters existed in MNF-W. They had seven brigades with twenty-one battalions. In addition, seven Department of Border Enforcement (DBE) battalions, and two Special Police Teams existed. In these numbered over 21,000 Iraqi soldiers and 1,700 police in the western Euphrates River valley.

The Marines and sailors of II MEF had accomplished a great deal during their year in country. The MEF had conducted over 4,500 offensive operations and nearly 1,000 combat patrols, its vehicles had driven over 800,000 miles, and its aircraft had accumulated over 100,000 flight hours. It had dropped over 194 tons of aviation ordnance and fired over six hundred counterbattery indirect-fire missions. Its actions resulted in detaining over ten thousand suspected insurgents, killing over 1,600 enemy fighters, and finding over two thousand IEDs before they exploded and over 1,700 weapons caches.

This had come at a cost. The enemy had launched over 2,400 attacks on the MEF with IEDs and over two thousand with small arms and rocket-propelled grenades. They had also conducted over 1,400 indirect-fire attacks against American forces using mortars and rockets. The MEF had lost over 240 Marines, soldiers, and sailors killed in action with over two thousand wounded to enemy action.

Reconstruction efforts continued during all of II MEF's combat operations. The Iraqi Relief and Reconstruction Fund employed over $120 million to rebuild destroyed homes and facilities. The MEF invested over an additional $26 million in the Development Fund for Iraq. Commanders also used over $87 million for local projects. Reconstructing an area is not easy during a war. Enemy forces conducted an average of 223 attacks against coalition forces per week, or nearly thirty-two attacks per day, across the MNF-W area. The most contested area in Al Anbar Province was the city of Ramadi, the provincial capital. Insurgents, organized under the new name of al-Qaeda in Iraq (AQIZ), launched complex attacks focused on Ramadi, but also occurring elsewhere across the region. However, working closely with the local population was starting to pay off.

Al Anbar Province is predominately composed of Sunni Muslims. The title Sunni comes from the Arabic word *Sunna*, meaning "tradition."[4] The Sunni are one of Islam's two main branches. The other group are the Shiite, who took their name from the word Shia, which means "partisan."[5] Sunnis and Shiites dispute the legitimacy of the heir to Muhammad. Sunnis believe in tradition and argue that the successor should be appointed by election and consensus. The Shiite believed that Muhammad's successors should come from his family line.

The 2003 invasion by coalition forces and the ousting of Saddam Hussein provided an opportunity for the Shiites after decades of marginalization by Hussein's corrupt government and the majority Sunni population. This turn of events led to Sunni claims that the first free elections held in Iraq in 2005 were neither fair nor free, a fact exacerbated when many Sunnis boycotted it. Sunnis soon realized they could no longer maintain power through strength alone. They now needed to be part of the democratic political process, if they wanted a voice in the government. Coalition forces helped to establish a secure-enough environment and 85 percent of the Sunni population voted in 2005.

The close interaction of coalition forces with the local population paid off in other ways. The coalition's efforts across the lines of operation promised to provide a secure environment, essential services, economic opportunity, and effective government, while the radical Islamists of AQIZ offered more fighting and suffering. Moreover, AQIZ's harsh methods convinced many moderate Sunnis to switch sides in what became known as the "Al Anbar Awakening," which began during my time with I MEF (Forward) in Iraq.

The Al Anbar Awakening occurred in the fall of 2006 when Sunni sheiks in Ramadi rejected AQIZ and joined the ISF and coalition forces in ousting the radical insurgents from the city.[6] Ramadi is strategically located in western Iraq. The Al Anbar ports of entry to Saudi Arabia, Jordan, and Syria provided access to foreign fighters, who subsequently used the extensive road network and Euphrates River, which passes through Ramadi to gain access to other provinces in Iraq. Controlling Ramadi denied AQIZ access to one of its most critical bases and therefore to other parts of the country. The awakening gained momentum in other parts of Al Anbar as well. One of I MEF's (Forward) main objectives was to facilitate these efforts.

One of the primary methods for winning in Al Anbar was to partner with and increase the skills and capacity of ISF. The 2nd Marine Division had made good progress in this regard. It established a training center in the city of Habbaniyah, just outside the Marine air base established at Al Taqaddum. Lt. Col. Wayne Sinclair, a future operations officer from I MEF who deployed with me as part of the advanced party, and I traveled to the training center in preparation for the I and II MEF turnover. Sinclair was later promoted to colonel and was director of the Marine Corps' School of Advanced Warfighting.

The 2nd Marine Division turned Habbaniyah into a rudimentary, but first-class, training facility. They established several classrooms and ranges of varied distances and purposes to train the ISF in an array of weapons systems and tasks. CWO 5/Gunner Terry Walker led a team of subject-matter experts in providing instruction to the ISF in such areas as marksmanship, security details, and patrolling. Walker was renowned in the Corps as a weapons expert and top instructor. He was the perfect man for the job. The instruction was good and focused on junior soldiers and noncommissioned officers (NCOs). Unfortunately, training is only productive if accepted and applied.

The Iraqi military at the time did not hold their noncommissioned officers or staff noncommissioned officers in high regard. The Deputy Military Transition Team (MTT) commander assigned to the 1st Iraqi Division explained to me why. During Saddam's rule, from 1979 to 2003, the Iraqi army held officers accountable and often punished them, some with death, for their units' failures. This produced a generation of officers who micromanaged every aspect of their soldiers' actions, for fear of retribution. The selection process also chose officers from the higher classes of society, who expected to be catered to.

The deputy MTT commander provided an example of one Iraqi officer's expectation of special treatment. He observed an officer get out of his vehicle, take two steps, and stop. He then held his arms out parallel to the ground; two soldiers came up on either side of him and removed his flak jacket and helmet. They then handed him a drink and a cigar, already lit. It was like something out of a movie. He claimed enlisted soldiers expected to be held in low esteem. This was a significant barrier that would have to be overcome before we could hope to raise the ISF's overall proficiency.

I asked one officer when he thought the Iraqi unit with whom he partnered could assume responsibility for its own battlespace as part of plans to transition control to the ISF. He responded, "Never." He explained that he felt Iraqis did not like to train or conduct long-term planning. His Iraqi partners stated, "We don't train, we only do missions." He also indicated that his partnered unit planned out to only twenty-one days at a time, because the unit shut down to provide "leave" to the soldiers every three weeks. I saw how it was easy for a Marine to become pessimistic in this environment. We had to coach and mentor our Marines to overcome such negativity.

Walker provided some unique insights into how to overcome some of these hurdles and maximize training value for the Iraqis. Effective training had to begin with building relationships and treating students with respect and dignity. Walker understood that the Iraqis frustrated his instructors at times, so he devised the "ten-second rule." He advised his instructors to step away and count to ten when something exasperated them. Failure to do so and losing one's temper or starting to think of the Iraqis as less than equal to Americans were grounds for removal from their positions. He understood that training lost its effectiveness after six hours of instruction in a day. He encouraged his people to learn Arabic and look past cultural differences. In every respect, Gunner Walker demonstrated care and concern for the students, to which they were not accustomed—for example, providing shade and ice water during the day's hottest times.

Walker also used psychology in getting the students to train. He observed them break beds and other furniture in the barracks until he made them sign for it. The fear of being held accountable had the desired effect. Whenever soldiers claimed they were too hot, cold, tired, hungry, etc. to train, he would respond, "Yes, yes, I understand . . . now if you will just give me your full name, I will let the general know you are too hot, cold, etc. to train." The soldiers inevitably always responded, "No, no, I will do it." They did not want their names on any lists.

Sinclair and I filed away these tactical lessons, as we traveled to Camp Blue Diamond in Ramadi to meet with the 2nd Marine Division staff to learn more about the plans for our mission. Camp Blue Diamond had gotten its name when the 1st Marine Division occupied it earlier in the campaign, and the name had stuck after the division returned home. Blue Diamond was the most beautiful area I had seen in Iraq. The camp surrounds one of Saddam Hussein's palaces on the Euphrates River just north of Ramadi. It had the affectionate nickname of the "JDAM" Palace, because it had received a direct hit from a joint direct attack munition (JDAM) bomb earlier in the war. Rumor was that Hussein only visited the palace once, giving it to his son Uday when he saw something about it he didn't like. The bomb only partially destroyed the palace, which became the headquarters for coalition forces operating in the Ramadi area. The 2nd Marine Division headquarters was in an outer building previously used by Uday for entertainment purposes. The palace itself was repaired for use as the new Iraqi 7th Division headquarters.

Sinclair and I met with the 2nd Marine Division G-3 operations officer, Colonel Holden. Holden and I connected as he had previously commanded the 1st Battalion, 4th Marines, the unit I was slated to assume command of after this deployment. He informed us that the MNC-I staff responsible for ground operations in Iraq was turning over. The Army's XVIII Airborne Corps under Lt. Gen. John Vines had passed responsibility for MNC-I to V Corps under Lt. Gen. Peter Chiarelli, the future thirty-second Vice Chief of

Staff of the Army. The 5th Corps staff was apparently much more demanding about staff work.

This concerned Colonel Holden, because Marine forces in Iraq were in the process of transitioning from having two senior-level staffs to only one responsible for MNF-W. Whereas the MEF staff up to this point focused on operational matters across the entire campaign, leaving the division staff to focus on tactical matters, the division now had to deal with both operational and tactical issues. Colonel Holden feared that feeding the MNC-I staff with what it wanted would consume his staff and leave it little time for supporting the Marines in the fight.

Holden provided insights and advice on moving forward. He advised against "putting the cart before the horse" of establishing policies or providing equipment before receiving units were ready. For example, MNC-I released a message directing that all older-generation up-armored vehicles be turned over to the Iraqis, because U.S. forces already possessed all the new "level-one" armored vehicles. This may have been true in Baghdad, but it certainly was not the case with the Marines out in the hinterland. In addition, the Iraqis had no maintenance system to care for and sustain the vehicles. They normally just drove them into the ground and then abandoned them. Holden also cautioned against standing up more Iraqi police until the support infrastructure was in place. Doing so risked hurting their credibility and recruiting efforts. He identified the need to choose and cultivate the right liaison officers to higher headquarters to educate the division's superiors about the realities on the ground.

Holden discussed upcoming operations, the relief in place and transfer of responsibility (RIP/TOA) between the 2nd Marine Division, which would gain responsibility as MNF-W from II MEF, and I MEF (Forward). Historically, enemy forces had attacked during RIP/TOAs. Incoming units are vulnerable until they have become acclimated to their new environment and have learned the ground and patterns of their area. The 2nd Marine Division developed Operation Patriot Shield to disrupt any enemy activities during the RIP. It also established an information operation plan to ensure that AQIZ did not interpret the division's departure from Ramadi to Fallujah as their success, when it was actually a transfer of responsibility for the area to the 7th Iraqi Division. Holden made it clear that this was not a division fight. Unlike that experienced by the 1st Marine Division in the march to Baghdad during OIF-1, the current phase of OIF was a fight of RCTs and battalion task force (BNTFs) in their areas of responsibility. The division's, and soon to be I MEF (Forward)'s, task was to support the RCTs and BNTFs.

Sinclair and I discussed this as we walked to the landing zone at 1:30 a.m. for a helicopter flight back to Fallujah. We ran into a firefight in progress. Artillerymen from Lima Battery, 3rd Battalion, 10th Marines, who manned a guard post on the camp perimeter wall, had engaged attacking insurgent forces. Tracer rounds filled the air as we checked into a hastily made plywood room for our flight. It was just another day in Iraq.

More outgoing artillery fire welcomed us back to Camp Fallujah. Bravo Battery 1/11 was responding to enemy mortar and rocket with counterbattery firing. Fortunately, the insurgents did not employ artillery. They preferred mortars and rockets, because with those weapons they could use "shoot and scoot" tactics. This entailed firing a small number of mortar rounds or rockets and then quickly departing the area, before Marine counterbattery fire ruined their day. Counterbattery is a precise process. Radars detect incoming rounds and automatically determine ten-digit grid coordinates for the points of origin (POOs) by computing the back azimuth of incoming rounds. This data is then electronically sent to the fire direction center (FDC), which verifies and approves missions. The FDC electronically sends computed control data by which the guns fire at the POO. The entire process happens quickly.

The artillerymen also fired "terrain denial" missions. These are preplanned missions on areas historically used by insurgents. Intelligence Marines study data of past enemy indirect-fire and IED attacks to determine patterns of the days, times, and locations. They used this data to make "best guesses" as to when and from where the enemy might attempt to fire on, or employ IEDs against, friendly forces. These missions did more to disrupt enemy activities than to achieve lucky shots killing insurgents in the act.

The 2nd Marine Division assumed responsibility as MNF-W from II MEF on 31 January 2006. Holden assumed responsibility as the unit's G-3 operations officer. He pulled together his Marines, the remaining G-3 Marines from II MEF and those of us in the I MEF G-3 advanced party, into a cohesive team until the RIP/TOA with I MEF (Forward) was complete.

The arrival of February brought with it members of our team. Colonel Schwankl and other members of the I MEF (Forward) staff arrived and started conducting left-seat/right-seat turnovers from the 2nd Marine Division team. Similar turnovers also occurred at the regimental and battalion levels across the region. I was happy to welcome Lt. Col. Dave Furness, my former boss, who was still commanding 1/1. He now served under the command of RCT-5, which, under Col. Larry Nicholson, assumed responsibility for operations in the Fallujah area. (Nicholson would later be promoted to general and assume command of the 1st Marine Division and III Marine Expeditionary Force. He was to be my future boss in the 1st Marine Division when I assumed command of the 5th Marines, the unit he commanded in Iraq.) I worked closely with both officers for the remainder of the deployment. The I MEF Marines fell under the command of Maj. Gen. Richard Huck, the 2nd Marine Division Commander, until Maj. Gen. Richard Zilmer, our own commanding general, assumed command of MNF-W on 28 February 2006.

General Huck shared with Colonel Schwankl, as part of the turnover, some lessons learned the hard way by infantrymen on the ground. He encouraged us to "get in the enemy's face, and to stay in it." He directed that we conduct "reset," reinforcement, and driver training with the Marines every two weeks to apply the lessons being learned in operations, as well as training on basic skills such as first aid, precombat checks, communications, and rules of engagement. He emphasized the need for Marines to wear all their personal protective gear—helmets, flak jackets with bullet-proof plates, gloves, goggles, and hearing protection—when operating outside friendly lines. He also cautioned us to stow pyrotechnics and grenades properly until needed.

The general was also clear on the actions he himself intended to take if needed. He promised to hold any violators of the law of armed conflict or rules of engagement accountable for their actions. He warned against increases in escalation-of-force (EOF) violations following IED attacks, after which Marines had heightened sensitivities. The general advised Marines who were interviewed by the media to "stay in their lane" and discuss only what they knew. He also reinforced the policy of no alcohol consumption in country and issued a firm warning to guard against complacency.

General Huck's final point to Colonel Schwankl was that there is no surrendering in this fight. It was common knowledge that AQIZ intended to take prisoners for propaganda purposes; the general emphasized that our Marines should go down fighting to avoid that. This was one word of advice on which I did not think he needed to convince any Marines.

I celebrated my thirty-eighth birthday on a rainy day at Camp Fallujah. The steady rain resulted in a condition well known to infantrymen; there was mud everywhere, although it did not matter much to me since my duties kept me in the battle square and the COC at most times. It only impacted my daily run around the base perimeter; I felt for the infantrymen operating in the field and yearned to be out there with them. Still, we all had our roles to play on this deployment and mine became clearer with the assignment of roles and responsibilities to those of us in G-3.

I assumed responsibility for a diverse set of duties as the ground combat operations officer for MNF-W. There was a lot to do, and I MEF (Forward) did not receive as many officers as expected. Lieutenant Colonels Mark Tull (the current-operations planner), Kevin Foster (the senior watch officer for the COC), and I split the tasks assigned to our section. My responsibilities entailed maintaining the battle rhythm (which drove the daily activities of the staff), publishing an operations tracker and update, confirming any boundary changes requested by subordinate units, maintaining the operations calendar, writing the MNF-W Situation Report (SITREP), sitting on the counter-IED and ISF working groups, addressing all training issues, processing urgent-needs requests, working with Tull to review and approve operation concepts and plans from our subordinate units, and acting as the liaison with the combined joint special operations task force in the area.

I attended a police-transition-team conference as part of my responsibility for ISF transition, which comprised the police as well as the army and border enforcement forces. The conference addressed several issues in growing the Iraqi Police (IP) in this proclaimed "Year of the Police." Many believed local problems required local solutions, rather than have national laws dictate actions in tribal areas. Some had concerns with a predominately Shiite central government dictating laws to the majority Sunni population in the province. Different interpretations of sharia (Islamic law) and tribal laws also complicated matters.

Establishing a secure environment that protected the population and enabled economic growth was essential in winning the counterinsurgency. This was a challenging prospect for Al Anbar Province in 2006. Insurgents attempted to assassinate the provincial governor twenty-seven times. In 2006, 650,000 of the 1.3 million people living in Al Anbar had no employment. This situation provided a ready pool of disheartened young men more than willing to raise arms and lay IEDs against coalition forces for the right price. Only 1,700 police existed in Al Anbar in 2006. The U.S. military needed assistance in recruiting and preparing more.

Recruiting police was no easy task. Coalition forces assisted the police in those efforts by providing security, manpower, and transportation during recruiting drives. The most effective method for advertising available positions was word of mouth by using local tribal sheiks who would gather candidates in a central location for screening, which normally consisted of a simple reading test to see if they met the standards for a police training class. Working with the sheiks proved successful until insurgents began intimidating cooperative sheiks with threats of harm or death. Insurgents also attacked gatherings of potential applicants to dissuade others from attempting to join the police. One attack at a factory in Ramadi being used as a recruiting station killed twenty and wounded eighty.

The police required additional assistance in training their new officers, once recruited. Assistance in training more police came in the form of the International Police Liaison Officers (IPLO). The IPLO was an organization of former police officers contracted by the Department of Defense through DynCorp International. The IPLO organized itself into regional offices, and our region consisted of approximately forty officers who operated from Iraqi police stations in five- to six-man teams. MNF-W had IPLOs operating in Al Asad, Fallujah, and Ramadi. Their duties consisted of mentoring, advising, guiding, and evaluating the Iraqi police. Unlike partnered military units, they did not accompany the police on operations. However, the work was still dangerous. Insurgents had killed six IPLOs shortly before the conference I attended.

Danger came in many different forms in Iraq. Marines faced difficulties in trying to identify enemy personnel operating among and dressing like locals. AQIZ was notorious for suicide tactics using innocent-looking individuals and vehicles employed as vehicle-borne IEDs (VBIED). Tactics, techniques, and procedures for conducting EOFs helped to mitigate the risk of unintended injury or death of innocent civilians approaching coalition forces. EOF procedures consisted of a sequence of actions as potential threats closed the distance, as vehicles approached coalition forces. The first line of defense was visual signals to approaching vehicles two hundred meters out from friendly positions. These included flags, signs, chemical lights, or other visual devices. Marines employed pyrotechnics including flares, flashbangs, and penlights if the perceived threat closed to within 150 meters. Marines fired warning shots to the side at a hundred meters and transition to vehicle-mobility kills if the threat advanced closer. Marines received authority to shoot to kill, having exhausted all other means if the threat had continued to advance to within meters of their position. This entire process might only take seconds, depending on the speed of approaching vehicles. Ultimately, it came down to the judgment of individual Marines to determine what action to take.

Although EOF procedures dealt with possible VBIEDs, it did not help defeat static IEDs laid to injure coalition forces. IEDs became the insurgents' weapon of choice. MNF-W ran a counter-IED working group to address the threat; I was a G-3 representative. We identified the first case of a cell phone–initiated IED attack in Al Anbar during the first week of February 2006. Insurgents had initiated this new method in response to the success Marines were having in discovering IEDs before they exploded. MNF-W had the highest rate of IED discoveries in all of Iraq. Although MNF-W experienced twice as many IED attacks as any other command, it was also the only command in country that discovered more IEDs than were successful. We attributed this to aggressive dismounted patrols and focused training for our Marines.

Training on IEDs was not sufficient. MNF-W took a holistic approach to defeating the IED threat and "getting to the left of the boom" (focusing on what happens before an explosion) by identifying and neutralizing IED emplacers before they laid the devices. This required extensive intelligence collection, analysis, targeting, and public-affairs messaging to convince Iraqis not to join the insurgency in placing such weapons. Marines reinforced the messaging by initiating efforts to grow the economy, so the population had alternatives for supporting their families other than taking money from AQIZ to place IEDs. MNF-W also initiated the extensive use of electronic countermeasures to defeat IEDs.

The insurgents adjusted their tactics as the coalition adapted its countermeasures, using long-range cordless telephones to detonate over half of the IEDs in Al Anbar in February 2006.[7] They also employed pressure switches and traditional mines and chose the type of device used based on the Marines' success in finding them. Thus, they increased the use of pressure-plate devices, which could not be jammed or initiated prematurely with electronic countermeasures and began to increase the lethal payloads of IEDs. Insurgents became more adept at camouflaging IEDs and began to daisy-chain them to attack people responding to an initial blast. Antitampering and antilift devices also became more common, as ways to injure or kill EOD technicians.

The leadership of MNC-I established a new direction for coalition forces, as the Marines and soldiers continued to address the threat of IEDs and insurgent fighters on the ground. Lieutenant General Chiarelli published a new mission statement and commander's intent. He identified four guiding principles for MNC-I actions. First, he called for a shift from kinetic to nonkinetic operations, to alienate the population less. Second, he directed preparation of an information-operations plan to articulate the government of Iraq's plans and accomplishments for a better future. Third, the general also voiced the need to shift further functions, facilities, and responsibilities to our Iraqi partners. The original 110 coalition FOBs had already declined to seventy-seven; the general wanted to reduce this figure to fifty by the end of 2006. Fourth, he directed MNC-I to support, within its capability nonsecurity Iraqi ministries (oil, electricity, etc.).

Chiarelli identified his desired end state for 2006. He wanted the Iraqi army to control most of the battlespace, while coalition forces remained in tactical and operational "overwatch." He intended for the Iraqis to take the lead for security with the coalition in support. The general also wanted all provinces to have achieved, or be on the way to achieving, provincial Iraqi control (PIC), in which Iraqis would control the government. He also wanted the conditions set for transition to phase II of the MNF-I campaign plan, which called for the restoration of civil authority throughout Iraq.

One Marine battalion was well on its way to achieving Chiarelli's goals. The 3rd Battalion, 6th Marines under the command of Lt. Col. Julian "Dale" Alford received the assignment to secure the Al Qa'im region along the Syrian border. Alford is a talented officer, who was later promoted to be a general officer. The Al Qa'im region had been known as the "Wild West" until 3/6, my old battalion 2/1, and partnered Iraqi forces conducted Operation Steel Curtain in November 2005 to clear the cities of Husaybah and Al Karabilah.[8] Alford followed the clearing of population centers with battalion-wide civic-action program. He had engineers build fourteen separate battle positions within the cities, right on the heels of the infantrymen clearing the area of insurgents. He embraced the concept of Marines living and operating among the people. His Marines quickly gained the confidence of the locals as they lived and operated side by side with their Iraqi partners in communities.

After the battle, Alford established nine lines of operation to further his unit's progress in Al Qa'im: rule of law, governance, civil administration, humanitarian assistance, local security forces, information management, economic development, security, and information operations. Alford often met with the local ISF and sheiks. His battalion partnered with the Iraqi 3rd Brigade, 7th Division and helped to recruit four hundred Iraqi Police, with more promised. The sheiks and other municipal leaders identified three projects to help the area recover. These included opening the POEs with Syria at Husaybah, repairing the railroad line running to a local phosphate plant and cement factory, and rebuilding a bridge destroyed by coalition forces.

I became intimately familiar with the Al Qa'im region and these projects, but later. My time in Iraq in support of OIF 05–07 came to an end before I knew it. My partners and I, from the I MEF (Forward) advanced party, set the conditions for a successful relief in place with the 2nd Marine Division, which took place on 28 February 2006. The MNF-W's new mission statement was to develop the Iraqi security force in Al Anbar, facilitate rule of law via democratic government reforms, and develop a market-based economy centered on Iraqi reconstruction.[9] Tull, Sinclair, and I departed Iraq early to return home to take command of our own battalions. I was to return to Iraq with mine in support of Operation Iraqi Freedom 06–08 (2006–2008) to continue the good work of Alford, and his successors, in Al Qa'im.

Perhaps our deputy commanding general (and future thirty-seventh Commandant of the Marine Corps) Brig. Gen. Robert Neller stated it best: "I don't know how this is all going to end up. I don't know if the Iraqi people will take advantage of this opportunity that they have. The historians will write that, and I don't know what they'll say. I can't necessarily control that. But what the history books have got to say is that our effort was noble, courageous, and honorable."[10]

CHAPTER

★

The China Marines, Sister Cities, and Counterinsurgency

1st Battalion, 4th Marines—The China Marines

After serving as the executive officer of 1/1, a company commander in 2/1, and the operations officer for 3/1, I was ecstatic to receive command of the 1st Marine Regiment's other battalion, 1st Battalion, 4th Marines (1/4). Although I started my career in the 7th Marines, I had come to appreciate the 1st Marines as my home in the operating forces. The 4th Marine regimental headquarters is stationed in Okinawa, Japan. It sources its subordinate battalions from regiments in the United States, which send battalions to Okinawa for six months as part of the Unit Deployment Program (UDP). The 1st, 2nd, and 3rd Battalions of the 4th Marines were permanently assigned to the 1st, 5th, and 7th Regiments of the 1st Marine Division, respectively—hence 1/4's assignment to the 1st Marines.

The 1st Battalion, 4th Marines has a historic past.[1] The battalion came into existence in 1911 to address civil unrest in Mexico. It landed in the Dominican Republic in 1916 to fight rebels and bandits and remained there for eight years. Marines from the battalion guarded the U.S. Mail across the western United States during the early 1920s before preparing again for overseas duty to China in 1927 to help protect American lives and property in the Shanghai International Settlement during the Chinese civil war. Tensions remained high, requiring the Marines to remain in China for fifteen years, until the outbreak of World War II. The long tour in China earned the 4th Marine Regiment the nickname "China Marines," a name they still use today.

The 1st Battalion, 4th Marines also had a rich combat history. The battalion transferred from China to the Philippines just prior to the bombing
of Pearl Harbor in 1941 and found itself defending the eastern half of Cor-
regidor Island. The battalion fought heroically against overwhelming odds
but eventually surrendered on the orders of Army general, Jonathan Wain-
wright, whom Gen. Douglas MacArthur had left in charge of the defense
of the Philippines. The battalion ceased to exist when it surrendered but
found itself reestablished two years later on Guadalcanal. The 1st Battalion,
1st Raider Regiment received orders to redesignate itself as the new 1/4.
The battalion fought on Guam and Okinawa and prepared for the invasion
of mainland Japan before the war ended. The battalion fought in Vietnam
1965–69, participated in Operation Desert Storm, and battled insurgents
in Nasiriyah, Al Kut, Baghdad, and Najaf from 2003 to 2004 in support of
Operation Iraqi Freedom.[2] Elements of the battalion supported the Hurricane Katrina disaster-relief efforts in Mississippi and Louisiana in 2005,
prior to my taking command in 2006.

I returned to my old job in the 1st Marine Division G-3 section pending
my assumption of command. Being back on Camp Pendleton provided
me an opportunity to gather my thoughts. I needed to think through how
I wanted to approach command and the preparation of the battalion for
deployment to Iraq. These preparations included determining the best
training areas to use in conducting small-unit exercises.

One Saturday morning, intending to kill two birds with one stone, I
decided to combine my daily run with a leader's reconnaissance of the
training areas I wanted to use for this purpose. I grabbed a map of the
base, staged my truck near a barracks, and started on my orienteering run
through the training area. I planned to remain on the unimproved roads
that traversed the rolling hills of the base, but things took a turn for the
worse when I found my path blocked about two miles from my truck.

I made a fateful decision. I took a shortcut over a hill to pick up another
trail. As I ran up the side of the hill, my bare legs were cut by the dry reeds
and branches of the bushes. The small spurts of pain I felt as the branches
scratched my legs paled in comparison to the sudden, sharp pain I felt in
my left ankle. I thought I had struck something sharp but immediately saw
a rattlesnake slithering off, then noticed two red dots forming on my white
sock. I had come upon the snake so quickly that it never had time to rattle
a warning.

A number of thoughts raced through my head. First the idea was to kill
the snake and take it with me. I quickly realized this was stupid, because

we did that only to identify whether a snake was poisonous, and I already knew the answer. I also realized that the snake would likely bite me again if I tried to catch it. My second thought was to suck the venom out of my ankle. I realized this was just as stupid and was not about to sit on the ground, only to be bit again. My final thought was to get my butt off the hill and to a hospital.

I turned and started making my way down the hill. More thoughts raced through my head as the venom started to take effect. The venom's potential effect on my respiratory system concerned me. I could no longer feel my left foot by the time I got to the bottom of the hill. I was limping as I approached the back of a warehouse and banged on the door. No one was working that early on a Saturday morning, so I moved around to the front looking for help, the venom working its way up my leg. It felt like pins and needles, or like novocaine wearing off. I hailed two Marines out on a run and asked if they had a car nearby. I let them go when they responded no, thinking I had a better chance of getting a ride by waving down a car on the nearby road.

I felt the venom flow across my torso and begin its way down my other leg as I limped to the road. I attempted to wave down cars, but they just drove by. More determined than ever to get assistance, I walked to the middle of the road and held both hands up to stop the next approaching vehicle. A young corporal stopped, and I explained that I had just been bitten by a rattlesnake.

My stubborn tendencies and pride got the best of me that morning. Rather than ask the corporal to drive me directly to the base hospital only a few miles away, I asked him to drive me back to my truck instead. This was not a smart decision, but it seemed right at the time. I was not concerned because the venom had not affected my ability to breathe. I thanked the corporal, got into my truck, and drove myself to the hospital.

By the time I pulled into the hospital parking lot, it felt like the skin on my face was being drawn back as I pulled into the hospital parking lot. I limped up to the emergency room nurses' station, still sweating from my run. Blood ran down both my legs from the scratches. The nurse on duty must have thought I had just sprained my ankle on a run and said, "Oh boy, what do we have here?" I responded, "Ma'am, I just got bit by a rattlesnake." She immediately perked up, her eyes wide, and she dragged me into the emergency room.

I expected to get a quick shot of antivenin and be on my way. It was not to be. The nurse explained that I needed to remain under observation for six hours and have my blood tested every hour. I accepted my fate, called my wife to let her know what happened, and asked her to bring me a book to occupy myself. Luckily, we lived in base housing close to the hospital. My wife was not happy, but she complied.

I felt fine for the first three hours, but my blood tests were not trending positively. I had received a bag of antivenom intravenously, but it did not help. My left leg started to swell and continued to do so as the nurse administered a second bag. The results of my blood tests continued to get worse, and the doctor admitted me to the intensive care unit (ICU).

I spent three days in the ICU. The pain was excruciating anytime I tried to apply pressure on my left foot. The swelling eventually went down, and in time the doctors released me. I had to use crutches for a few days, and couldn't get my foot back into a boot until the day I assumed command of 1/4. Because I still felt the pain, I put most of my weight on my right foot as I stood in formation in front of the battalion and accepted our unit colors. A unit's "colors" is a flag representing the unit, adorned with battle streamers to signify the battles and operations in which it has participated.

I was proud now to be a China Marine and wondered what the Marines under my command thought of me as I walked through the barracks. I had heard a rumor among my Marines that the new commanding officer had just escaped death from a snakebite by crawling miles on his hands and knees to the hospital for treatment. Marines like to embellish stories, but I let it go.

Preparing for Iraq

The China Marines commenced training in preparation for assignment to Regimental Combat Team Six (RCT-6) to conduct counterinsurgency operations in the Fallujah area. We developed a predeployment training plan that began with individual training; transitioned to small-unit training at the fireteam, platoon, and company levels; and concluded with battalion-level exercises and participation in the capstone training event, Mojave Viper, in Twentynine Palms.

The plan seemed well coordinated and going fine, when things changed. Progress was not going well in Iraq, and President G. W. Bush had developed a new strategy. In January 2007 he announced that he intended to deploy 30,000 additional American troops to Iraq in what became known as "the Surge."[3] I received word that 1/4, and 2/5 from the 5th Marines, would deploy early as the Marines Corps contribution.

Although exciting, the decision diminished our preparation time by four months and changed our mission. The reduction in training time resulted in an expedited plan that provided only two weeks each for fireteam-through-battalion training before our participation in Mojave Viper and deployment. It was a fast ride. Our assignment also shifted from working for RCT-6 in Fallujah to working for RCT-2 in Al Qa'im.

Although short, our predeployment training was fruitful, thanks to the Marine Corps' investment in training aids. One of the advantages of being stationed in southern California is the proximity to Hollywood. The Corps had approached Stu Segall, a movie and TV producer and president/founder of a company called Strategic Operations.[4] Strategic Operations provides "hyper-realistic" training for the military and law enforcement by creating tactical scenarios in great detail, controlling and manipulating both the physical and sensory environments.[5]

Strategic Operations offered two training venues for 1/4's predeployment training. Segall operates a production studio in the San Diego area where he created "movie sets" of Iraqi villages, fully equipped with actors playing the roles of Iraqi citizens.[6] Marines in combat gear trained in these facilities and interacted with role players to simulate the types of operations being conducted in Iraq. Special effects, pyrotechnics, and simulated injuries added realism. Segall's studios built another training village on the grounds of Camp Elliott, part of Marine Corps Air Station Miramar in San Diego County. This larger venue offered an urban environment with the same amenities but for training larger units. The China Marines took full advantage of both facilities in training prior to Mojave Viper.

Mojave Viper was the Marine Corps' premier training event in 2007. It provided the right balance of live-fire combined-arms training with stability and support operations in urban environments. The month-long exercises took Marines through live-fire training events starting at the individual level and concluding with battalion-level fire and maneuver. It then transitioned into a two-week SASO program, executed in venues similar to that of Segall's studios but on a much grander scale. The villages created at Twentynine Palms supported an entire battalion of over a thousand Marines operating simultaneously in an urban environment. The environment was so realistic that I actually felt like I was back in Twentynine Palms, when I arrived in Iraq with 1/4.

The commanding general of Multi-National Force West at the time, Maj. Gen. Walter Gaskins, and the ground combat element commander, Brig. Gen. Charles Gurganus, provided guidance for our review prior to deploying.[7] General Gaskins identified stability in Al Anbar Province as our contribution to legitimate Iraqi governance and development. He indicated that will and determination on the part of the Iraqi people were prerequisites to achieving and sustaining the mission and tasked us with focusing our efforts on fueling the resolution and resilience Iraqis needed to achieve legitimate control as well as their political and economic aspirations. He identified his desired endstate as achieving provincial Iraqi control in Al Anbar.

The general further defined PIC as a condition wherein legitimate civil authorities in Al Anbar possessed the will and ability to govern. He mandated that the way to achieve this was legitimate, organized force to secure the people and effectively manage counterinsurgency operations. Governing effectively would require a comprehensive and enforceable rule of law. It would also entail a government that provided basic essential services for the people and fostered a vibrant economy.

He further laid out stability operations and, to help shift our thinking from fighting to development and transition, a concept that he named "multiagency operations." These would involve all instruments of national and multinational power and action. Such operations would start by establishing security to facilitate humanitarian and reconstruction efforts, while setting conditions for reconciliation between warring elements of the population. He tasked us with helping to establish a political, social, and economic architecture that would facilitate the transition to legitimate local governance.

General Gaskins listed challenges we faced. The psychological impact of decades of dictatorship and command economy had resulted in social, governmental, and economic dysfunction throughout Iraq, exacerbated by the disenfranchisement of a majority-Sunni population in Al Anbar. A scarcity of resources and an active insurgency being executed by AQIZ added to the problem. According to him, the citizens of Al Anbar would be the operational center of gravity for Marine operations. The Marines had to mobilize the populace by marginalizing and defeating insurgent fighters, while deterring active insurgent supporters. He implored us to dissuade insurgent sympathizers and to persuade those uncommitted or neutral. He tasked us with protecting government sympathizers while consolidating and strengthening active government supporters. A nontraditional combined-effects approach addressing security, governance, and the economy was the only way to achieve this.

General Gaskin defined security as defeating AQIZ, neutralizing the insurgency, and creating order in the region. This required a close partnership between the ISF and coalition forces, with the Iraqi army initially in the lead. It was hoped that the Iraqi police would continue to grow and develop until prepared to assume the lead in internal control of the region, with border enforcement units securing the borders. A secure environment would allow development of governance, including civilian control of the security apparatus to reform the justice system and enforce the rule of law. It would include holding fair and credible public elections of politicians who would provide the essential services needed by the people. It also would establish a system for public infrastructure improvements. Economic development would be necessary to provide the government with the funds needed to govern effectively. Facilitating economic development would require domestic and international investment, banking reform, and agricultural development. Corporate laws also needed to support industrial renewal and development while commercial telecommunications and transportation infrastructures facilitated sales and trading.

A strong social foundation was the glue that would hold the population together. Marines had to understand and respect the tribal organization and norms in Iraq. A civil law system, health services infrastructure, and public education reform would eventually facilitate the growth of thriving communities. They would also provide an environment where child care and development programs and women's interest groups flourished. General Gaskin cautioned us to operate with a long-term outlook. This growth and these reforms would not happen overnight. Marines would be required to engage with the Iraqi people with professionalism, respect, and dignity at all levels simultaneously. We were to use every opportunity to assist the ISF in achieving primacy in the region, while fostering the credibility and confidence of the government "by and for the people."

Laguna Niguel—The Sister City

The realization that our battalion did not possess the requisite skill sets to achieve much of what General Gaskins called for struck me as we continued preparations for deployment. The Marine Corps understood these shortfalls too and developed organizations to assist battalions with achieving the goals of the overall campaign plan. These organizations consisted of military personnel with requisite skills in civil affairs, contracting, engineering, construction, and legal matters. It also included civilians assigned from the State Department and other organizations with similar skills to work with Marines. Unfortunately, these experts were spread thin and had varying levels of experience. I needed something more and found it in our battalion's adopted community.

The battalions of the 1st Marine Division were privileged to be adopted by communities in southern California following the tragic events of 11 September 2001. I first experienced this with the city of Newport Beach while serving as executive officer for 1/1. Newport Beach outdid itself showering the Marines, sailors, and their families with love and support manifested in many ways, from hosting family events and providing gifts to the children of Marines during the holidays to financial support to families in need when their loved ones deployed, and more. The China Marines of 1/4 were fortunate to have the city of Laguna Niguel as its adopted community.

Laguna Niguel provided much of the same type of support I remember from Newport Beach, but I asked for more. I asked Mayor Paul Glaab and the city council to assist us in accomplishing our mission in Iraq by partnering with the local government and municipal leaders of the Al Qa'im region of Iraq. I explained to Mayor Glaab that, in essence, I was to perform the duties of a mayor in helping our Iraqi partners run numerous cities, towns, and villages. My staff and I lacked the experience to perform these functions, but Mayor Glaab and his staff did. I asked the mayor and leaders of Laguna Niguel to be subject-matter experts to whom we could communicate our ideas and challenges for their input. I also offered to put Laguna Niguel and Iraqi government counterparts in communication with each other, providing any translation needed. Some were a little apprehensive about the idea, but Laguna Niguel voted on the concept and embraced it. My idea was not new. I was not aware at the time that a formal "sister city" program already existed.

Sister Cities International was the creation of President Dwight D. Eisenhower's 1956 White House conference on citizen diplomacy.[8] Its mission was to "promote peace through mutual respect, understanding, and cooperation—one individual, one community at a time."[9] Eisenhower had created sister cities to facilitate bringing different cultures together to celebrate and appreciate their differences. He reasoned that building partnerships would lessen the chance of new conflicts. My view was a little different; I was trying to end a current conflict. Laguna Niguel's acceptance of my proposal provided a higher level of confidence as 1/4 departed for Al Qa'im, Iraq.

Counterinsurgency

The Al Qa'im region is approximately 250 miles west of Baghdad and shares a border with Syria. The Euphrates River flows from Syria to Baghdad through the region and waters farmers' fields along its banks. The Euphrates also nourishes the many cities, towns, and villages spread from west to east along its shores. Al Qa'im's terrain is lush and green along the Euphrates but quickly turns to desert the farther north or south one moves from the river. Most of Al Qa'im's 150,000 inhabitants live close to the river, but many Bedouins and goat herders live throughout the desert region. The region's strategic location has made it a hotbed for smuggling for centuries. Not surprisingly, it has fostered the introduction of foreign fighters into Iraq during OIF as well as what would later be the fight against the Islamic State of Iraq and the Levant (ISIL). Fighters entering Iraq through Al Qa'im moved down the Euphrates River valley to the key cities of Ramadi, Fallujah, and Baghdad.

The region's importance also ensured an American presence there. The U.S. Army 3rd Armored Cavalry Regiment was the first to occupy the area, turning it over to the 3rd Battalion, 7th Marines in March 2004. Al Qa'im remained contested and became the site of Operation Matador to clear insurgents out of the key cities of Husaybah, Al Karabilah, Ramana, and Al Ubaydi in May 2005.

The fighting was fierce and resulted in 125 insurgents and 9 Marines being killed.[10] Cpl. Jason Dunham of Kilo Company, 3/7, received the Congressional Medal of Honor posthumously for deliberately covering an enemy grenade with his body to save nearby Marines in Al Qa'im.[11] Maj. Rick Gannon, with whom I served in 3/9, received the Silver Star posthumously; he was killed leading his Marines in this battle.[12] In November 2005, over 2,500 Marines and 1,000 Iraqi soldiers conducted Operation Steel Curtain in the area to restore security and establish a permanent presence of coalition and Iraqi forces among the people.[13] One of the camps established in Husaybah after the battle was named in honor of Major Gannon. Another close friend and 3/9 alumnus, Capt. Ray Mendoza, died in the area leading his company during Operation Steel Curtain.

The China Marines of 1/4 inherited Camp Gannon and thirteen battle positions that our predecessors had erected throughout the region. Each battle position received its name from a historic Marine battle, like Belleau Wood, Tarawa, and Beirut. Our battalion, reinforced with other capabilities and designated Task Force 1/4, assumed the command post vacated by 3rd Battalion, 4th Marines, the battalion we had relieved. Our predecessors had established the command post at Al Qa'im's inoperable train station, in the desert south of the Euphrates. Trains from this station had previously supported the economy of the region.

Three industrial facilities now fed the Al Qa'im region's economy. The Belgians had opened a phosphate plant in 1976 to produce fertilizer from minerals extracted from mines in the nearby town of Akashat. The Iraqis had built a uranium extraction facility on the same site in 1984.[14] American aircraft destroyed that facility during Operation Desert Storm out of fear of the possible uses for the uranium, but the phosphate plant remained. There was also a local cement plant. Iraqis built a railroad to connect the mines at Akashat with the phosphate plant, the cement plant, and other parts of Iraq. Groups of Romanians and Indians leased and ran the cement plant before the wars.[15] These three facilities provided opportunity for spurring the economy in Al Qa'im and became a focus of our reconstruction efforts to help the local population.

The people of Al Qa'im are predominately Sunni and belong to over twenty different tribes. The tribes comprise related clans that further break down into families led by sheiks. Many Iraqis identify more strongly with, and are more loyal to, their tribes than the national government. This posed challenges to the Marines as we worked to create legitimacy for the Iraqi government. The sharia and tribal laws also posed problems as we assisted the Iraqis in establishing the rule of law and a judicial system. Revenge killings and other solutions imposed by clan sheikhs to settle tribal disputes nearly derailed our efforts later, but this was just one of many challenges in working with our Iraqi partners.

Task Force 1/4 established partnerships with several different groups. I spent much of my time with, and befriended, Mayor Farhan Ftehkhan. Mayor Farhan was a former general in Saddam Hussein's army and had had responsibility for the air defense of Baghdad at one time. Coalition and Iraqi officials had vetted him prior to his assumption of responsibility as the senior civilian administrator in Al Qa'im. I found the mayor to be a hard-working and committed man, dedicated to aiding the local population. I often traveled throughout the region with him and gave him credit for any progress achieved. The Iraqi Security Forces also provided the mayor assistance in providing for the population.

Task Force 1/4 partnered with the ISF's 3rd Brigade, 7th Iraqi Division under the command of Brigadier General Ayad Ismael. I primarily engaged with Ismael, my company commanders with his subordinate battalion commanders. General Ismael established his headquarters near the Task Force 1/4 headquarters, his battalions established bases at Combat Outposts (COPs) North and South on either side of the Euphrates River. Marines and Iraqi soldiers lived, trained, and operated side by side. In fact, Iraqi sergeants led the patrols our Marines conducted toward the end of our deployment. The army remained poised to defend the borders and

Task Force 1/4 and 3rd Brigade staffs worked closely together in defeating a counterinsurgency in the Al Qa'im region of Iraq in 2007. *Author collection*

generally conducted operations on the outskirts of the population centers, while the Iraqi Police provided internal security.

The Al Qa'im police chief, Colonel Jamal Mohammed was General Ismael's brother. Colonel Jamal commanded over 1,500 police, who operated out of stations located within the local communities. His fledgling force continued to grow as we assisted with his recruiting efforts. All police recruits trained at a centralized police academy in another part of Iraq before returning to assume duties in Al Qa'im. The police and army received support from the Border Defense Enforcement (BDE) battalions. The BDE manned several border forts along the Syrian border in our battlespace and faced challenges similar to those of the army and police in recruiting, arming, and sustaining its force. As the battlespace owner for Al Qa'im, I received assistance from transition teams in facilitating the growth, training, and sustainment of the BDE, army, and police.

The coalition created military transition teams (MTTs), police transition teams (PTTs), and border defense transition teams (BDTTs) to assist in the administration and training of the ISF. The Marine Corps found

The China Marines of 1st Battalion, 4th Marines were partnered with the 3rd Brigade, 7th Iraqi Division, commanded by Brigadier General Ismael (*center*) and the Al Qa'im police, commanded by Ismael's brother, Colonel Jamal (*second from right*). *Author collection*

personnel from across the force to man these teams. Like our Marines in the rifle companies, these Marines ate, lived, and operated side by side with their Iraqi counterparts and coached and mentored them to succeed. They also acted as lifelines to the firepower, logistics, and medical support the task force provided when needed.

We also partnered closely with the tribal sheiks. The sheiks represented, and in many ways controlled, the actions of the people. They possessed the ability to assist, or resist, depending on how well one established relationships with them. One of the most powerful tribes in the region was the Albu Mahal. I made it a point on arriving in the region to build a strong relationship with the tribe's sheik, Kurdi Raffa Farhan, as well as sheiks from other tribes. We formed mutually beneficial friendships that helped facilitate progress in the region. However, building relationships is not always enough. One must also understand the culture of one's partner. Lack of cultural understanding can lead to animosity, misunderstanding, and mission failure. Our Marines received hours of cultural training on topics ranging from how to greet Iraqis, what hand to eat with, and actions that might be considered offensive. But we also had to understand aspects of the Arab culture unacceptable in many Western cultures. For example, one of the primary leverage points we had over our Iraqi friends was the power of the purse.

Coalition forces controlled the reconstruction funds to which local Iraqi power brokers and businessmen wanted access. Arabs do not play by the same ethical business rules that those in the West supposedly do. It was not uncommon for sheiks or government employees to expect baksheesh for connecting two individuals who then do business. Arabs see baksheesh as a tip, where many Westerners see it as a bribe. What the Arabs see as the cost of doing business, some Westerners see as corruption. Other cultural differences can also lead to problems.

A sanctioned execution nearly ended Task Force 1/4's efforts to develop the Iraqi police in Al Qa'im. I found myself shocked when visiting Colonel Jamal one day to learn from him that a local tribe had conducted a public execution that morning with his and Mayor Farhan's approval. Jamal handed me a video of the hearing held by the tribe the night before when tribal leaders had decided on the execution. We had experienced progress in developing the rule of law and had just completed refurbishing the local courthouse. Nevertheless, the tribes did not yet have faith in the legal system. They handled this case the way they had handled similar cases for centuries. The sheiks did not involve the police or local judicial system in the process. Mayor Farhan explained to me what occurred later that day at a joint security meeting.

A local policeman had proposed marriage to a young woman in his tribe. She had accepted, but her two brothers, who were both insurgents, disapproved. They sent a false message to the policeman that their sister wanted to see him and on his arrival ambushed and killed him. All participants came from the same tribe, but different families. Arab culture states that clan or tribal members must avenge the death or harm done to one of their members by someone outside of the clan or tribe.[16] Tribal elders feared the possibility of tit-for-tat revenge killings, resulting in more tribesmen killed, if they did not immediately deal with the situation. Although perfectly normal in Arab culture, many Westerners had issues with this approach. A Reuters reporter, Peter Graff, who attended the security meeting, wrote a story on the incident.[17]

MNF-W and others were not happy. Graff's news story raised questions by people far removed from the situation about the legitimacy of our mission, if actions like this one continued to occur. I understood their position, but I also understood why the tribe took the action they did. I in no way justified or condoned the action but tried to explain that the tribes had little confidence in a judicial system not yet fully developed. The judges in Al Qa'im were authorized to adjudicate only minor cases. Any major felony cases had to be tried in the provincial capital of Ramadi, where the courts had hardly begun to operate. The tribes believed the central courts incapable of hearing any such case.

This explanation was not sufficient for MNF-W. Although he backed my position, my RCT commander, Col. Stacy Clardy, informed me that it was cutting off all funding for the police in Al Qa'im as punishment for having allowed the execution to occur. I was concerned about losing the initiative to the enemy if our police stopped performing their duties and thought this was a step in the wrong direction. Wiser heads advocating on our behalf eventually prevailed after further discussions with Clardy. The police mission continued. (Clardy later attained the rank of lieutenant general and still serves on active duty today.)

The counterinsurgency operation conducted by Task Force 1/4 was a decentralized fight with centralized support. Squad- and platoon-sized units were the points of action. They departed their battle positions located in the many towns and villages across the region daily to engage with the public alongside their Iraqi Security Force partners. My headquarters supported other efforts by providing direction, guidance, and the resources.

The task force headquarters also initiated a number of high-level projects throughout the entire region. These projects were numerous and varied in support of our lines of operation—security, rule of law, governance, information, and economics. We continued to invest in security infrastructure, weapons, vehicles, and equipment to support the Iraqi army and to follow an aggressive reconstruction plan that repaired many of the buildings destroyed or damaged during previous battles. We worked with the Iraqis to reestablish television and radio stations and provided funding for a new newspaper in the region. We assisted the government in providing essential services by repairing water pumping stations and hospitals. We aided the Iraqis in issuing local driver's licenses for the first time, helped to establish microfinance projects, and began an automated teller machine (ATM) system. We opened schools and clinics in the area and, when possible, tied multiple projects together so as to achieve the greatest return on our investment.

One project provides a particularly good example. We worked with our partners in opening a vocational-technical (VOTEC) school. The school taught eleven essential skills for carpentry, masonry, plumbing, and more.

These skills were only useful if our graduates had somewhere to apply them, so we added a clause to the contracts with the companies we hired. The clause stipulated that a percentage of the workers on any project had to be graduates of the VOTEC school. This agreement benefited the security, economics, and governance LOOs. It diminished the available pool of young men wanting to join the insurgency, because they now had employment to provide for their families. The money earned by the graduates went back into the local economy, and the establishment of the school added credibility for the local government. We thought it could also help with the information LOO.

We realized that the Arab culture blocked us from communicating with nearly half of the Iraqi population. For Western men to engage with Arab women was frowned upon, but we knew that in many cases the women were the decision makers in their families. We addressed this by establishing a construction project to build a women's engagement center, using our VOTEC graduates to assist with the project. Once it was completed we brought in female Marines and Navy nurses and doctors to provide medical information to the women of the community. However, we needed another draw to attract the local women.

I asked Laguna Niguel, Al Qa'im's new sister city and 1/4's adopted community, to donate sewing machines and materials for the women's use at the engagement center so they could make clothes for themselves and their families. We took this idea a step further and had the VOTEC start to teach seamstress classes as well. It was my intent to establish a business venture through which these women could send clothes they made in Iraq back for sale in boutiques in southern California. We went as far as determining that there was actually an Iraqi diaspora living in southern California. Unfortunately, we ran out of time before fully implementing the plan.

We achieved much in Al Qa'im, thanks to the efforts of all the coalition forces that had fought for and secured the area with our Iraqi partners since 2003. Those of us deployed to the area in 2007 reaped the benefits of their hard work and sacrifices and vowed to set the conditions for the success of those who followed us. The progress made in Al Qa'im and other parts of Al Anbar was recognized by others too. I received a phone call from my higher headquarters, RCT-2, late one evening while sitting in my command post. The officer on the other end asked if I could get two of the senior sheiks from our area on a helicopter to go to an undisclosed place, at an undisclosed time, to meet an undisclosed person. I responded, "What? You need to give me more than that." The officer responded that he could not. I told him that I would try. It was at times like this that relationships paid off. My friends Sheiks Kurdi and Murdi boarded a CH-46 helicopter at Camp Al Qa'im at 7:00 the next morning and flew off.

I received word that the sheiks were returning later that afternoon. I went out to meet them at the landing zone, curious to know where they had gone. I could not help smiling when Sheik Kurdi got off the helicopter with hydraulic fluid spilled down the front of his dishdasha, the long white robe traditionally worn by men in the Middle East. He was not happy that the helicopter had leaked on him but quickly forgot about it when he pulled out a picture of him shaking hands with President George W. Bush.

President Bush had secretly departed the White House to conduct a surprise visit to Al Asad Air Base on 3 September 2007. The president met with military commanders, Iraqi leaders including our two sheiks, and approximately 10,000 American troops stationed at the base. He was nearing a decision on deploying future troop levels in Iraq. The national security advisor, Stephen Hadley, stated, "This gives the president an opportunity first hand to hear from people directly involved and make his own assessments."[18] This visit gave the sheiks enormous *wasta* (social clout).

Although great for the sheiks, the president's visit had an unintended consequence. Many other commanders and I had worked hard to build the credibility of our local Iraqi government officials. I intentionally put Mayor Farhan at the forefront of all progress in the region, but the president (or more likely his staff) did not ask for government officials. He asked for sheiks. The problem became painfully obvious, as I met with the sheiks and Mayor Farhan in the front parlor of Sheik Kurdi's house for our morning *chai* (tea) and cigarettes. I noticed the picture of Sheik Kurdi with President Bush displayed near the door as I entered.

It did not take Sheik Kurdi long to begin nagging Mayor Farhan. As I took a sip of chai, I saw Kurdi puff out his chest and say, "Hahh, Farhan, you are a second-class citizen. Our good friend George Bush called for us. He did not call for you." I watched as Mayor Farhan slumped in his seat dejectedly. I knew I had to do something quickly to restore the mayor's credibility. I said, "Mayor Farhan, do not worry. The sheiks got to meet the president; you are going to meet Mickey Mouse." Everyone in the room immediately knew what I meant; I would help Mayor Farhan visit the United States. I had no idea at that point how I was going to do it, but I would figure it out. Mayor Farhan straightened up in his chair as the sheiks looked on, shocked. Sheik Kurdi asked, "What is with this Mickey Mouse? How will you do this?" I responded, "Let me worry about that."

Sheik Kurdi of the Albu Mahal tribe (*left*) and Mayor Farhan of Al Qa'im, Iraq (*right*). Sheik Kurdi got to meet President Bush, but Mayor Farhan got to meet Mickey Mouse. *Author collection*

It took a year to accomplish, but we did it. By that time stationed in Washington, D.C., I worked with Col. Nick Marano, another former battalion commander who had worked with Mayor Farhan, and the good people of Laguna Niguel to get the mayor to the United States. Farhan spent two weeks here. Nick and I hosted him for a week in Washington, D.C., where he met members of Congress, visited the Department of Agriculture and the headquarters of Sister Cities International, and even had time for a steak dinner with Nick and me at Ruth's Chris Steak House. He also spent a week in California, hosted by Laguna Niguel. The city put a parade on for him and took him to Disneyland, where he finally got to meet Mickey Mouse. I'm sure he flaunted a picture of himself with Mickey to the sheiks when he returned home.

Not all was fun in Al Qa'im though. It was still a very dangerous place. Coalition efforts reduced but did not eliminate insurgent activity. Having learned that going head to head with Marines did not end well, they found other options to inflict casualties. IEDs were still killing and injuring Marines. This fact struck home with me on a hot July day in 2007.

Task Force 1/4 had responsibility for an expansive area. Every one of our companies had its own battlespace to manage and Iraqi units with which to partner. The companies focused on the population centers and main lines of communication through the area, which left us little manpower to address other requirements. For this reason I employed the battalion's 81-mm Mortar Platoon as a quick reaction force and my personal security detail (PSD) as a separate maneuver element.

The 81-mm Mortar Platoon and security platoon possessed the mobility, manpower, and firepower to make a difference whenever they arrived on scene. The 81-mm Mortar Platoon was the largest in the battalion and trained as a cohesive team. I created my security platoon by pulling Marines together from across the battalion to provide transportation and protection across the battlespace. Sgt. Maj. Carlos Perez, the battalion sergeant major, selected GySgt. Mike West to lead the security platoon. (Perez later retired and published a book called, *Mass Exodus: The Story of an Illegal Immigrant*. West attained the rank of sergeant major and continues to serve on active duty.) West chose several former FAST Company Marines to join the platoon, because of the special skills they possessed. Gunny West trained the Marines well in the time he had. They became a tight and effective unit.

The security platoon quickly gained a reputation as a professional, no-nonsense organization. I always shed my personal protective gear during key leader engagements with Iraqis in order to present a less threatening posture, with full confidence that the security platoon had my back. Sgt. Zack Hammons and Cpl. Jeremy Allbaugh were my personal bodyguards. Both Hammons and Allbaugh had joined the Marines after high school, Hammons from Florida and Allbaugh from Oklahoma. Both had great and caring personalities but could become deadly serious when they needed to. Several "green on blue" incidents had recently occurred, where supposed Iraqi friends turned on and killed or injured their coalition partners. I went into every meeting with complete confidence, knowing that my "shadows" stood poised and ready close by if I needed assistance.

On this particularly hot day, Sergeant Hammons and Corporal Allbaugh led the security platoon in the lead vehicle of a motorized patrol through the southern half of our area of responsibility. Gunnery Sergeant West was in the number-two vehicle, and Sergeant Major Perez and I followed in the third vehicle. We had just departed the T-1 oil pumping station, originally built by the British in years past, and were following a road that ran along a rail line toward Hadithah. We stopped at an

Task Force 1/4 personal security detail (PSD), commanded by GySgt. Mike West, that was not only employed to provide protection for the task force commander and sergeant major but also as a maneuver element when and where needed. The platoon is standing in front of a mine resistant ambush protection (MRAP) vehicle. *Author collection*

abandoned train station and found spent 7.62 bullet casings scattered about the ground. I decided to continue the patrol to search some nearby Bedouin camps and rustic villages.

Sergeant Hammons and his driver, LCpl. Cory Jameson, noticed some painted rocks at the side of the road. Insurgents were known to use painted rocks as markers to alert other insurgents to the presence of IEDs. Sergeant Hammons led the patrol off to the side of the road and called me on the radio to recommend we search this area during our return trip. He marked the location on his Blue Force Tracker, a real-time battlespace and communication system.

There was nothing further significant to report until we returned to investigate the area with the painted rocks. The platoon dismounted and conducted 5-25 checks as Sergeant Hammons and Corporal Allbaugh, with Cpl. Daniel Klein following "in trace" (close behind) to provide security, scanned some distance to the patrol's front for anything unusual. They stopped at the top of a knoll and scanned the surrounding area with rifle-mounted optics but saw nothing to give them concern. The patrol remounted and continued on its way.

The patrol's HMMWVs bounced down the road for some distance traversing a maze of potholes. Sergeant Hammons joked with Corporal Allbaugh about how they were being banged around and directed Lance

Corporal Jameson to move off the dirt road to smoother sand. The front passenger tire of Sergeant Hammons' vehicle rolled uneventfully through a pothole as the vehicle turned off the road, but the rear passenger tire hitting the same pothole initiated a pressure-plate IED.

A large explosion lifted the HMMWV three to five feet in the air. It appeared the vehicle might flip over, but it did not. Sergeant Hammons' head slammed forward and his rifle smashed the Blue Force Tracker mounted in front of him. All electronics shut down in the vehicle. Sergeant Hammons noticed that Lance Corporal Jameson was unconscious. He shook his arm, and Jameson awakened. Hammons then looked to his left rear and saw Corporal Klein grimacing with pain; his legs had been driven into the vehicle's mid brace bar. Hammons gave the order for the Marines to dismount and saw that the explosion had thrown the gunner, LCpl. Adam Lewis, approximately fifteen feet from the vehicle. Lewis was unable to move due to pain in his back. Corporal Klein tried to run to him but fell from his leg injuries. Undeterred, he crawled to Lewis' aid. These Marines were family. They cared more for each other than they did for their own health and safety.

Sergeant Hammons assessed the situation and saw that Allbaugh had not exited the vehicle. He ensured that Jameson provided security to the front and ran to Allbaugh's aid. Hammons noticed diesel fuel leaking as he opened the vehicle door and saw Allbaugh patting his chest and gasping for air. The explosion had pinned Allbaugh's feet beneath the front passenger seat. Hammons turned and waved to the second vehicle to move forward to assist. Gunnery Sergeant West approached to help extract Allbaugh, as Doc Hannon, our platoon corpsman, raced to the scene with his medical bag. The Marines removed Allbaugh from the vehicle and carried him a safe distance away in case the vehicle exploded.

The platoon established a 360-degree security perimeter around the blast site to guard against possible follow-on attacks. Sergeant Kohler moved his vehicle from the number-four position to provide security to the front, as Doc Hannon attempted to help Allbaugh breathe. As Gunnery Sergeant West established a secure perimeter, I yelled for my vehicle's crew to get the satellite radio set up and I ran to the lead vehicle.

Miraculously, it did not appear that any of the Marines had received serious injuries, although Allbaugh had issues breathing. I inspected the vehicle and determined that the IED had exploded directly under Allbaugh's seat. I walked up to Allbaugh, as Doc Hannon continued to work on him. It amazed me that Allbaugh did not have a scratch on him, although he was unable to talk. I told Allbaugh that it would be all right and returned to my vehicle to ensure my crew called in a casualty evacuation request. Lance Corporal Roysdon was getting radio checks with the SATCOM (satellite communications radio), and I sent a casualty evacuation request over my vehicle's Blue Force Tracker as a backup.

The Army UH-60 "Dustoff" helicopter arrived quickly from Al Qa'im and flew Corporal Allbaugh, Corporal Klein, and Lance Corporals Lewis and Jameson back to Al Qa'im, to our waiting Shock Trauma Platoon. The remainder of the security platoon conducted a deliberate search of the area and quickly determined we had driven into an IED field. We discovered five additional IEDs to our front. Our Navy EOD and Marine vehicle recovery teams arrived, and the security platoon protected them. It was dusk before the IEDs were cleared and the platoon and others could move. I ordered a halt and the establishment of a secured perimeter when the darkness made it too difficult to locate other IEDs. It had been a long stressful day, but it appeared all was fine now.

I received a radio call from my executive officer, Maj. Jay Zollmann, as I sat in my vehicle going over the day's events in my head. Cpl. Jeremy Allbaugh had succumbed to his wounds. Although he showed no physical external injuries, the blast had been so powerful that it caused severe internal damage. I was devastated. The task force had just lost its first Marine on this deployment. I pulled Sergeant Major Perez and Gunny West aside and told them the bad news. I also ordered them not to share the information with anyone, because we needed the Marines' "heads in the game." It was a quiet and uneventful ride to Camp Al Qa'im the next morning. I pulled the security platoon into a tight group after parking our vehicles in front of the command post and informed them of our brother's passing. It was hard, but this story was not yet over. We had yet another hand to play.

A U.S. Army Special Operations group, Operation Detachment Alpha (ODA), a Green Berets "A-Team," also operated from Camp Al Qa'im. They had received the mission of training Iraqi Police Special Weapons and Tactics, or "SWAT," teams. It took a little time to build trust between our units, but the barriers broke down when our Marines provided some critical information the Special Forces troops needed for conducting a raid on a suspected insurgent in the area. This opened the door to a close working relationship and an opportunity for a combined operation. Our intelligence told us that a known terrorist in the area, named Jabbar Jassim, led the IED cell that had likely employed the IED that killed Corporal Allbaugh. I intended to capture Jassim or kill him if necessary. Unfortunately,

Jassim proved to be elusive, so Task Force 1/4 and the ODA partnered in an operation to find and neutralize him.

The Marines of the task force executed an information plan against Jassim intended to solicit a response that would help us find and target him. I put the word out to all the sheiks and ISF that I wanted to talk to Jassim. Marines from our Alpha Company patrolled past his home, where his mother and wife still lived. They questioned these women often, always with respect but making clear we wanted to find him. We sent vehicles with loudspeakers through Jassim's neighborhood, calling him out, stating that he was a coward for leaving his family, and declaring that he wore women's dresses to hide. All of this was aimed at getting him to make a move we could exploit. It worked. It took four months of tactical patience, but Jassim finally contacted a friend whom we had developed into a source. We now knew where he was.

We established a combined team consisting of the 81-mm Mortar Platoon, ODA with their Iraqi SWAT team, and air support to track and capture Jassim or kill him if he resisted. I controlled the operation from our combat operations center. All units were put in motion toward Jassim's suspected location. A helicopter flew too close to his position and spooked him; he and two other men jumped into a pickup truck and sped across the desert. We vectored the ground units, and they surrounded the insurgents in a quarry. Jassim and the others parked their truck and ran into the quarry, in which a maze of seven-foot piles of rocks was strewn about. The ODA and SWAT followed Jassim through the front of the quarry, as the 81s platoon raced around the back to block the escape.

I watched the live feed from the helicopter as the 81s platoon positioned their vehicles. The platoon commander jumped out with the corpsman in tow and ran toward the rock piles to locate the insurgents. They quickly froze in place as one of the insurgents appeared in front of them. There was a second of hesitation, and then the lieutenant and doc turned to run. The corpsman pushed the lieutenant to the ground just as the insurgent erupted in an explosion. He was wearing a suicide vest. Marines off to the right flank stopped another insurgent and had him raise his clothing to confirm he was not wearing a suicide vest as well. A machine gunner on one of the vehicles spotted and engaged the third insurgent, who, after being hit, dropped behind a pile of rocks.

The Marines held in place to prevent getting caught in another suicide blast, as the ODA and SWAT approached from the other direction. They spotted Jassim on the ground and ordered him to stand and raise

Cpl. Jeremy Allbaugh (*top*) and LCpl. Jeremy Burris (*bottom*) of 1st Battalion, 4th Marines gave the ultimate sacrifice in the service of their country and brother Marines in Al Qa'im, Iraq, 2007. *Author collection*

his dishdasha. The SWAT team, which later claimed Jassim made a sudden move, riddled him with bullets. The job was done. The team recovered the body and brought it back to Camp Al Qa'im to confirm his identity and properly handle the remains. The Marines did not take any pictures, because they were under strict orders from higher headquarters not to do so. Too many photos of gory battle casualties were making their way onto social media, and senior leaders wanted it stopped.

I met with the senior sheiks, General Ismael, and Colonel Jamal the next morning to announce the result. I was solemn and serious in my presentation, so I was surprised when Sheik Kurdi smiled and responded, "Yes, we know, see," as he handed me full-color photos of Jassim's corpse. The Americans were sensitive about pictures of corpses, but the Iraqis were not. The Iraqi SWAT team had proudly posed with Jassim's body to show their achievement.

Unfortunately, casualties on both sides persisted. Thirty-three China Marines received wounds during the deployment, and we lost another Marine in October. LCpl. Jeremy Burris of Weapons Company was on a patrol when the seven-ton truck in which he was riding hit an IED. The seven-ton was our most survivable vehicle against IEDs, but everyone in the vehicle received minor injuries except Burris. Weapons Company called in a casualty evacuation, as the Marines swept the area for other IEDs. They found none. Lance Corporal Burris went back to the cab to retrieve some items, jumped to the ground, and landed right on top of a pressure-plate IED. He died instantly. Burris' death hit many Marines particularly hard, because he was a man of great faith who often volunteered at our chapel and played guitar to worship with and entertain his fellow Marines.

We all mourned for Corporal Allbaugh and Lance Corporal Burris. We conducted memorial services for them both in country and after we returned home. We still remember them today. They and the other Marines, sailors, and soldiers of Task Force 1/4 could be justifiably proud of what they had accomplished during this deployment. They moved the ball farther down the field and helped Iraq to stand on its feet a little more firmly. Many of us wished our Iraqi brothers the best as we returned home, thinking this would likely be the last time any of us stepped foot in that country again. That is not how it would be. Unfortunately, I found myself back again seven years later leading some of the first conventional forces to go back into the country to fight a new enemy.

CHAPTER

★

The Fighting Fifth, Special Purpose MAGTF, and the Fight against ISIL

The National War College

It was time for a break after three back-to-back deployments. I received orders to attend the National War College (NWC) in Washington, D.C., as a member of the class of 2009. The NWC is located at Fort Lesley J. McNair. The Continental Army first established the base as a post in 1781, in the middle of the American Revolution. The post hosted the first federal penitentiary and gained notoriety in 1865 when Union soldiers imprisoned and then hanged on its grounds the conspirators in the assassination plot that killed President Abraham Lincoln. The NWC became part of the National Defense University in 1976 and assumed the mission of educating strategic leaders.

The NWC is one of five primary top-level schools (TLSs) for officer-level professional military education. Each of the military branches has its own war college, but the NWC belongs to the chairman of the Joint Chiefs of Staff. All the war colleges host a mix of students from each of the services, as well as from interagency and international partners. I chose to sponsor an international officer, as I had at the Infantry Officer Advanced Course as a captain and the Marine Corps Command and Staff College as a major. Now as a lieutenant colonel, I had the privilege of sponsoring Air Commodore Syed Hassan of the Pakistani air force and his family with my wife. Hassan was a fighter pilot by trade but was expected to rise within the ranks of the Pakistani armed forces.

Hassan and I enjoyed our studies and gained a greater appreciation for the imperative of PME. The passage of a military professional from the tactical through strategic levels requires increased understanding of the close linkage between the armed forces and their civilian leaders. Senior leaders must also recognize the capabilities that all government and nongovernment organizations contribute to a nation's national defense, while learning how to employ these capabilities skillfully in developing strategies to match ends, ways, and means. There is no substitute for real-world experience, but opportunities to gain such experiences are fleeting. PME fills the void. The year spent focused on one's studies, away from the distractions of a full-time job (for those fortunate enough to attend a resident school), is also invaluable. The time allows one to think, read, and write at levels far beyond what can be achieved when assigned to the operating forces. Attending PME also provides many military professionals an opportunity to recharge their batteries and reconnect with families after long periods of separation.

My family and I had a wonderful year. I received the honor of selection as a research fellow for the school and wrote a thesis titled, "A Central Role for America's Ground Forces in Whole-of-Government Approaches to National Security." I leaned heavily on my recent experiences in Iraq in writing the paper. The opportunity to conduct a focused study and to visit a specific geographic location of the world was another highlight of the year. I chose Indonesia, Singapore, and Malaysia, because I saw enormous potential for the United States to engage more fully in that area. Indonesia is the most heavily populated Muslim country in the world, and I thought it important to strengthen America's connection to it. My frustrating experiences with Indonesia during the tsunami relief also influenced my decision.

Nine students and a faculty adviser traveled to the three countries. The trip included visits to military, government, and social venues. On arriving in Indonesia, the U.S. ambassador requested we visit the city of Yogjakarta, on the island of Java. Yogjakarta was apparently a hotbed of Islamic fundamentalism in years past, but the mayor of the city had quelled the unrest. The ambassador wanted to recognize the mayor's efforts with a visit. The mayor graciously hosted us as we followed a deliberate and preplanned agenda authorized by the embassy. All was going well, and then the mayor changed the plan. He drove us to a mosque where approximately a thousand Muslims sat in prayer.

Our faculty adviser became nervous as the worshippers sensed our presence. The imam exited the mosque, introduced himself, and asked our faculty adviser to address his followers. Our adviser was clearly uncomfortable and graciously declined. I stepped forward as the student leader for the trip and said, "I'll do it." I did not want to let such an opportunity for goodwill pass. I followed the imam into the mosque and climbed the podium, where a microphone was waiting. I looked across the segregated crowd—the women sat on one side, the men on the other—and listened as the imam made introductory comments in a language I did not understand. The imam handed me the microphone, and the Muslims parishioners listened intently.

I reverted to what my cultural training and experience had taught me. I placed my right hand over my heart and said, "Assalamu alaikum" (peace be upon you)" in the best Arabic I could muster. The worshippers jumped up and cheered. I then spoke about the common ground between our people, the imam translating. I declared in general terms, without discussing specifics, that we were all believers. This appeared to work, and the crowd seemed pleased. It was an experience I will never forget. I received word of my next assignment on our return home. Although I had avoided it for the first nineteen years of my career, I had received orders to the Pentagon.

The Joint Staff

My orders assigned me to the Directorate of Strategic Plans and Policies (J5). The J5 "proposes strategies, plans, and policy recommendations to the Chairman of the Joint Chiefs of Staff (CJCS) to support his provision of 'best military advice' across the full spectrum of national security concerns to the President and other national leaders."[1] I initially served as a strategic planner but quickly transitioned to the front office to serve as the director's deputy executive assistant (DEA). Navy captain Rick Snyder, the executive assistant, and I initially served Vice Adm. James "Sandy" Winnefeld, later his successor, Lt. Gen. Charles Jacoby of the Army. (Snyder was a Navy helicopter pilot who had commanded an amphibious warship. He later achieved the rank of admiral and still serves on active duty today.)

Winnefeld and Jacoby were stellar examples to follow and learn from. Winnefeld left when he received a promotion and assumed command of the U.S. Northern Command (NORTHCOM), responsible for the conduct of homeland defense, civil support, and security cooperation to defend and secure the United States and its interests.[2] He later returned to the Joint Staff as vice chairman. Jacoby followed Winnefeld and relieved him as the NORTHCOM Commander, prior to retiring. For my part, in addition to serving as the DEA, I stood up a Strategic Initiatives Group (SIG) for Jacoby and had the opportunity to travel around the world with him and Adm. Michael Mullen, at the time the chairman of the Joint Chiefs of Staff. Much of the work we did, however, was classified and cannot be discussed in this book.

The House of Representatives

My two years with the Joint Staff ended quickly, and I prepared to return to the operating forces. Again, however, the Marine Corps had other plans. I received orders as the director of the Marine Corps Liaison Office to the U.S. House of Representatives. This position fell under the Headquarters Marine Corps Office of Legislative Affairs (OLA). Our mission was to facilitate a shared understanding between the Marine Corps and the members of the House of Representatives to ensure support for the commandant's legislative priorities and to maintain the Corps' unique role as the nation's premier force in readiness.[3]

Our liaison office served as a go-between linking Headquarters Marine Corps and the members of Congress. We had a fireteam-sized (four people) staff and ten congressional fellows, who served on specific representatives' staffs. Our duties included facilitating meetings among congressional members, staff, and senior Marine leaders; giving briefings; providing information; participating in various functions; and supporting congressional travel around the world. These activities allowed us to educate and inform Congress about the contribution and needs of the Marine Corps, while providing access and influence to ensure their support of Marine Corps priorities. Each of the military branches had such offices in both the House and the Senate. Like the Joint Staff, OLA was an extraordinary learning experience and provided me a new perspective, as I prepared to return at last to the operating forces.

The Fighting Fifth Marines

After having served five years in Washington, D.C., I had to return to the fleet. I received the honor of assuming command of the Fighting 5th Marines, the Marines Corps' most decorated regiment.[4] The Marine Corps established the regiment in June 1917 in preparation for joining the fight in Europe during World War I. The regiment fought so effectively in this war that it became known as "the Fighting Fifth," and helped all Marines earn the nickname, "Devil Dogs." After receiving three awards of the French Croix de Guerre for heroism in battle, Marines from the 5th and 6th Regiments earned the honor of forever wearing the French Fourragère (a braided, knotted cord and spike), a tradition still followed today.

The regiment's exploits were far from being over. It guarded the U.S. mail in the 1920s and fought in Nicaragua during the Banana Wars. It fought on Guadalcanal, New Guinea, Peleliu, and Okinawa during World War II, and at Pusan, Inchon, the Chosin Reservoir, and along the Demilitarized Zone in the Korean War during the 1950s. The regiment deployed to Vietnam in 1966 and remained there until April 1971. It added Rung Sat, Chu Lai, Phu Bai, Hue, Khe Sanh, An Hoa, Tam Ky, and Da Nang to its long list of battle honors.

But there was more. The regiment fought in Operation Desert Storm and captured Ahmed al-Jaber Air Base in Kuwait, a base it would return to in the coming years. The regiment was the first to cross the line of departure in the march to Baghdad during Operation Iraqi Freedom I, under the command of the future chairman of the Joint Chiefs of Staff, Col. Joe Dunford, with my mentor and first company commander, Lt. Col. Fred Padilla, as one of his battalion commanders.[5] The following years saw the regiment deploy as a RCT headquarters to Iraq and Afghanistan, while its four battalions deployed separately in support of these operations and as the ground combat elements of MEUs.

The regimental staff returned from its last combat deployment to Afghanistan just prior to my assumption of command. The regiment, like all Marine units, had received tough assignments over the previous decade of combat deployments. The regimental staff and battalions did not expect to conduct any further combat deployments in the near future. President Barack Obama had pulled American forces out of Iraq in 2011 and was drawing down forces in Afghanistan. The staff went about reconciling supply accounts, conducting much-needed maintenance, and reinstituting normal peacetime practices that had slackened in favor of wartime requirements. The regiment's battalions settled into a scheduled deployment cycle of rotating through Okinawa as the ground combat element of the 31st MEU. It appeared indeed that the regiment had earned a hiatus from fighting. Nevertheless, as has always been the case, the enemy gets a vote.

Terrorists attacked the U.S. mission in Benghazi, Libya, on 11 September 2012, killing Ambassador Chris Scott and three other Americans.[6] Pundits continue to debate the details surrounding the incident and question the lack of a more robust military response. However, the fact is that no rapidly deployable and credible crisis-response force existed in the area at the time.

MEUs provide premier crisis-response forces. However, the lack of adequate amphibious warships had caused the Marines to reduce the MEU presence in the region. As a result of the Benghazi attack, the secretary of defense directed the establishment of additional crisis-response forces to mitigate the risk of further attacks. The Marine Corps responded with the Special Purpose Marine Air Ground Task Forces–Crisis Response (SPMAGTF-CR).

The SPMAGTF-CRs are land-based, expeditionary MAGTFs capable of conducting crisis-response and contingency operations in support of combatant commanders. The Marine Corps established the first SPMAGTF-CR, to cover Europe and Africa, in April 2013. II MEF sourced the personnel and equipment to establish what became known as Special Purpose Marine Air Ground Task Force–Crisis Response–Africa (SPMAGTF-CR-AF) and based it in Morón, Spain. It quickly proved its worth when it successfully evacuated noncombatants from the American embassy in South Sudan in January 2014.

The commandant directed the establishment of a second SPMAGTF-CR to cover the twenty countries of the CENTCOM area of operations. I MEF received the task of manning and equipping this force. It delegated responsibility for the headquarters element to its ground combat element, the 1st Marine Division. The division's commanding general (CG), Maj. Gen. Larry Nicholson, faced the challenge of earmarking a significant portion of his combat power to this new mission while maintaining the division's fighting ability in case it received the call to war. (Nicholson received a third star and is the commanding general of the III Marine Expeditionary Force based in Okinawa as of the writing of this book.) Each of the division's subordinate units was already heavily tasked, and the Fighting Fifth was no exception.

It already had a lot on its plate. It had received orders as the GCE for the 1st Marine Expeditionary Brigade (MEB) and also was assigned as an air contingency force (ACF). The regiment received the additional tasks of providing a regimental staff to lead an integrated training exercise (ITX— the successor of Mojave Viper) in Twentynine Palms and participate in a division-level exercise and separate MEB large-scale exercise (LSE). The regiment also had responsibility for manning, training, and equipping its four battalions (1/5, 2/5, 3/5, 2/4) for their own deployments. Although busy, I had my staff begin initial planning in anticipation of receiving the mission for what became known as Special Purpose Marine Air Ground Task Force–Crisis Response–Central Command (SPMAGTF-CR-CC).

Special Purpose Marine Air Ground Task Force–Crisis Response–Central Command

My first request on receiving confirmation that the 5th Marines was to stand up SPMAGTF-CR-CC was to get relief from some of our other commitments. The 7th Marines eventually assumed responsibility for the ITX and LSE, which helped greatly. I also split the 5th Marines' headquarters into an "Alpha" and a "Bravo" command. I led the Alpha and took some of my principal staff officers with me to stand up and deploy with the SPMAGTF. My executive officer, Lt. Col. Jer Garcia, led the Bravo command and would remain in the rear to continue the battalions' care and feeding. He also assumed responsibility as the area commander for Camp San Mateo, home of the 5th Marines and 1st Combat Engineer Battalion at Camp Pendleton. (Garcia, a former enlisted reconnaissance Marine who served as an infantry officer once commissioned, performed exceptionally well leading Bravo and later received his own command, an LAR battalion.)

This new arrangement required me to wear two hats at once. I remained the commanding officer of the 5th Marines and maintained an office at Camp San Mateo, on the north side of Camp Pendleton, while my SPMAGTF staff maintained a second command post at Camp Del Mar, on the base's southern side. This also meant I was working for three different bosses at the same time. Maj. Gen. Nicholson remained my boss as the CG of the 1st Marine Division, while I still reported to the commanding general of the 1st MEB, Brig. Gen. Sam Mundy, in my capacity as the MEB's GCE. (Mundy moved on to command Marine Forces Central Command [Forward], and became my future boss while deployed with the MAGTF. He later received a second star and command of Marine Forces Special Operations Command.) I also now began reporting to the Commander Marine Forces Central Command (MARCENT), Lieutenant General Neller.

Initial guidance directed SPMAGTF-CR-CC to be fully operationally capable (FOC) in the CENTCOM theater no later than 1 February 2015. This was an onerous task, since it was already March 2014 and SPMAGTF-CR-CC was still nothing more than a concept and a blank piece of paper. Our challenge increased when we received word that Headquarters Marine Corps had pushed the deployment timeline forward, now requiring FOC by 1 October. This only gave us six months from a cold start to develop, man, train, equip, and deploy a 2,500-man MAGTF across the globe.

We had gone from a plate with a lot on it to a full plate, to say the least. We still had to define our mission and develop a mission-essential task list to determine the type of force we had to build. We needed to train and equip the force in accordance with the skills required to accomplish its mission. The MAGTF also had to develop a predeployment training plan and determine the venues at which to conduct this training. We needed to decide what gear and equipment the mission required to support our operations and then find and obtain it from across the Marine Corps. We still had to determine the "bed-down" locations—that is, the places where the force would operate in theater—and receive authorizations from those countries. But before we could do any of these things, we needed to build and man the team that would develop, and eventually execute, these plans.

The 5th Marines' regimental staff provided the foundation. Additional Marines and sailors from the I MEF major subordinate commands (MSC– 1st Marine Division, 3rd Marine Air Wing, 1st Marine Logistics Group) filled out the rest of the staff. We established a stand-alone ACE staff under Lt. Col. Chris "Cliff" Henger. Henger was a fighter pilot who was commanding an F/A-18 training squadron when chosen to lead the ACE. The ACE consisted of: (Medium Tilt-Rotor Squadron) VMM-363; a MV-22 Osprey squadron, (Marine Attack Squadron) VMA-211; an AV-8B Harrier squadron, (Marine Tactical Electronic Warfare Squadron) VMAQ-4; an EA-6B Prowler squadron, an initial detachment from (Marine Refueler Squadron) VMGR-234 and a later detachment from VMGR-352 of four KC-130s; and detachments from a Marine Wing Support Squadron (MWSS), Marine Air Command Group (MACG), and a Marine Air Logistics Squadron (MALS). The GCE formed around the 2nd Battalion, 7th Marines (2/7) reinforced with combat engineers and commanded by Lt. Col. Sean Hankard. (Hankard and his team were hoping for a deployment to Afghanistan, but the emergence of ISIL helped change their plans.) Combat Logistics Battalion Five (CLB-5), commanded by Lt. Col. Brian Ecarius, provided the Logistics Combat Element. The CLBs normally provide small detachments in support of other deploying units, so CLB-5 was ecstatic to get the chance to deploy as a cohesive unit.

The MAGTF maximized the time, people, and resources available to prepare for its mission. In addition to crisis-response force for the CENT-COM region, we also assumed responsibility for three existing missions currently being executed in theater. These included that of Marine Air Group-50, which was flying combat missions supporting American forces in Afghanistan, an embassy reinforcement mission in Sana, Yemen, and a theater security cooperation (TSC) mission in Jordan.

This knowledge assisted us in devising our mission statement. It read, "SPMAGTF-CR-CC 15.1 (2015 first iteration) conducts crisis response, contingency operations, Theater Security Cooperation, Enabling Operations, and all other mission as may be directed throughout the CENTCOM area of operations in order to support the Commander Central Command's requirements in the 'New Normal' environment." "New Normal" referred to the unrest experienced in the Middle East and the introduction of a new threat—the Islamic State of Iraq and the Levant (ISIL).[7] The appearance of ISIL in the theater two months after we began preparations for SPMAGT-CR-CC guaranteed profound changes to our mission on arriving in theater but did not diminish our other responsibilities.

We identified ten mission-essential tasks (MET) the SPMAGTF had to prepare to perform on arriving in theater:

1. Conduct enabling (the introduction of larger units) operations.
2. Attack targets.
3. Facilitate foreign humanitarian assistance.
4. Conduct/support TSC activities.
5. Provide security.
6. Conduct embassy reinforcement.
7. Conduct tactical recovery of aircraft and personnel (TRAP).
8. Conduct NEOs.
9. Develop partner-nation forces.
10. Integrate and operate with joint, interagency, intergovernmental, and multinational (JIIM) organizations.

During its deployment, the SPMAGTF conducted every one of these tasks and also, as our mission statement stated, "all other missions as may be directed." We trained the Marines to be the flexible, adaptable problem solvers described in Marine Corps Doctrinal Publication 1 *Warfighting*. We explained to them that "we do windows"—whatever our nation needs us to do, we do, whether we received specific training to conduct the mission or not. However, we attempted to train to as many skills as possible in the time remaining.

The SPMAGTF-CR-CC conducted a condensed predeployment training program from May to September 2014. The command element and subordinate MSEs each conducted independent training until able to join together for select events toward the end of the training cycle. Some of the major training events included rapid-response planning, security cooperation planning, command-post and fire-support exercises, tilt-rotor operations, adviser training, information operations, humanitarian assistance, and medical training. We conducted a mission rehearsal exercise (MRX) as our capstone training event.

The MRX was the first and only time the SPMAGTF could train as a cohesive team prior to deploying. The exercise used five different locations across southern California and Arizona simultaneously to replicate its expected bed-down in theater. We used Naval Air Station El Centro and Marine Corps Air Station Miramar, California, to represent Ahmed al-Jaber Air Base in Kuwait, where we intended to establish the SPMAGTF's crisis-response operations center (CROC) and base many of our aircraft. Camp Pendleton simulated Yemen; we established a mock embassy there. We established another mock embassy and TSC site at Twentynine Palms, which stood in for both Jordan and Iraq. Marine Corps Air Station Yuma simulated Sheik Isa Air Base in Bahrain. Practicing moving people, gear, and equipment over long distances was one of the key training objectives for the MRX, but we still lacked most of the gear and equipment needed to execute our mission.

Equipping the SPMAGTF was a major undertaking. No table of equipment (TOE) existed for the newly established unit. I MEF was the primary bill payer. Units across the MEF were directed to provide some of their own gear to the SPMAGTF. We established a marshaling yard on Camp Pendleton and set up a receiving section that inspected, received, tagged, and packaged gear for shipment overseas. The short time available to build, train, and equip the team left little or no time to work with the gear we inherited. This had to wait until we arrived in theater.

The deployment arrived before we knew it. I sent an advance party forward on 4–5 September, the same time that 84 percent of our gear and equipment departed the Port of Galveston, Texas, on board the *Alliance Richmond,* a civilian vehicle carrier. The gear the "black bottom" (government-contracted) ship carried was essential to the SPMAGTF's ability to declare itself fully mission capable by 1 November, as directed. Our higher headquarters defined FOC as all personnel present and all our gear and equipment present and fully functioning. The *Alliance Richmond* first had to stop in Florida to pick up a heavy crane needed by the ACE for aircraft maintenance; it arrived in Kuwait over a month later. We projected we would need another week to unload and transport the equipment to al-Jaber on the ship's arrival.

The remaining 16 percent of the SPMAGTF's gear shipped by air 11–13 September. We chose to fly the gear essential for establishing command

and control of the unit across the CENTCOM area of operation, to ensure its early arrival. The SPMAGTF needed this gear to be able to declare itself "initially operational capable" (IOC) no later than 1 October, a month before FOC. Higher headquarters defined IOC as one infantry platoon (thirty-five to fifty Marines) to act as a crisis-response force, four MV-22s, and one KC-130 present, operational, and ready for employment.

Our main body deployed 14–19 September on contracted aircraft, and our Harrier squadron left on 27 September. The Harriers experienced some minor maintenance issues en route and decided to have six of its twelve aircraft lay over in Rota, Spain, and arrived later in Bahrain. We expected to have the month of October to receive and check our gear from the *Alliance Richmond* before declaring ourselves fully operational capable on 1 November. Instead, we received orders to join the bombing campaign against ISIL in Iraq the day after our Harriers arrived. The game was on.

The SPMAGTF-CR-CC engaged the day it started arriving in theater. We established the MAGTF headquarters at Ahmed al-Jaber Air Base in Kuwait. The 5th Marines had captured al-Jaber twenty-four years earlier during Operation Desert Storm, so it was fitting that it was now our base of operations. The Kuwaiti air force operated three F/A-18 Hornet squadrons from the air base. The headquarters of the air, ground, and logistics combat elements also operated from al-Jaber, to facilitate planning and coordination. The GCE Headquarters and Service Company provided security for our compound—once again, "every Marine a rifleman."

Echo Company 2/7 was designated as a crisis-response company and remained on a six-hour alert to respond to any crisis or contingency in the theater. The "Lucky Red Lions" of VMM-363, commanded by Lt. Col. Dave Lane, provided the lift for Echo Company with their MV-22s. (Coincidently, Lane had been my radio operator twenty-two years earlier, when I was a lieutenant and he was a lance corporal in the original Bohm's Bastards.) Echo Company also provided a platoon on "a short tether" to act as a TRAP team. The TRAP team received the mission of recovering downed pilots or flight crews and assisting with the recovery of downed aircraft, if necessary.

The MAGTF provided a casualty evacuation capability for the CENTCOM area as well. We provided trained special Navy medical enroute care teams (ECTs) and received reinforcement from a combined Army/Air Force Tactical Critical Care Evacuation Team (TCCET). Our medical teams remained on alert to deploy on MV-22s or KC-130s if necessary, to stabilize patients prior to delivering them to our shock trauma platoon at al-Jaber or to a higher level of medical treatment.

The operational lift provided by the MV-22 Osprey, combined with the KC-130 refueling aircraft, was a game changer. The MV-22 can fly twice as far and twice as fast as any helicopter, but to do so it must refuel in flight. Partnering the MV-22 with the KC-130 enabled the SPMAGTF to touch the entire CENTCOM area of operations. The SPMAGTF operated from eleven different countries on its deployment. One cannot underestimate what possessing its own organic aircraft means for the support and sustainment provided by a MAGTF.

The SPMAGTF supported more than just its own MV-22 squadron and half of the KC-130 detachment at al-Jaber. The self-supporting and self-sustaining capability of the MAGTF enabled it to support other coalition partners as well. Although the U.S. Air Force maintained senior airfield authority (SAA) for al-Jaber, initially it was unable to support other coalition partners participating in the air campaign against ISIL from al-Jaber. SPMAGTF did so, with bulk fuel, ordnance, security, medical, engineering, and other services to our Canadian, Danish, Italian, and U.S. Air Force partners, until the Air Force assumed these responsibilities.

SPMAGTF's aircraft operated from two other locations. The "Wake Island Avengers" of VMA-211, our AV-8B Harrier squadron, commanded by Lt. Col. Cory "Gene" Simmons, and the other half of our KC-130 detachment operated from Sheik Isa Air Base in Bahrain. (Simmons was later recognized for commanding the top attack squadron and the 3rd Marine Air Wing's top overall squadron of the year before retiring.) Bravo Battery, 3rd Light Anti-Air Defense (LAAD) Battalion provided security for the squadron, its aircraft, and facilities, once again validating the ethos of every Marine being a warfighter. Agreements with the Bahraini government stipulated that we could not employ infantry Marines in their country. Accordingly, our Harriers, which conducted a sustained bombing campaign against ISIL in Iraq and Syria throughout the deployment, were guarded by their support personnel.

The "Seahawks" of VMAQ-4, commanded by Lt. Col. Dave Mueller, operated from Al Udeid Air Base in Qatar. They provided electronic warfare, leaflet drops, and nontraditional intelligence, surveillance, and reconnaissance (ISR) missions over Iraq, Syria, and Afghanistan with their EA-6B Prowlers. Mueller had the honor of leading one of the EA-6B's last operational deployments; the aircraft is being phased out and replaced with the F-35 Joint Strike Fighter. The SPMAGTF also established a liaison element at Al Udeid to coordinate our aircraft's operations across the CENTCOM area of operations with the Combined Air Operations Center (CAOC), which had responsibility for the overall air campaign in theater.

An EA-6B Prowler from VMAQ-4 of SPMAGTF-CR-CC 15.1 sits on the ramp at Al Udeid
Air Base, Qatar, preparing for other missions in support of Operations Enduring Freedom
and Inherent Resolve. *Courtesy of 1st Lt. Matthew Finnerty*

The SPMAGTF established a theater security cooperation element
(TSC-E) at the Joint Training Center (JTC) in Amman, Jordan. The 2/7
Bravo command group and the battalion's Golf Company joined forces
with Marines from the Marine Corps Reserve, who were already in country assisting the Jordanians to train units for deployment to Afghanistan. I
gave the lieutenant colonel leading the reserve Marines overall command
of the combined TSC-E. This combined force partnered with elements of
the Jordanian armed forces in establishing a battalion-sized quick-reaction
force at the request of the king of Jordan. They also partnered with the
Jordanian 77th Marine Battalion, which operated from Acqaba with access
to the Red Sea.

The SPMAGTF received the mission to reinforce two embassies.
Marines from the 1st Marine Division augmented security at the diplomatic mission in Sanaa, Yemen, because of the internal strife created by
Houthi rebels. Houthi influence in Yemen had spread following the 2012
ouster of Yemeni president Ali Abdullah Saleh, and the Houthi had taken
over the capital in September 2014.[8] We assigned Weapons Company 2/7 to
secure the American embassy and the diplomatic transient facility (DTF)
located approximately a half-mile away in Sanaa. Both positions were tenu-
ous. High ground surrounded the compounds and offered adversaries good
visibility and clear fields of fire into the two positions. A special operations
colonel was the senior American military official in country and received

tactical control of our weapons company under the ambassador, with the SPMAGTF maintaining operational control.

The security situation deteriorated to the point that the Department of State ordered evacuation of the embassy in Yemen in February 2015. The Houthis had begun harassing diplomats, and they controlled the airport and ports. The Marines received orders to destroy their weapons, gear, and equipment in place before evacuating to prevent their capture. Officials made the decision to leave using a third country's commercial airline, rather than American military capabilities poised nearby. Marine Corps officials questioned the need to destroy the weapons and gear, but the decision ultimately belonged to others and we complied with orders.

Marines from Fox Company 2/7 reinforced the Baghdad Embassy Complex (BEC) in Iraq, while its weapons company guarded the embassy in Yemen. A FAST platoon originally reinforced the American embassy in Baghdad, following ISIL's offensive into Iraq. After watching ISIL capture Iraqi armored vehicles and weapons, the RSO at the embassy requested heavier firepower than the FAST Marines had brought. A full infantry company from 1st Battalion, 6th Marines (1/6) deployed with the 22nd MEU to relieve the FAST Marines, and Fox Company 2/7 relieved the Marines from 1/6. The RSO, responsible for the security of the embassy and embassy personnel, assumed tactical control of Fox Company, with the SPMAGTF maintaining operational control. The threat from ISIL in Iraq was real.

The origin of ISIL goes back to Operation Iraqi Freedom in 2006. Al-Qaeda in Iraq combined with other extremist groups in Iraq following the death of its leader, Abu Musab al-Zarqawi, and renamed itself the Islamic State of Iraq.[9] The group attempted to spread its influence, but the Sunni tribes that Task Force 1/4 and others had worked with in western Iraq rejected them during the "Al Anbar Awakening" due to their brutal tactics. Abu Bakr al-Baghdadi assumed leadership of the group in 2010 following his release from a five-year prison sentence. His influence spread into Syria as civil war raged in that country. He announced the establishment of the Islamic State in Iraq and the Levant in April 2013.

ISIL launched offenses in both Syria and Iraq from its stronghold in Raqqah, Syria. It attacked through the China Marines' old home in Al Qa'im, Iraq, in January 2014 and continued down the western Euphrates River valley, securing Fallujah and Ramadi in its push toward Baghdad. ISIL then shifted its focus northward and captured Iraq's second-largest city, Mosul, in June. News reports showed hordes of Iraqi soldiers surrendering to or retreating before ISIL's advance. Commentators displayed maps showing seas of red representing ISIL's gains across Iraq. Nevertheless, there was hope. Some Iraqi units held firm.

Not all of western Iraq had fallen to ISIL. The 7th Iraqi Division, the unit the Marines had trained and partnered with during OIF, was fighting back. The division and its corps headquarters, referred to as the Jazeera and Badia Operations Command (JBOC), held positions in the city of Hadithah and at Al Asad Air Base. Al Asad had been a significant Marine base during OIF. It was the location of Task Force 1/4's higher headquarters, Regimental Combat Team Two, and the location President Bush had visited when he asked to meet with our sheiks. Other locations in Iraq also held but needed help in fighting ISIL.

Help came in the form of a coalition of nations that joined an American-led combined joint task force. Ten nations met in a NATO conference in September 2014, just as SPMAGTF-CR-CC arrived in theater. They agreed that ISIL posed a threat to Iraq and the international community and committed themselves to forming a "broad international coalition to degrade and ultimately destroy ISIL."[10] These nations immediately began providing air support, training, and munitions to the Kurdistan Regional Government as well as the government of Iraq. The SPMAGTF actively participated in these airstrikes, but it did more.

Senior leaders also decided the coalition would have to support the Iraqis on the ground by establishing "building partnership capacity" (BPC) enclaves throughout the country to reconstitute units for the Iraqi army, as well as establish new ones. Locations for these BPC sites first needed to be assessed to determine suitability for use. Criteria for selection of the sites included the presence of an Iraqi unit to partner with, adequate facilities to house coalition and Iraqi forces, a functioning airfield to sustain the force, adequate training areas, and defensible terrain since ISIL forces surrounded most locations.

The SPMAGTF partnered with special operations forces to conduct these assessments. Special operations forces possess unique qualifications for this type of mission, but those in theater did not yet possess either sufficient organic lift or the heavier firepower Marines can provide. The SPMAGTF provided Marine squads and platoons, MV-22s, and KC-130s to work closely with Army special forces. It also maintained its crisis-response force, TRAP, CASEVAC, and strike aircraft packages on alert to rapidly respond in support of the assessment teams, if necessary. The BPC sites selected included Arbil, Bismayah, At Taji, and Al Asad.

The Department of Defense designated U.S. and coalition operations against ISIL, Operation Inherent Resolve (OIR) on 15 October 2014. Overall responsibility for the operation belonged to Central Command. The command stated that the code name Inherent Resolve was "intended to reflect the unwavering resolve and deep commitment of the U.S. and partner nations in the region and around the globe to eliminate the terrorist group ISIL and the threat they pose to Iraq, the region, and the wider international community."[11]

Central Command designated the commander of U.S. Third Army and Army Forces Central Command as commander of CJTF-Operation Inherent Resolve. He received the task of establishing a combined, and joint, headquarters to oversee operations to degrade and ultimately defeat Daesh. ("Daesh" is an Arabic acronym for ISIL with negative connotations. Our Iraqi partners interpreted it to roughly mean "dirty dogs.")

The CJTF based its headquarters at Camp Arifjan, Kuwait, and organized into functional components to execute the operation. These included combined forces (CF), land (CFLCC), air (CFACC), and maritime (CFMCC) component commands (CC). Personnel and equipment for the component commands came from the service component commands for CENTCOM: the Army (ARCENT), Navy (NAVCENT), Air Force (AFCENT), and Marine Corps (MARCENT).

The SPMAGTF-CR-CC fell under the operational control of MARCENT, now under command of Lt. Gen. Kenneth McKenzie. (McKenzie later served as the Joint Staff Director of Strategic Plans and Policies [J5] and director of the Joint Staff, prior to being nominated to assumed command of Central Command.) MARCENT's headquarters was at MacDill Air Force Base, Florida, beside the CENTCOM headquarters. It established a forward headquarters in Bahrain, designated MARCENT (Forward), under command of Brig. Gen. Sam Mundy, who wore three hats: the deputy commanding general for MARCENT, and as the commanding general of both MARCENT (Forward) and Combined Task Force 51, with command and control of amphibious forces in the region.[12] He reported to the commanders of both MARCENT and NAVCENT in these capacities. This dynamic helped foster mutually supportive relationships between the SPMAGTF and the MEUs rotating through theater.

Although I worked directly for General Mundy, I also answered to other senior leaders. The CFACC controlled all strike missions conducted by our Harriers, as part of the larger air campaign. The SPMAGTF's rifle companies guarding the embassies in Baghdad and Sanaa fell under the tactical control of American ambassadors at those locations but remained under our operational control. The Theater Special Operations Command (TSOC) led several of the missions that we conducted with them throughout the theater. The SPMAGTF augmented several MEUs conducting TSC events that fell under NAVCENT. The CENTCOM (Forward) staff in Jordan controlled operations in that country, and there were others. I soon found myself reporting directly to the CFLCC as well.

Task Force Al Asad

The SPMAGTF received orders to establish an expeditionary BPC site at Al Asad Air Base, one of the locations we had previously assessed. Soldiers of the U.S. Army and other coalition partners were to establish BPC sites at Arbīl, Bismayah, and At Taji. This was part of a "bridging" strategy, until permanent advise and assist (AA) teams formed in the United States and deployed forward.

The CJTF intended to sustain current Iraqi Security Forces efforts in battling ISIL, while buying time for the further reconstitution of ISF units and the building of new ones. The Marine Corps committed to providing two AA teams, which initially fell under the command of SPMAGTF-CR-CC. I MEF provided a team, led by Col. Joseph Russell, that I intended to partner with the 7th Iraqi Division. Russell was an AAV officer by trade and was serving as the 1st Marine Division Headquarters Battalion commander. II MEF provided a team, commanded by Col. John McDonough, that was to partner with the JBOC. McDonough, an infantry officer, was the 2nd Marine Division Headquarters Battalion commander. It was some time before these teams arrived.

I tasked Lt. Col. Sean Hankard, the SPMAGTF GCE commander, with establishing what became known as Task Force Al Asad. The tasks assigned to Hankard and his battalion fully committed it across the CENTCOM area of operations. His Marines already reinforced the embassies in Yemen and Iraq, while providing the crisis-response company and TRAP force from Kuwait. His Marines also guarded Ahmed al-Jaber Air Base in Kuwait. They provided the forces conducting joint operations with the special forces in Iraq, and they sourced the TSC in Jordan. Now I was relying on them to establish Task Force Al Asad in Iraq.

This required some selective maneuvering of existing forces and reinforcement from other sectors. We pulled half of the battalion's Golf Company, assigned to Jordan, and joined it with Hankard's Alpha Command group with augmentation from across the MAGTF. Another platoon from the GCE deployed forward with two Army Green Beret A-teams to establish a tribal engagement mission at Al Asad, and a company of Danish soldiers under the command of Lieutenant Colonel Bo Overgaard joined Task Force Al Asad under Hankard. The CFLCC informed us that additional logistics and communications support was forthcoming. The CFLCC assumed tactical control of Task Force Al Asad, with SPMAGTF maintaining operational control.

The CJTF established the CFLCC under the "Big Red One"—the U.S. Army 1st Infantry Division, commanded by Maj. Gen. Paul Funk. (Funk, the son of an Army lieutenant general, received his own third star and corps command following this deployment. He later returned in overall command of Operation Inherent Resolve.) Funk established his headquarters at the BEC, guarded by SPMAGTF's Fox Company. The SPMAGTF moved quickly when given authorization from Funk to establish the task force. However, I became concerned when he informed me that the forward logistics element (FLE), medical teams, and communications detachment promised by the other services could not make agreed-upon timelines. The general stated we needed to delay the mission, but I told him not to worry. I already deployed organic capabilities forward to support the task force until the other capabilities arrived. He was surprised at the versatility of the MAGTF and asked how long I could sustain the support. I informed him that the support was there for as long as he needed it. He asked us to maintain it until March.

I agreed to cover the gap, knowing this would take capability away from the remainder of the SPMAGTF. I bled assets off the command element and LCE to support Task Force Al Asad in this priority effort. However, the SPMAGTF quickly approached its culmination point—beyond which a military unit begins to experience diminishing returns. We had fully committed our Marines at this point, although the SPMAGTF still maintained the crisis-response (CR) company, TRAP, and CASEVAC capabilities. I requested authority up the Marine chain of command to employ the CR Company if needed in Iraq as well and received permission, with the acknowledgment that the fight against ISIL was a crisis. Lieutenant Colonel Hankard established Task Force Al Asad at the air base and prepared to accept ISF units in support of the BPC mission. He assumed control of a fenced compound that had last hosted a MALS in 2009, prior to President Obama's pulling American forces out of the country. Hankard designated the area Camp Havoc, in recognition of 2/7's radio call sign.

A Danish soldier assigned to Task Force Al Asad works closely with Iraqi Security Forces on a tactical planning exercise in preparation for the fight against ISIL in Iraq, January 2015. *Courtesy of LCpl. Skyler Treverrow*

Returning to Al Asad Air Base for the first time in five years was like something out of *The Twilight Zone,* the classic TV show. It appeared that American forces had just picked up and departed when the president ordered them to leave the country. In some offices Marines found newspapers of the date the Marines had departed five years previously. While the base looked much like it had in 2009, the buildings showed varying states of disrepair, and the once-busy facility was now eerily quiet.

The Iraqi Air Force had assumed control of Al Asad, but very few aircraft operated from the field. Iraqi air force security personnel guarded the miles of perimeter fence and gates to the base, while Task Force al Asad now established a secure compound within the base to guard against threats that might get past the ISF. The 7th Iraqi Division headquarters and some of its subordinate units also resided on the air base. Other ISF lived at a military housing complex located off base near the town of al Baghdadi, just outside the front gate. ISIL had control of much of the area surrounding the base except for a corridor that connected Al Asad to Hadithah approximately thirty-four miles north along Highway 12. ISIL routinely rocketed the base and began to target Camp Havoc once we had established our presence.

Task Force Al Asad received several tasks. It assumed responsibility for advising and assisting both the 7th Iraqi Division under the command of Staff Major General Majid, and the JBOC (under Staff Major General Diya) until the Marine AA teams arrived from the United States. Marines and Danish soldiers worked side by side in the BPC mission. The Iraqi 71st Brigade, part of the newly formed 15th Division, arrived with nine hundred soldiers to be trained. They established themselves at a former Marine Logistics Support Area (LSA) called "Gettysburg." The task force worked with the Army special forces team in tribal engagement, and an Australian task group operated on base to train special Iraqi police forces. Task Force Al Asad also played a critical role in combating ISIL.

President Obama opted for a deliberate and minimalist approach to fighting ISIL. He placed a cap on the number of American forces permitted in Iraq, against which both SPMAGTF Marines reinforcing the embassy and those constituting Task Force Al Asad counted. In addition, although he authorized the establishment of the BPC sites, he forbade American forces from leaving the confines of the established bases. I equated this to fighting a war looking through a soda straw, because the only view of the battlefield we received was what we saw from unmanned aerial vehicles (UAVs) and manned aircraft feeds. Americans provided intelligence, logistics, and fire support but no maneuver units to engage ISIL. The ISF were the maneuver units in this fight.

Task Force Al Asad assisted the ISF in planning, coordinating, and executing operations using ISR platforms, armed UAVs to locate ISIL targets for strike aircraft dropping bombs to destroy. Colonel Hankard and his team performed their role well, but higher headquarters wanted more weight behind the effort. MARCENT directed me to deploy to Iraq to take command of Task Force Al Asad, while still commanding the remainder of the SPMAGTF across the CENTCOM region. This delighted General Funk at first, because he thought my assignment to Task Force Al Asad meant he gained control of all the SPMAGTF's assets. I had to explain this was not the case. He only had tactical control of those forces on the ground assigned to the task force, but not the remainder of the MAGTF's assets operating across the region.

I advised against my being in direct command of Task Force Al Asad, because I believed I could best lead my unit by providing command and control for the entire SPMAGTF, using the infrastructure established for

Marines from SPMAGTF-CR-CC 15.1 and Iraqi Security Forces work side-by-side to defeat ISIL forces at Al Asad Air Base, Iraq, January 2015. *Courtesy Cpl. Carson A. Gramley*

this purpose at al-Jaber in Kuwait. Engaging ISIL on the ground in Iraq with a small force risked consuming my focus and efforts at the expense of the remainder of the SPMAGTF. However, I understood my orders and their rationale, and I complied. I once again split my command element into Alpha and Bravo elements, just as I had back in Camp Pendleton with the 5th Marines, and deployed forward. The SPMAGTF executive officer, Lt. Col. Dave Handy, remained in Kuwait and continued to coordinate the SPMAGTF's many other missions. (Handy was a versatile and competent officer who later received battalion command. He remains on active duty today.)

My first task on arriving in Al Asad was to form what became known as the "Combined Force." The 7th Division did not have the manpower it needed to accomplish its tasks. The division had possessed less than 50 percent of its authorized strength in June 2014, when ISIL had attacked. Months of sustained combat with ISIL had further degraded its numbers. It had enough soldiers to recapture areas lost to ISIL, but not to hold them. We eventually found a solution by working with the tribes and Iraqi police (IP).

The author welcomes senior leaders of the Iraqi Ground Forces Command to the Task Force Al Asad headquarters in Iraq, while with SPMAGTF-CR-CC 15.1. *Courtesy of LCpl. Skyler Treverrow*

The Iraqi army, tribes, and police and their coalition partners had worked in a "stovepiped," independent manner up to this point. The result had been an incoherent strategy in the western Euphrates River valley. That, in turn, resulted in American forces arguing over the limited ISR and fire assets available to prosecute operations in support of our partners. We pulled Task Force Al Asad, the Army special forces, and Australian special forces together; no formal command relationships existed among these groups, but we agreed to work together in defeating our common enemy.

Each organization had a key role to play in this fight. Task Force Al Asad remained partnered with the conventional Iraqi army. The Army special forces recruited, trained, equipped, and planned operations with unconventional forces comprising tribal fighters. The Australian special forces did similar work with special police teams. I later requested and received authority from CFLCC to partner with the conventional police as well. We developed a strategy to gain and maintain the initiative from ISIL while systematically recapturing areas lost to the terrorists. This helped stop the flow of foreign fighters into Iraq and set the conditions for clearing western Iraq of ISIL influence and conducting a counteroffensive to recapture Mosul.

U.S. Marines and Danish soldiers from SPMAGTF-CR-CC 15.1 worked closely together to train Iraqi forces at Al Asad Airbase, Iraq. *Courtesy of Cpl. Tony Simmons*

The combined force established a battle rhythm whereby the 7th Division would conduct a major operation to recapture lost ground approximately once every week or two with the tribal fighters and IP in support. The conventional forces captured the ground; the tribes and IPs held the liberated territories, enabling the soldiers to rearm and refit in preparation for the next large battle. The tribal fighters conducted numerous smaller raids and other operations in between these larger operations to keep ISIL guessing as to where we would strike next, while further degrading their forces and sources of supply. In order to prevent the type of infighting that earlier occurred, we agreed that priority of fire and ISR belonged to the lead unit conducting an operation.

The arrival of Shia militia at Al Asad complicated matters. A company-sized Shia militia force arrived in Al Asad and demanded to join our operations. Officials in Baghdad had apparently sent this force. It was commonly understood that the militia had ties to Iran, and many of the Sunni ISF officers feared for the safety of their families who had moved to Baghdad when ISIL first attacked the area. Some believed Iranian influence in Baghdad would result in threats to their families if they did not comply with the militia's demands. The ISF gave the Shia militia "a seat at the table" and key roles during some of the earlier battles, although I never permitted them to enter Camp Havoc when we planned operations. The Shia militia's credibility began to drop as time went on and their heavy-handed approach with the ISF wore thin. By the time I departed, the militia had been relegated to serving as the reserve for operations.

The combined force was quickly put to the test. In January 2015, ISIL fighters attempted to block Highway 12, the lifeline between the 7th Division at Al Asad and the JBOC at Hadithah. We responded by developing Operation *Thar Abtal* (Hero's Revenge). The 7th Division's mission was to disrupt ISIL fighters in the towns of Alus and Albu Hyat to deny the enemy the ability to control Main Supply Route Bronze (Highway 12) between Hadithah and Al Asad. Task Force Al Asad helped set the conditions for the operation by calling in Air Force A-10 Warthogs to destroy nine boats and a barge being used by ISIL to ferry reinforcements and supplies to the western side of the Euphrates River.

The operation was a success. The combined efforts of Iraqi ground maneuver and coalition air strikes resulted in twenty-two enemy killed in action (EKIA) and a vehicle-borne IED destroyed. Tribal fighters from the Jaghayfa and Albu Nimur tribes accounted for twenty-four additional EKIA, as they mopped up following the 7th Division's clearing operation. The overall cost to the combined force was three Iraqi soldiers and three tribal fighters wounded. No soldiers died, although half of the force's twenty vehicles in the operation sustained damaged and had to be towed back to Al Asad.

This was a recurring theme throughout the combined force's operations. ISIL small-arms fire and IEDs took their toll on ISF vehicles. The Task Force Al Asad mechanics worked closely with their Iraqi partners to put Band-Aids on these vehicles and get them back into the fight. Eventually, the supply chains for the CFLCC and Iraqi government started providing replacements. The most sought-after vehicle was the Buffalo variant of the Mine Resistant Ambush Protected (MRAP) armored vehicles used by Iraqi EOD teams. The 7th Division rated twenty-five MRAPs but only had eight, half of which were always in the shop being repaired. The Iraqis constantly rotated these four with the other vehicles, which inevitably returned from operations damaged. The MRAPs proved critical as ISIL fighters modified their tactics to survive and became more lethal.

Operations like Thar Abtal taught us much about ISIL's tactics, techniques, and procedures. ISIL fighters quickly learned not to expose themselves unnecessarily to observation. If we could see them and positively identify them as adversaries, we could kill them. ISIL countered by "shooting and scooting," employing indirect fires to prevent us from obtaining positive identification. They preferred to engage us during periods of inclement weather, when UAVs and strike aircraft did not fly or their observation was impaired. ISIL fighters often conducted diversions to draw ISR assets away from their main efforts. They avoided being observed and targeted in other ways as well.

Whereas ISIL fighters had previously openly brandished weapons when fighting the ISF, they began to understand that our rules of engagement required positive identification before we could engage targets. Accordingly, they now kept weapons hidden and out of sight. They started covering weapons they carried or transported in vehicles or boats. Some ISIL fighters wore camouflaged ghillie suits or tan burlap bags to blend in with the landscape. They also stopped moving when in the middle of battle, to prevent their being targeted. They learned to leave weapons inside buildings, fire from deep inside rooms to prevent muzzle flashes from being seen by UAVs, and walk calmly from one weapons cache to another in a nonthreatening posture to confuse our targeting.

In addition, ISIL changed from openly attacking urban areas from the outside in to fighting from the inside out. Rather than conduct a traditional linear attack from the outside of an urban area to clear it of coalition forces, ISIL now demonstrated tactical patience. They took the time needed to establish numerous hidden weapons caches inside of urban areas before initiating battles by striking from inside the towns or villages. This provided our friendly forces little or no time to react, which further challenged targeting. The lack of an effective human-intelligence apparatus and of U.S. presence on the ground beside our coalition partners enabled this tactic to be effective.

ISIL also became better at hardening their vehicles while improving the lethality of their weapons. ISIL created armored VBIEDs and used them to great effect. I watched as a captured M113 armored personnel carrier raced toward an ISF position guarding the far side of a bridge spanning the Euphrates River. Iraqi army soldiers fired frantically with their small arms trying to stop the vehicle, but it crashed into their position and exploded, killing most of the soldiers. The few survivors ran to the near side of the bridge as ISIL fighters attacked behind them and secured the area. ISIL also became more reliant on IEDs to slow and stop our advances, as we became more adept at targeting. I am convinced that many of the improvements made by ISIL resulted from the assistance of foreign fighters.

The combined force identified foreign fighters from Europe, Africa, Asia, and elsewhere in the Middle East in our area of operations. We observed an ebb and flow in the skill and professionalism of those we engaged as we killed off the more experienced and knowledgeable fighters, and then, after a time other experienced terrorists replaced them. Foreign fighters pushed less experienced locals into the breach to draw our fire, remaining back themselves and more deliberately attacking our partners. For our part, these battles also taught us valuable lessons about how to best employ the combined force.

We learned to use several planning factors when developing combined-force operations. The limited resources available to the ISF made it imperative that we preserve their resources by conducting only well-planned and relevant operations worth the risk and possible costs. We learned to play to ISF and coalition strengths while maximizing ISIL's exposure. We learned to mass forces and effects better and at critical times and places while appropriately weighing the main effort of the operation. We also learned not to conduct complex operations with the combined force. We focused on limited and achievable objectives, concentrating on a priority axis of advance to prevent splitting limited ISR and fire assets in support of ISF maneuver. We also reinforced the importance of employing cohesive units to the greatest extent possible, rather than building ad hoc arrangements when conducting combined-force operations.

Another valuable lesson learned was to never let one's guard down. This became evident in February when a squad of ISIL fighters infiltrated Al Asad Air Base and attacked the 7th Division Headquarters. The fighters cut through the perimeter fence and penetrated to the headquarters wearing Iraqi army uniforms before they attacked with suicide vests, automatic weapons, and hand grenades. We believe all, if not most, of them died in the attack, but not before taking some ISF soldiers with them.

Task Force Al Asad intently watched the attack play out using UAVs as we prepared for the attack against Camp Havoc. We had ISR watching the battle from overhead and pushed other platforms to screen the air base perimeter to ensure that no larger attack was forthcoming. We also alerted our quick-reaction force and had it poised to support the 7th Division, if needed. I held them back out of concern for the possibility of fratricide, because of the confusion caused on the ground by ISIL fighters attacking in army uniforms. We had attack aircraft "stacked up" above Al Asad, waiting for clear targets to engage if needed and alerted our medical staff to prepare for casualties.

Our medical staff did extraordinary work in Al Asad. The CFLCC provided Army surgical teams to provide shock trauma, if needed. Fortunately, no American personnel received wounds during our time at Al Asad, but plenty of Iraqis did. The first casualty to arrive at Camp Havoc was a five-year-old boy with a blown-off hand, a blown-out eye, and shrapnel wounds across half his body. ISIL did not discriminate in its targeting.

Our Army doctor was hesitant to treat the boy at first. He interpreted the medical ROE as forbidding him to treat Iraqis. I interpreted them differently and told him I took full responsibility. This appeased the doctor; he treated the boy and never looked back. He and other doctors skillfully and compassionately treated numerous Iraqi citizens and soldiers. I initially caught some flak from doctors at senior levels for treating the Iraqis, but they backed off once I got General Funk's approval.

Funk supported us also in two other big ways. First, he provided Task Force Al Asad with an organic Army Shadow Platoon.[13] The RQ-7 Shadow is a lightweight UAV with an array of sensors to identify targets from up to eight thousand feet and from as far as 125 kilometers away from ground-control systems. The platform can operate by day or night, although it had some difficulty in inclement weather.

Senior leaders and staff informed me that the intended use of the Shadow was to loiter over known enemy rocket points of origin to identify and target rocket teams as a force-protection measure. The task force established POO patterns using counterbattery radars to establish Shadow search boxes, but I saw other uses for the Shadows as well.

Marines are offensively minded, and this use of the Shadows was defensive in nature. Rather than have our Shadows loiter in one place waiting for the enemy, we employed them to hunt the enemy. This did not sit well with some in higher headquarters, and I received a call from a senior officer who told me he did not want the Marines using the Shadows to "chase rainbows and unicorns." I convinced the officer to allow us to test our method. We never discussed it again once we started demonstrating success in hunting the enemy.

The Shadow did have limitations. The problem it and other aircraft had with inclement weather led me to request an all-weather indirect-fire asset. ISIL historically increased the number of indirect fire attacks against us during bad weather, and we needed a way to address this since we were not permitted to leave the base to observe the enemy directly. The second big way the general supported Task Force Al Asad was in acquiring an Army M-109 Paladin Platoon for us for this purpose.[14] The M-109 is a self-propelled 155-mm howitzer that can fire an artillery shell more than twenty-four kilometers. Again, there were opposing views on the employment of this capability.

Although thankful for the delivery of the M-109s, I received pushback on how I intended to employ them. Senior staff officials notified my Fire Effects Cell that the M-109s were only for use in counterbattery fires for force protection. This, like the intended use of the Shadows, limited the M-109s to the defense. Marines are taught the value of combined-arms operations in their earliest lessons, and I intended to use our newly acquired artillery to support the offensive maneuver of our ISF partners. My intent was to push ISIL outside the effective range of their rockets using offensive operations, rather than wait for them to fire on us so we could employ counterbattery fires. The best defense is a good offense. The counterbattery fire provided by the howitzers was an added benefit, but not their sole purpose. This also took some convincing and several practice missions against open terrain before we were authorized to employ these weapons as we saw fit. That authority could not have come at a better time.

ISIL forces conducted a surprise attack and captured the town of Albaghdadi right outside the front gate of Al Asad Air Base. Their forces had infiltrated across the Euphrates River in the middle of the night and quickly overran the lightly defended town. This caused more than one problem for us. The arrival of ISIL in al Baghdadi caused approximately a thousand Iraqi civilians to flee and arrive at Al Asad's doorstep. The ISF now had a humanitarian crisis to deal with that required our assistance. Matters got worse when ISIL, having captured the water pumping station in Al Baghdadi, turned off the fresh water to the base. The strength of the MAGTF proved its worth once again.

The combined efforts of the SPMAGTF ACE and LCE helped us through this crisis. Most supplies arrived at Al Asad by air, because ISIL controlled much of the land surrounding the base. Although CFACC tasked transport aircraft to deliver goods to Al Asad, this method was neither flexible nor timely. For example, we needed a repair part from Kuwait for one of our Shadows. The Shadow Platoon used the proper channels through CFACC and received word that it would take a week for the part to arrive. I made a quick phone call, and we flew the part in that same day using SPMAGTF MV-22s. This type of flexibility is only possible when a unit possesses its own assets, like a MAGTF does. This flexibility and adaptability assisted in other ways as well.

Task Force Al Asad had responsibility for running the Al Asad Airfield. Inherent with this responsibility was the task of keeping the runway operational. The SPMAGTF assisted here as well by employing engineers from its Marine wing support squadron to make runway repairs. This facilitated Iraqi aircraft flying in humanitarian supplies for the internally displaced people from Albaghdadi, who now lived on the base. The SPMAGTF also employed its aircraft to deliver water purification systems to the base.

The SPMAGTGF LCE provided logistical support not available to the Iraqis. They ran two SPMAGTF lightweight water purification and two CFLCC-provided tactical water purification systems to provide clean drinking water to the entire base. The water came from four wells that Marines had dug in years past during Operation Iraqi Freedom. We retapped the wells when ISIL shut the water off. The LCE assisted the ISF in providing food, fuel for cooking and heat, and even delivered three babies among the displaced personnel.

The combined force planned to oust ISIL from Albaghdadi, as we brought the humanitarian situation under control. The operation was dubbed *Wathba Al Asad* (Lion on the Prowl). It was our largest operation to date and required reinforcements from Baghdad. Help came in the form of an Iraqi police counterterrorism force, which was one of the most effective fighting units in the ISF, and a tank platoon. Three Cold War–era T-55 main battle tanks joined our ranks, though two broke down before the battle began. I was surprised to see these tanks joined by a short but heroic tribal leader driving another Cold War–era vehicle—a BMP-1 armored personnel carrier, with a 73-mm smooth-bore main gun.

The fighting was fierce, but the combined force came into its own. The ISF, tribal fighters, and IP fought shoulder to shoulder, clearing Albaghdadi one building at a time. Although the task force experienced some frustrations in getting the missions we requested approved in a timely manner, coalition fire proved decisive. The force recaptured Albaghdadi, got the water flowing back to Al Asad, and helped the displaced citizens return to their homes. It cost ten soldiers killed, but our combined efforts killed over a hundred ISIL fighters and destroyed nine boats, a 120-mm mortar, and multiple SVBIEDs.

The fight was not over. ISIL infiltrated more fighters across the Euphrates. The combined force had to conduct clearing operations over the coming days in the towns of Jubbah, Walid, Albu Hyat, and Alus south of the Euphrates to destroy this menace and keep Highway 12 open to Hadithah. Focus then shifted to the southeast toward the major city of Hit. Hit was the next major objective we planned to secure.

The Marine advise-and-assist teams arrived in the meantime and prepared to assume leading roles. I turned Task Force Al Asad over to Col. Joe

Russel and the I MEF AA team at the end of March. The II MEF AA team deployed from Al Asad to Baghdad to set conditions for standing up another task force in the Euphrates River valley at Al Taqaddum (TQ) Air Base. TQ was another major air base run by Marines in OIF.

SPMAGTF-CR-CC 15.1's deployment was coming to an end. The advanced party of the 7th Marines who were to relieve us as the lead for SPMAGTF-CR-CC 15.2 (i.e., 2015 second iteration) began arriving as I returned to al-Jaber. We spent the first two weeks of April 2015 turning over with the 7th Marines. I toured the area of operations with Col. Jay Bargeron, the CO of the 7th Marines. (Bargeron later attained a promotion to general officer and remains on active duty today.) We visited each of the locations where the SPMAGTF operated, for which his Marines and sailors assumed responsibility. Our transfer of authority for the SPMAGTF mission occurred on 19 April 2015.

I had time to reflect on the year-long sprint we had just completed and was justifiably proud of all that our young Marines and sailors accomplished. They had taken a concept and put it into action. They had formed, trained, and executed in short order and delivered a blow to an enemy that our nation had not even known it had a short time before. An enormous amount of effort had gone into this task.

During this deployment the SPMAGTF sustained a crisis-response company, TRAP force, and CASEVAC capability to cover the entire CENT-COM region for over 3,500 hours, or 150 straight days. The ACE flew over 7,350 flight hours, conducting over 2,360 sorties without a mishap. Our KC-130s delivered over 575,000 gallons of fuel, 3,500 passengers, and 3.2 million pounds of cargo. We conducted four major SC exercises across the region and bilateral training with our partners in Iraq, Jordan, Bahrain, Kuwait, Saudi Arabia, and the United Arab Emirates. We assisted Jordan in establishing its own crisis-response force, secured two diplomatic missions, conducted a successful withdrawal from a hostile country, and in the end destroyed over seven hundred ISIL fighters, a hundred enemy vehicles, sixty ISIL fighting positions, and ten indirect-fires assets.

Reflection

Soviet-era T-55 tanks and BMP-1 employed by our Iraqi friends reminded me just how far our country had come in the last thirty years. What started as lessons for a young midshipman on how to defeat the Soviets morphed into a journey of changing missions as the strategic environment evolved.

The U.S. national military strategy continued to shift as our nation adjusted to become the world's sole superpower, with a perceived responsibility for policing the world. Many small-state and nonstate actors filled the void left by the loss of the checks and balances of a once bipolar world. They grasped the opportunity to forward their agendas, often at the expense of others. This new world order presented ample work for the men and women in uniform.

America's armed forces met, and will continue to meet, the many challenges of adjusting to this changing world. They succeeded across the entire spectrum of conflict, from providing humanitarian assistance to prosecuting conventional wars and everything in between. They took on Mother Nature, bandits, pirates, insurgents, terrorists, and conventional armies, and they always came out on top. They did so at a cost, though.

Many soldiers, sailors, airmen, and Marines made the ultimate sacrifice in securing our freedoms and American way of life. It is an important fact that those of us who serve, and our families, must embrace and that the nation should not forget.

Evil still exists in this world. Threats to our livelihood and the safety of our families continue to emerge and evolve, but all Americans can take heart. I spent my entire adult life watching our young men and women accomplish extraordinary feats under extreme circumstances. They are the best our nation has to offer. Regardless of future challenges, I am confident that when the nation next calls, our service men and women will deliver . . . just as they always have.

God bless and Semper Fidelis.

Afterword

t has been said that history has a way of repeating itself. This is certainly proving true in the twenty-first century. Although our nation's national military strategy has evolved over the last thirty years following the fall of the Soviet Union, we now find ourselves once again preparing for high-end conflict against peer competitors. The changing missions that continued to shift in response to the changing times have come full circle with the arrival of a resurgent Russia, now joined by a rising China.

America finds itself having to relearn many of the skills needed to succeed on the high end of the spectrum of conflict after predominantly focusing on fighting terrorists, conducting counterinsurgencies, and performing other tasks on the low end for nearly two decades. Many of these critical skills have atrophied and are now made more difficult by the rapid proliferation of technology and the establishment of two new warfighting domains—cyber and space. Small-state and nonstate actors now possess many of the tools of war once only available to the strongest nations, adding levels of complexity to future battlefields and demanding more of our service men and women.

America's armed forces are responding like they always have in times of need. They are adapting, developing, and testing new and innovative operational concepts, acquiring new and improved platforms, and increasing the overall knowledge, skills, and capabilities of the individual fighting man and woman to remain a step ahead of our would-be adversaries.

Although the character of war is changing, the nature of war is enduring. As the Marine Corps improves its ability to shoot, move, and communicate, it also maintains a firm foundation in its warfighting doctrine. Marine Corps Doctrinal Publication-1, *Warfighting*, is as relevant today as it was when first published at the beginning of my journey as a Marine.

Time-tested and evolving concepts and doctrines and the advantages offered by modern technology, combined with more capable men and women, are essential to success on future battlefields. When my colleagues and I first joined the service, we learned from the Vietnam generation. It is now our responsibility as the Desert Storm/Iraqi Freedom/Enduring

Freedom generation to pass on our knowledge and skills to the next generation. They will most assuredly need them as they experience their own operations in many of the same distant lands that helped to shape my fellow Marines, soldiers, sailors, airmen, and Coast Guardsmen and me.

As I write these words, Marines are once again deploying to Norway after years of absence to work with other NATO allies to deter and, if necessary, defeat Russian forces. American special forces are back in Somalia to prevent that country from becoming a safe haven for extremist organizations. Marines were sent back to reinforce the U.S. embassy in Haiti yet again as violence erupted once more in that country. Although under new operational names, Marines also continue operations in Iraq and Afghanistan.

Some may look at the above list and ask, if we need to return to these countries after investing so much in them in the past, what have we really accomplished? To me, the answer is clear: By forward deploying to assure our allies and partners and deter and, when necessary, defeat our adversaries, my fellow service men and women have preserved our freedoms and the American way of life. The real question that should be asked is: What would the world look like if America had not sent its sons and daughters forward to defend our nation?

I am honored to continue to wear the uniform today and am proud to welcome new generations of Americans to our ranks. Many of the names remain the same. In fact, many of them are the sons and daughters of those with whom I have been privileged to serve over the years, including one of my own daughters. In many ways, they are better equipped than my peers and I were when we first joined. They will need to be in order to confront the many challenges of changing missions during the coming changing times.

Acknowledgments

I need to acknowledge and thank God before all others, because I know that I owe all that I have and all that I am to Him. Only through God's grace have I been permitted to share the many experiences, and survived many a close call, with my brothers and sisters in uniform. I have faith that those whom He has taken from us so early in life are in a better place. For that, I am eternally grateful.

I also want to thank my wife and children. I could not have continued to wear the uniform of our nation without their love, support, and sacrifice all these years. My wife is my best friend. She has shared my joys, successes, failures, and heartbreaks during every step of our journey together over these thirty years. Our children have grown into strong and independent adults who understand the meaning of service and sacrifice. We could not be prouder of them.

I owe a special debt of gratitude to the many coaches, trainers, and mentors who helped shape me into the Marine and man I am today—both enlisted and officer, in uniform and out. I have experienced many failures in my life, and they used these as opportunities to help me grow. I try to pay that forward by using these lessons to help others succeed and meet their full potential.

Two mentors who have been particularly helpful in seeing the publication of this book through to completion are Dr. Williamson "Wick" Murray and Dr. Charles Neimeyer. Dr. Murray is an American historian, professor emeritus of history at Ohio State University, and author of over twenty-five books, numerous articles, and other writings. He has a passion for professional military education (PME) and has taught at all the military services' senior schools. I first met him while serving as the director of the Marine Corps Expeditionary Warfare School. Dr. Murray graciously gave of his own time to educate and mold select groups of high-achieving captains with a passion for learning. He also continues to pay it forward and was extremely helpful in guiding me as a nascent author. Dr. Neimeyer is a retired Marine lieutenant colonel, former director of the Marine Corps History Division, and published author of many works. Dr. Neimeyer is not only the preeminent expert on Marine Corps history, but he also shares a passion for PME and has assisted me numerous times over the years in my capacity as a student, school director, and author. I owe both gentlemen many thanks for their assistance and friendship.

Jim Dolbow, senior acquisitions editor for professional development content; Caitlin Bean, production editor; Ann Boyer, copy editor; and other staff at the Naval Institute Press have also been invaluable in helping to see this project through to fruition. The Naval Institute Press has contributed to the preservation and sharing of naval history for more than one hundred years. They provide an important service for which I am grateful.

Five other organizations serve an invaluable service to Marines, sailors, and their families. It is for this reason that to them I will be donating a portion of any proceeds I receive from the sale of this book. The Semper Fi Fund provides direct financial assistance and vital programming for combat wounded, critically ill, and catastrophically injured service members and their families during hospitalization and recovery.[1] The Navy and Marine Corps Relief Society provides financial, educational, and other assistance to members of the U.S. Navy, eligible family members, and survivors when in need.[2] The Marine Corps Association and Foundation is the professional association for Marines. It disseminates knowledge of military arts and science, provides professional development opportunities, fosters the spirit and preserves the traditions of the Marine Corps, and recognizes the professional excellence of Marines through a robust awards program.[3] The Marine Corps University Foundation supports the professional military education of active duty and reserve officers and enlisted Marines by underwriting and enhancing their educations.[4] The Marine Corps Heritage Foundation preserves and promulgates the history, traditions, and culture of the Marine Corps and educates all Americans in its virtues.[5] My Marines and sailors, our families, and I have benefitted greatly from these organizations, and through this book's readers' help, I hope to assist them all in their missions.

Finally, I must thank the many Marines, sailors, soldiers, airmen, and Coast Guardsmen to whom this book is dedicated. The opportunity to raise a family and serve beside these men and women of honor is the primary reason I still wear the uniform today.

God bless and Semper Fidelis.

Notes

Introduction

1. "Geographic Prepositioning Force, Norway Air-Landed Marine Expeditionary Brigade (NALMEB), Norway Air Landed Marine Air Ground Task Force (NALMAGTAF)," Global Security, http://www.globalsecurity.org/military/facility/nalmeb.htm.
2. Vojtech Mastny, Sven S. Holtsmark, and Andreas Wenger, *War Plans and Alliances in the Cold War: Threat Perceptions in the East and West* (Abingdon, UK: Routledge, 2006), 104.
3. "Geographic Prepositioning Force."
4. Aled-Dilwyn Fisher and Nina Berglund, "Cold War Defense Included Plans to Sacrifice Finnmark in the North," *News in English, Views and News from Norway,* http://www.newsinenglish.no/2011/02/04/cold-war-defense-included-plans-to-sacrifice-finnmark/.
5. Col. Ivar Hellberg (Ret.), Royal Marines, in discussion with the author, 3 February 2016.
6. Goldwater-Nichols Department of Defense Reorganization Act of 1986, Pub. L. No. 99-433, 100 Stat. 992 (1986).
7. Ronald Reagan, *National Security Strategy of the United States* (Washington, DC: White House, January 1987), 2.
8. See Jason Bohm, "Complacency Kills: The Need for Improvement in the Way the Marine Corps Prepares for Future Conflict" (master's thesis, United States Marine Corps Command and Staff College, 2001), 2.
9. Colin Powell, *National Military Strategy of the United States* (Washington, DC, January 1992), 1.
10. Dennis P. Mroczkowski, *Restoring Hope: In Somalia with the Unified Task Force, 1992–1993, U.S. Marines in Humanitarian Operations* (Washington, DC: United States Marine Corps History Division, 2005), 8.
11. Charles C. Krulak, "The Strategic Corporal: Leadership in the Three Block War," *Marines Magazine,* January 1999.

12. Mark Bowden, *Blackhawk Down: A Story of Modern War* (New York: Atlantic Monthly Press, 1999).

13. John Shalikashvili, *National Military Strategy of the United States* (Washington, DC, 1995).

14. Shalikashvili.

15. David D. Kirkpatrick, "Saudi Arabia Said to Arrest Suspect in 1996 Khobar Towers Bombing," *New York Times*, 26 August 2015, https://www.nytimes.com/2015/08/27/world/middleeast/saudia-arabia-arrests-suspect-khobar-towers-bombing.html.

16. Richard M. Meinhart, "National Military Strategies: 1990 to 2009," chap. 7 in *U.S. Army War College Guide to National Security Issues, Vol. II: National Security Policy and Strategy* (Carlisle, PA: U.S. Army War College, 2010), 112. Discussion that follows on this strategy is from this source.

17. Meinhart.

18. Meinhart.

19. "Operation Resolute Response," Global Security, http://www.globalsecurity.org/military/ops/resolute_response.htm.

20. SETAF Public Affairs, "SETAF Through the Years, Today," *SETAF Outlook*, October 25, 2005, 5.

21. Richard B. Myers, *National Military Strategy of the United States of America: A Strategy for Today; A Vision for Tomorrow* (Washington, DC, 2004), 4.

22. "Tsunami 2004 Facts and Figures," http://www.tsunami2004.net/tsunami-2004-facts/.

23. Michael G. Mullen, *The National Military Strategy of the United States: Redefining America's Military Leadership* (Washington, DC, 2011), 21.

Chapter 1. Marine Culture, Warfighting, and Desert Storm

1. Victor H. Krulak, *First to Fight: An Inside View of the U.S. Marine Corps* (Annapolis, MD: Naval Institute Press, 1984), xx.

2. An Act to Fix the Personnel Strength of the United States Marine Corps, and to Establish the Relationship of the Commandant of the Marine Corps to the Joint Chiefs of Staff, Pub. L. No. 82-416, 66 Stat. 677 (1952).

3. Charles C. Krulak, *Marine Corps Doctrinal Publication 1, Warfighting* (Washington, DC: Headquarters U.S. Marine Corps, 1997), 3.

4. Office of U.S. Marine Corps Communication, *Marine Corps Communications Playbook* (December 2015).

5. Allan R. Millett, *Semper Fidelis: The History of the United States Marine Corps* (New York: Free Press, 1991), 633.

6. Alfred Gray, *Fleet Manual Force Manual 1, Warfighting* (Washington, DC: Headquarters U.S. Marine Corps, 1989); Krulak, *Warfighting*.

7. Krulak, *Warfighting*, 72.

8. Krulak, *Warfighting*, 73.

9. Krulak, "Strategic Corporal."

10. The Infantry Officer Course has been extended to a thirteen-week course today.

11. Paul W. Westermeyer, *U.S. Marines in the Gulf War, 1990–1991, Liberating Kuwait* (Quantico, VA: History Division, U.S. Marine Corps, 2014), 21.

12. Westermeyer, 19–20.

13. Charles C. Krulak, *Marine Corps Doctrinal Publication 3, Expeditionary Operations* (Washington, DC: Headquarters U.S. Marine Corps, 1998), 70.

14. Westermeyer, *U.S. Marines in the Gulf War*, 37.

15. II MEF G3 Operations/Maritime Prepositioning Force (MPF) Cell, *MPF Planning Guide* (Camp Lejeune, NC: II MEF, 1998), 4.

16. H. Avery Chenoweth and Brooke Nihart, *Semper Fi: The Definitive Illustrated History of the U.S. Marines* (New York: Sterling Reprint, 2010), 399.

17. Millett, *Semper Fidelis*, 637.

18. Westermeyer, *U.S. Marines in the Gulf War*, 42.

19. Westermeyer, 43.

20. Chenoweth and Nihart, *Semper Fi*, 405.

21. Chenoweth and Nihart, 409.

Chapter 2. The Infantry, Okinawa, and "Bohm's Bastards"

1. Marine Corps Base Camp Pendleton official website, http://www.pendleton.marines.mil/. All information on Camp Pendleton to follow was derived from this website.

2. Ray Tessler, "Oceanside's Big Parade to Hail Marines' Return," *Los Angeles Times*, 24 April 1991.

3. A. J. Baker, *Okinawa* (London: Bison Books, 1981), 9. Facts and statistics discussed in this paragraph are derived from this source.

4. Millett, *Semper Fidelis*, 438.

5.   U.S. Marine Corps, *NAVMC 3500.42B, Tactical Air Control Party Training and Readiness Manual* (Washington, DC, 2014), 20.

Chapter 3. Restore Hope and the Three Block War

1.   *Encyclopedia Britannica*, 15th ed., s.v. "Eastern Africa, Somalia," 834.
2.   Mroczkowski, *Restoring Hope*, 4.
3.   *Encyclopedia Britannica*, "Eastern Africa, Somalia," 834.
4.   Mroczkowski, *Restoring Hope*, 5.
5.   United States Central Command, *Country Information Guide, Somalia, Operation Restore Hope* (locally produced, 1992), 1.
6.   R. R. Keene, "Operation Eastern Exit: Night Mission to Mogadishu," (originally published March 1991), https://www.mca-marines.org /leatherneck/operation-eastern-exit-night-mission-mogadishu.
7.   "Operation Provide Relief," Global Security, http://www.globalsecurity .org/military/ops/provide_relief.htm.
8.   Mroczkowski, *Restoring Hope*, 9.
9.   Mroczkowski, 11.
10.   Mroczkowski.
11.   Gary W. Cooke, "81mm Mortar Ammunition and Fuzes," *Gary's U.S. Weapons and Ammunition Reference Guide* (10 May 2006), http:// www.inetres.com/gp/military/infantry/mortar/81mm.html.
12.   Cooke, "81mm Mortar."
13.   "Food," MyMemory, http://mymemory.translated.net/en/English/Somali /food.
14.   Mroczkowski, *Restoring Hope*, 55.
15.   Mroczkowski, 70.
16.   William H. Rupertus, "My Rifle—The Creed of a United States Marine," (1942), https://www.marineparents.com/marinecorps/mc-rifle.asp.
17.   Regimental Combat Team 7, *Somalia Information Handbook* (Twentynine Palms, CA, 1992), 9.
18.   Mroczkowski, *Restoring Hope*, 43.

Chapter 4. Steel Rain, Amphibious Operations, and Korea

1.   Michael G. Mullen, *Joint Publication 5-0, Joint Operation Planning* (Washington, DC: Joint Chiefs of Staff, 2011), III-38. The discussion on the six phases of military operations is derived from this source.

2.   Charles Smith, *Marines in the Revolution: A History of the Continental Marines in the American Revolution, 1775–1783* (Washington, DC: History and Museums Division, Headquarters, U.S. Marine Corps, 1975), 50.

3.   Tony Guerra, "What Is the Marine Corps Ship Sea Duty Detachment?," *Career Trend*, 5 July 2017, http://everydaylife.globalpost.com/marine-corps-ship-sea-duty-detachment-13801.html.

4.   Dirk A. Ballendorf and Merrill L. Bartlett, *Pete Ellis, an Amphibious Prophet, 1880–1923* (Annapolis, MD: Naval Institute Press, 1997).

5.   Ballendorf and Bartlett.

6.   Millett, *Semper Fidelis*, 331.

7.   Millett, 332.

8.   Holland M. Smith, "The Development of Amphibious Tactics in the U.S. Navy," *Marine Corps Gazette* (October 1946), 31.

9.   Krulak, *Doctrinal Publication 3*, 2–14.

10. "Armored Amphibious Vehicle," Marines.com, http://www.marines.com/operating-forces/equipment/vehicles/aav-7.

11. "Landing Craft, Air Cushion-LCAC," *United States Navy Fact File*, http://www.navy.mil/navydata/fact_display.asp?cid=4200&ct=4&tid=1500.

12. "Landing Craft, Mechanized and Utility-LCM/LCU," *United States Navy Fact File*, http://www.navy.mil/navydata/fact_display.asp?cid=4200&tid=1600&ct=4.

13. *Encyclopedia Britannica*, 15th ed., s.v. "Korea, History."

14. Millett, *Semper Fidelis*, 106.

15. Bevin Alexander, *Korea: The First War We Lost* (New York: Hippocrene Books, 1986), 11.

16. T. R. Fehrenbach, *This Kind of War: The Classic Korean War History*, 2nd ed. (Washington, DC: Brassey's, 1998), 32.

17. Lee Ballenger, *The Outpost War: U.S. Marines in Korea*, volume 1, *1952* (Washington, DC: Brassey's, 2000).

18. "This Day in History, July 27, 1953, Armistice Ends the Korean War," History.com, http://www.history.com/this-day-in-history/armistice-ends-the-korean-war.

19. "U.S. Forces Korea—Exercises," *Global Security*, http://www.globalsecurity.org/military/ops/ex-usfk.htm.

20. James Sheehan, "Foods of War: Hardtack," *War on the Rocks*, http://warontherocks.com/2015/04/foods-of-war-hardtack/.

21. Marine Corps Installation Camp Mujuk official website, http://www.mcipac.marines.mil/Installations/CampMujuk.aspx.

Chapter 5. Antiterrorism, Haiti, and Embassy Reinforcement

1. "Terrorism: Definitions of Terrorism in the U.S. Code," Federal Bureau of Investigation, https://www.fbi.gov/about-us/investigate/terrorism/terrorism-definition.

2. "The Iranian Hostage Crisis," United States Department of State, Office of the Historian, https://history.state.gov/departmenthistory/short-history/iraniancrises.

3. "Lebanon, Bombing of U.S. Embassy and Marine Barracks," *Encyclopedia of Espionage, Intelligence, and Security* (2004). Quoted in Encyclopedia.com, http://www.encyclopedia.com/doc/1G2-3403300454.html.

4. "Target America, Terrorist Attacks on Americans 1979–1988," *Frontline*, Public Broadcasting Service, http://www.pbs.org/wgbh/pages/frontline/shows/target/etc/cron.html.

5. Shannon Schwaller, "Operation Just Cause: The Invasion of Panama, December 1989," *Army Heritage and Education Center*, 17 November 2008, http://www.army.mil/article/14302/operation-just-cause-the-invasion-of-panama-december-1989/.

6. International Organization for Migration, *The UN Migration Organization*, https://www.iom.int/ambassador-william-lacy-swing.

7. "Marine Corps Embassy Security Group, 'Vigilance, Discipline, Professionalism,'" Marines.mil, http://www.mcesg.marines.mil/About/MCESGHistory.aspx.

8. "Haitians Seize Equipment of U.S. Marines," *New York Times*, 13 June 1994, http://www.nytimes.com/1994/06/13/world/haitians-seize-equipment-of-us-marines.html.

9. John R. Ballard, *Upholding Democracy: The United States Military Campaign in Haiti, 1994–1997* (Westport, CT: Praeger, 1998), 3.

10. Ballard, 3.

11. Ballard, 1.

12. *Encyclopedia Britannica*, 15 ed., s.v. "West Indies, History," 749.

13. James H. McCrocklin, *Garde D'Haiti: Twenty Years of Organization and Training by the United States Marines Corps* (Annapolis, MD: Naval Institute Press, 1956), v.

14. *Encyclopedia Britannica*, "West Indies, History," 749.

15. *Encyclopedia Britannica*, 750.

16. "Intervention in Haiti, 1994–1995," United States Department of State, Office of the Historian, https://history.state.gov/milestones/1993-2000/haiti.

17. Shawn Dorman, ed., *Inside a U.S. Embassy: How the Foreign Service Works for America* (Washington, DC: American Foreign Service Association, 2005), 2.

18. Dorman, 8.

19. "Welcome to Defense.Gov," U.S. Defense Department, https://www.defense.gov/ ; and "Mission," U.S. Department of State Careers Representing America, https://careers.state.gov/learn/what-we-do/mission.

20. "LAV-150 Commando," *Army Guide,* http://www.army-guide.com/eng/product1149.html.

21. "Revolutionary Front for Haitian Advancement and Progress (FRAPH)," *Global Security,* http://www.globalsecurity.org/military/world/haiti/fraph.htm.

22. Benjamin Radford, *Voodoo: Facts About Misunderstood Religion,* Live Science (30 October 2013), http://www.livescience.com/40803-voodoo-facts.html.

23. James Brady, "Get the Marines Out of Haiti," *AdAge,* (26 September 1994), http://adage.com/article/news/marines-haiti/89994/.

24. Bradley Graham, "Marine Unit Deploys to Sea in a Hurry," *Washington Post,* 8 July 1994, https://www.washingtonpost.com/archive/politics/1994/.

25. Graham, "Marine Unit Deploys."

26. William C. Mayville Jr., Joint Publication [JP] 3-68, *Noncombatant Evacuation Operations* (Washington, DC: Government Printing Office, 18 November 2015), ix.

27. Mayville, ix.

28. Associated Press, "U.S. Ready for Invasion, Congressman Tells Haitian Leaders," *Deseret (UT) News,* 19 July 1994, http://www.deseretnews.com/.

29. Associated Press.

Chapter 6. Upholding Democracy

1. *Encyclopedia Britannica,* s.v. "Hydra," http://www.britannica.com/topic/Hydra-Greek-mythology.

2. Jason Bohm, notes taken from the author's personal diary kept during Operation Uphold Democracy.

3. Bohm.

4. David Hackworth and Julie Sherman, *About Face: The Odyssey of an American Warrior* (New York: Simon and Schuster, 1989).

5. David Hackworth with Tom Matthews, *Hazardous Duty* (New York: William Morrow Company, 1996).

6. Bohm, diary.
7. "OH-58D Kiowa Warrior Armed Reconnaissance Helicopter," *Army Technology*, http://www.army-technology.com/projects/kiowa/.
8. "USS Cyclone PC-1," *Military Factory*, http://www.militaryfactory .com/ships/.
9. UN Security Council, Security Council Resolution 940 (1994) [UN Mission in Haiti], 31 July 1994, S/RES/940 (1994), https://www.refworld .org/docid/3b00f15f63.html.
10. Krulak, *Warfighting*.
11. *USS* Comte De Grasse *(DD 974)*, http://www.navysite.de/dd/dd974.htm.
12. "PSYOP Expert Discusses Military Information Support Operations," *Institute of World Politics*, 9 March 2011, http://www.iwp.edu /news_publications/.
13. Eric Schmitt, "8 Haitians Killed by Marine Patrol," *New York Times*, 25 September 1994, http://www.nytimes.com/1994/09/25/world/8 -haitians-killed-by-marine-patrol.html.

Chapter 7. Migrants, Special Security Missions, and Stopping Terrorism

1. David Bentley, "Operation Sea Signal: U.S. Military Support for Caribbean Migration Emergencies, May 1994 to February 1996," *National Forum* #73 (Washington, DC: National Defense University Institute for National Strategic Studies, May 1996), 1.
2. Bentley, 1.
3. Eric Schmitt, "Cuban Refugees Riot in Panama," *New York Times*, 8 December 1994, http://www.nytimes.com/1994/12/09/world /cuban -refugees-riot-in-panama.html.
4. Schmitt.
5. *USS* Austin *(LPD 4)*, http://www.navysite.de/ships/lpd4.htm.
6. *USS* La Moure County *(LST 1194)*, http://www.navysite.de/lst/lst1194 .htm.
7. The Marine Corps Security Force Battalion was later redesignated a regiment and the Marine Corps Security Force Companies at Kings Bay and Bangor were later redesignated battalions.
8. *USS* Dallas *(SSN 700)*, https://www.navy.mil/submit/display.asp?story _id=105059.
9. "820th Red Horse Squadron," Nellis Air Force Base, 12 July 2012, http://www.nellis.af.mil/AboutUs/FactSheets/.

10. "Seabees: 'We Build, We Fight,'" http://www.navy.mil/navydata /personnel/seabees/seabee1.html.
11. David L. Patton, "Operation Uphold Democracy: Use of Military Police and Non-Lethal Weapons in Haiti" (Powerpoint presentation, 14 April 1999).
12. Drew Fellman, "Club Med Reopens Magic Isle on Haiti," *Los Angeles Times,* 7 January 1996, http://articles.latimes.com/1996-01-07/travel /tr-22083_1_club-med.
13. "USO Show Troupe," United Services Organization (USO), https:// metrony.uso.org/programs/uso-show-troupe.
14. *Encyclopedia Britannica,* s.v. "John Shalikashvili, United States Army Officer," https://www.britannica.com/biography/John-Shalikashvili.
15. "Moments in U.S. Diplomatic History, The Khobar Towers Bombing," Association for Diplomatic Studies and Training, http://adst .org/2015/02/the-khobar-tower-bombings/.
16. "Khobar Towers Bombing."
17. Naval Support Activity Bahrain official website, http://www.cnic.navy .mil/regions/cnreurafswa/installations/nsa_bahrain.html.
18. NSA Bahrain.
19. Jason Bohm, "Antiterrorism Mission, Manama, Bahrain, Fleet Antiterrorism Security Team (FAST) Company, Marine Corps Security Force Battalion, 2 July 1996 to 19 October 1996," (student monograph, U.S. Army Infantry Officer Advanced Course 2-97, 27 May 1997), 7.
20. Bohm, 10.
21. Thom Shanker, "Gen. Wayne A. Downing, 67, Special Operations Leader, Dies," *New York Times,* 19 July 2007, http://www.nytimes.com /2007/07/19/washington/19downing.html.
22. "New Anti-Terrorism Officials Announcement," *C-SPAN,* 9 October 2001, http://www.c-span.org/video/?166573-1/new-antiterrorism -officials-announcement.
23. Bohm, "Antiterrorism Mission," 20.
24. "USS Cole Bombing," National September 11 Memorial Museum, http://www.911memorial.org/uss-cole-bombing.

Chapter 8. Terrorist Attacks, Company Command, and Recruiting the Force

1. Office of the Secretary of Defense, *Force Protection, Global Interests, Global Responsibilities, Secretary of Defense Report to the*

President (Washington, DC: U.S. Department of Defense, September 1996), 17.

2.   Secretary of Defense.

3.   Mark J. Reardon and Jeffery A. Charlston, *From Transformation to Combat: The First Stryker Brigade at War* (Washington, DC: Government Printing Office, 2007), 11.

4.   "Marine Corps Systems Command; Equipping Our Marines," Marines.mil, https://www.marcorsyscom.marines.mil/Portfolios-and -Programs /LAV/.

5.   "USS Boxer (LHD 4)," Navy.mil, http://www.navy.mil/local/lhd4/.

6.   "Sgt. Jesse Aligana," Marine Embassy Guard Association Historical Archives in Memoriam, http://www.msg-history.com/historicalitems /hp_nairobi_1998_aliganga.html.

7.   "USS Harpers Ferry (LSD-49)," NavSource Online: Amphibious Photo Archive, http://www.navsource.org/archives/10/12/1249.htm; "USS Cleveland (LPD 7), http://www.navysite.de/ships/lpd7.htm.

8.   "SEATF Southern European Task Force," USASADF Net, Worldwide Radio Direction Finding Net, http://www.usasadf.net/usarmy-setaf .html.

9.   The points discussed in this paragraph are derived from Bernard D. Rostker, "The Evolution of the All-Volunteer Force," RB-9195-RC (Santa Monica, CA: RAND, 2006), http://www.rand.org/pubs/research _briefs/RB9195.html.

10. "Grundy, Virginia Population," CensusViewer, http://censusviewer .com/city/VA/Grundy.

11. Toys for Tots, http://www.toysfortots.org/Default.aspx.

Chapter 9. Battalion Landing Team XO, the Tsunami, and Operation Iraqi Freedom

1.   Nathan S. Lowrey, *U.S. Marines in Afghanistan, 2001–2002, From the Sea, U.S. Marines in the Global War on Terrorism* (Washington, DC: U.S. Marine Corps History Division, 2011), 20.

2.   Lowrey, iii.

3.   "Fedayeen," Dictionary.com, http://www.dictionary.com/browse /fedayeen.

4.   Bing West, and Ray L. Smith, *The March Up: Taking Baghdad with the 1st Marine Division* (New York: Bantam Books, 2003), 36.

5.   Jason Bohm, "Complacency Kills: The Need for Improvement in the Way the Marine Corps Prepares for Future Conflict" (master's thesis, U.S. Marine Corps Command and Staff College, 2001).

6.   National Defense University, *Joint Vision 2020: America's Military— Preparing for Tomorrow*, 2000, www.dtic.mil/dtic/tr/fulltext/u2 /a526044.pdf.

7.   "US Marines 'Mojave Viper' Combat Training," https://www.youtube .com/watch?v=lmOPveWfHS0.

8.   "USS *Bonhomme Richard*," *America's Navy*, http://www.public.navy .mil/surfor/lhd6/Pages/default.aspx#.WB4w1C3x6M8.

9.   "USS *Rushmore*," *America's Navy*, http://www.public.navy.mil/surfor /lsd47/Pages/default.aspx#.WB4xkS3x6M8.

10. "USS *Duluth* (LPD 6)," http://www.navysite.de/ships/lpd6.htm.

11. Ray Mabus, *A Cooperative Strategy for the 21st Century Seapower* (Washington, DC: March 2015); Robert Neller, *The Marine Corps Operating Concept: How an Expeditionary Force Operates in the 21st Century* (Washington, DC, September 2016).

12. "Navy SERE Training: Learning to Return with Honor," *The Balance Careers*, https://www.thebalance.com/navy-sere-training-3356100.

13. Jeremy Wilson, *Lawrence of Arabia; The Authorized Biography of T.E. Lawrence* (New York: Atheneum, 1990).

14. "The Deadliest Tsunami in History?," *National Geographic News*, https:// news.nationalgeographic.com/news/2004/12deadliest-tsunami-in -history/.

15. "The Deadliest."

16. *15th Maine Expeditionary Unit (SOC), WESTPAC 2–04*, cruisebook, 2004.

17. Angel Rabasa and John Haseman, *The Military and Democracy in Indonesia: Challenges, Politics, and Power*, MR-1599-SRF (Washington, DC: RAND, 2002,) 139.

18. "Camp Buehring Army Base in Udari, Kuwait," Militarybases.com, https://militarybases.com/camp-buehring-army-base-in-udari -kuwait/.

Chapter 10. 1st Marine Division, I MEF (Forward), and Iraq Again

1.   David Galula, *Counterinsurgency Warfare, Theory and Practice* (St. Petersburg, FL: Hailer, 1964).

2. Galula, 31.
3. M. P. Caufield, *Fleet Marine Forces Reference Publication 12–15, Small Wars Manual* (Washington, DC: Headquarters U.S. Marine Corps, 1990); and Galula, *Counterinsurgency Warfare*.
4. "Muslim," "Shi'ite," and "Sunni," Dictionary.com, http://www.dictionary.com/.
5. "Muslim," Dictionary.com.
6. Timothy McWilliams and Kurtis Wheeler, eds., *Al Anbar Awakening; Vol 1, American Perspectives, US Marines and Counterinsurgency in Iraq, 2004-2009* (Quantico, VA: Marine Corps University, 2009).
7. Statistics taken from the author's personal journal written during this deployment.
8. Bill Roggio, "Operation Steel Curtain in Husaybah," *FDD's Long War Journal*, 5 November 2005, http://www.longwarjournal.org/archives/2005/11/operation_steel_1.php.
9. *I MEF (Forward), Operation Iraqi Freedom 05–07, Al Anbar, Iraq,* cruisebook, 2007.
10. *I MEF (Forward),* cruisebook.

Chapter 11. The China Marines, Sister Cities, and Counterinsurgency

1. Lonnie Young, "History of the First Battalion, Fourth Marines," 1969, http://1stbn4thmarines.net/history-of-14.html.
2. "The History of the 1st Battalion, 4th Marines," the official website of the U.S. Marine Corps, http://www.1stmardiv.marines.mil/Units/1ST-MARINE-REGT/1st-Battalion-4th-Marines/History/.
3. "Timeline: The Iraq Surge, Before and After," *Washington Post*, http://www.washingtonpost.com/wp-srv/nation/thegamble/timeline/.
4. "Stu Segall," *Strategic Operations*, http://www.strategic-operations.com/team/stu-segall/.
5. "Stu Segall."
6. "Studio Services: San Diego Studio," Stu Segall Productions, http://www.stusegall.com/studio_services/san_diego.shtml.
7. The information concerning guidance from Generals Gaskin and Gurganus was derived from an unclassified brief provided to the author prior to his deployment in support of OIF 06-08.
8. "History and Mission," *Sister Cities International*, https://sistercities.org/.

9. "History and Mission."

10. Jim Garamone, "Operation Matador Ends, Marines Continue to Monitor Area," American Forces Press Service, 14 May 2005, quoted from Marines.mil, https://www.hqmc.marines.mil/News /News -Article-Display/Article/551923/operation-matador-ends-marines -continue-to-monitor-area/.

11. "Medal of Honor Citation for Cpl. Jason L. Dunham," the official website of the U.S. Marine Corps, 12 January 2007, http://www .hqmc.marines.mil/News/News-Article-Display/Article/551570 /medal-of-honor-citation-for-cpl-jason-l-dunham/.

12. Military Times, *Honoring the Fallen*, https://thefallen.militarytimes .com/marine-capt-richard-j-gannon-ii/257208.

13. Roggio, "Operation Steel Curtain."

14. "Al Qa'im, City in Iraq," *Mygola*, http://www.mygola.com/al-qaim -d1234103/train-station.

15. "Al Qa'im."

16. TRADOC DCSINT Handbook No. 2, *Arab Cultural Awareness: 58 Fact-sheets* (Ft. Leavenworth, KS: Office of the Deputy Chief of Staff for Intelligence US Army Training and Doctrine Command, January 2006), 29.

17. Peter Graff, "Harsh Justice Where U.S. Relies on Iraq Tribes," Reuters, 4 September 2007, http://www.reuters.com/article/us-iraq-justice -idUSL0376971420070904.

18. Missimo Calabresi, "Bush's Surprise Iraqi Visit," *Time*, 3 September 2007, http://content.time.com/time/nation/article/0,8599,1658499 ,00.html.

Chapter 12. The Fighting Fifth, Special Purpose MAGTF, and the Fight against ISIL

1. "J5 Strategy, Plans and Policy," Joint Chiefs of Staff, http://www.jcs .mil/Directorates/J5%7CStrategicPlansandPolicy.aspx.

2. U.S. Northern Command (website), http://www.northcom.mil/.

3. "Office of Legislative Affairs, Headquarters Marine Corps," Marines .mil, http://www.hqmc.marines.mil/Agencies/Office-of-Legislative -Affairs/.

4. "5th Marine Regiment, 1st Marine Division," Marines.mil, http:// www.1stmardiv.marines.mil/Units/5TH-MARINE-REGT/History/.

5. "General Joseph F. Dunford Jr., Chairman of the Joint Chiefs of Staff," U.S. Department of Defense, https://www.defense.gov

/About-DoD/Biographies/Biography-View/Article/621329/general
-joseph-f-dunford-jr.

6. "Benghazi Mission Attack Fast Facts," CNN Library, 4 September 2018, http://www.cnn.com/2013/09/10/world/benghazi-consulate -attack-fast-facts/.

7. Marina Ottiway, "The New Normal in the Middle East," *Real Clear World*, 20 July 2016, http://www.realclearworld.com /articles/2016/07/20/the_new_normal_in_the_middle_east.html.

8. Alastair Jamieson, "Who Are Yemen's Houthis and What Do They Want?," *NBC News*, http://www.nbcnews.com/news/world /who-are-yemen-s-houthis-what-do-they-want-n665636.

9. *Encyclopedia Britannica*, s.v. "Islamic State in Iraq and the Levant (ISIL)," https://www.britannica.com/topic/Islamic-State-in-Iraq-and -the-Levant.

10. Operation Inherent Resolve (website), http://www.inherentresolve .mil/.

11. Operation Inherent Resolve (website).

12. "Task Forces, U.S. Naval Forces Central Command," U.S. Naval Forces Central Command, Combined Maritime Forces–U.S. 5th Fleet, http:// www.cusnc.navy.mil/Task-Forces/.

13. "Shadow 200 RQ-7 Tactical Unmanned Aircraft System," Army Tech- nology, http://www.army-technology.com/projects/shadow200uav/.

14. "Paladin M109A6 155mm Artillery System," Army Technology, http:// www.army-technology.com/projects/paladin/.

Acknowledgments

1. Semper Fi Fund, https://semperfifund.org/.

2. Navy Marine Corps Relief Society, http://www.nmcrs.org/.

3. Marine Corps Association and Foundation, https://www.mcafdn .org/.

4. Marine Corps University and Foundation, https://www.marinecorps universityfoundation.org/.

5. Marine Corps Heritage Foundation, https://www.marineheritage .org/.

About the Author

Brig. Gen. Jason Q. Bohm, USMC, an infantryman by trade, has served in many command and staff positions in his nearly thirty years of service. Bohm commanded at every level from platoon to Marine Air Ground Task Force and has served in key staff positions including the Joint Staff and director of the Expeditionary Warfare School.